SALT WATER TAFFY

⌐ THE SEASIDE ADVENTURES OF ⌐

JACK AND BENNY

IN

A CLIMB UP MT. BARNABAS

Written & Illustrated by

MATTHEW LOUX

Lettered by DOUGLAS E. SHERWOOD
Design by MATTHEW LOUX *&* KEITH WOOD
Edited by RANDAL C. JARRELL

Published by Oni Press, Inc.
JOE NOZEMACK, publisher
JAMES LUCAS JONES, editor in chief • RANDAL C. JARRELL, managing editor
CORY CASONI, sales & marketing • KEITH WOOD, art director
JILL BEATON, assistant editor • DOUGLAS E. SHERWOOD, production assistant

ONI PRESS, INC.
1305 SE MARTIN LUTHER KING JR. BLVD.
SUITE A
PORTLAND, OR 97214
USA

www.onipress.com • www.actionmatt.com

First edition: October 2008
ISBN-13: 978-1-934964-03-3

3 5 7 9 10 8 6 4 2

PRINTED IN U.S.A.

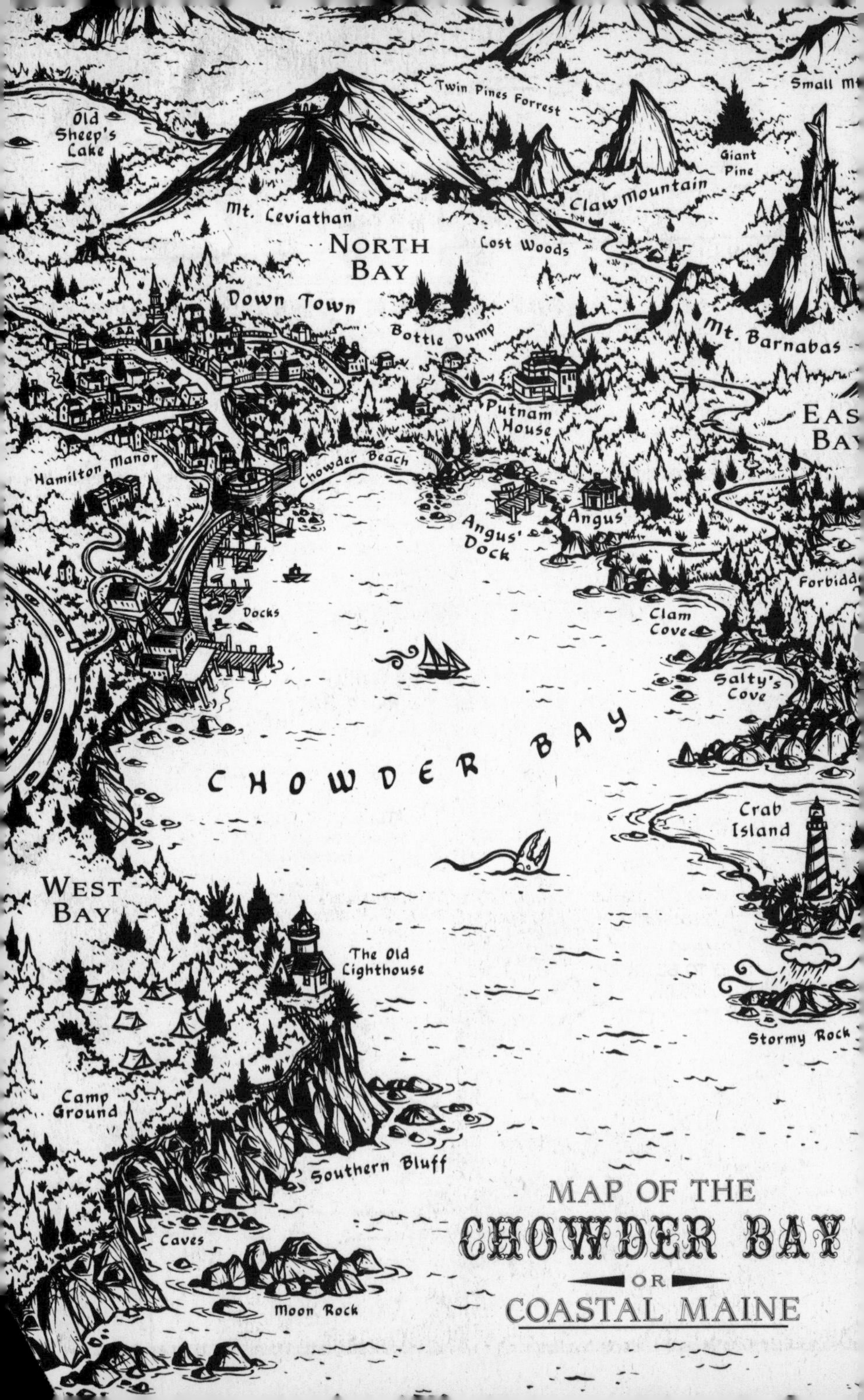
Old Sheep's Lake
Twin Pines Forrest
Giant Pine
Claw Mountain
Mt. Leviathan
NORTH BAY
Lost Woods
Down Town
Bottle Dump
Mt. Barnabas
Putnam House
Hamilton Manor
Chowder Beach
Angus' Dock
Angus'
Docks
Clam Cove
Salty's Cove
CHOWDER BAY
Crab Island
WEST BAY
The Old Lighthouse
Stormy Rock
Camp Ground
Southern Bluff
Caves
Moon Rock
MAP OF THE
CHOWDER BAY
OR
COASTAL MAINE

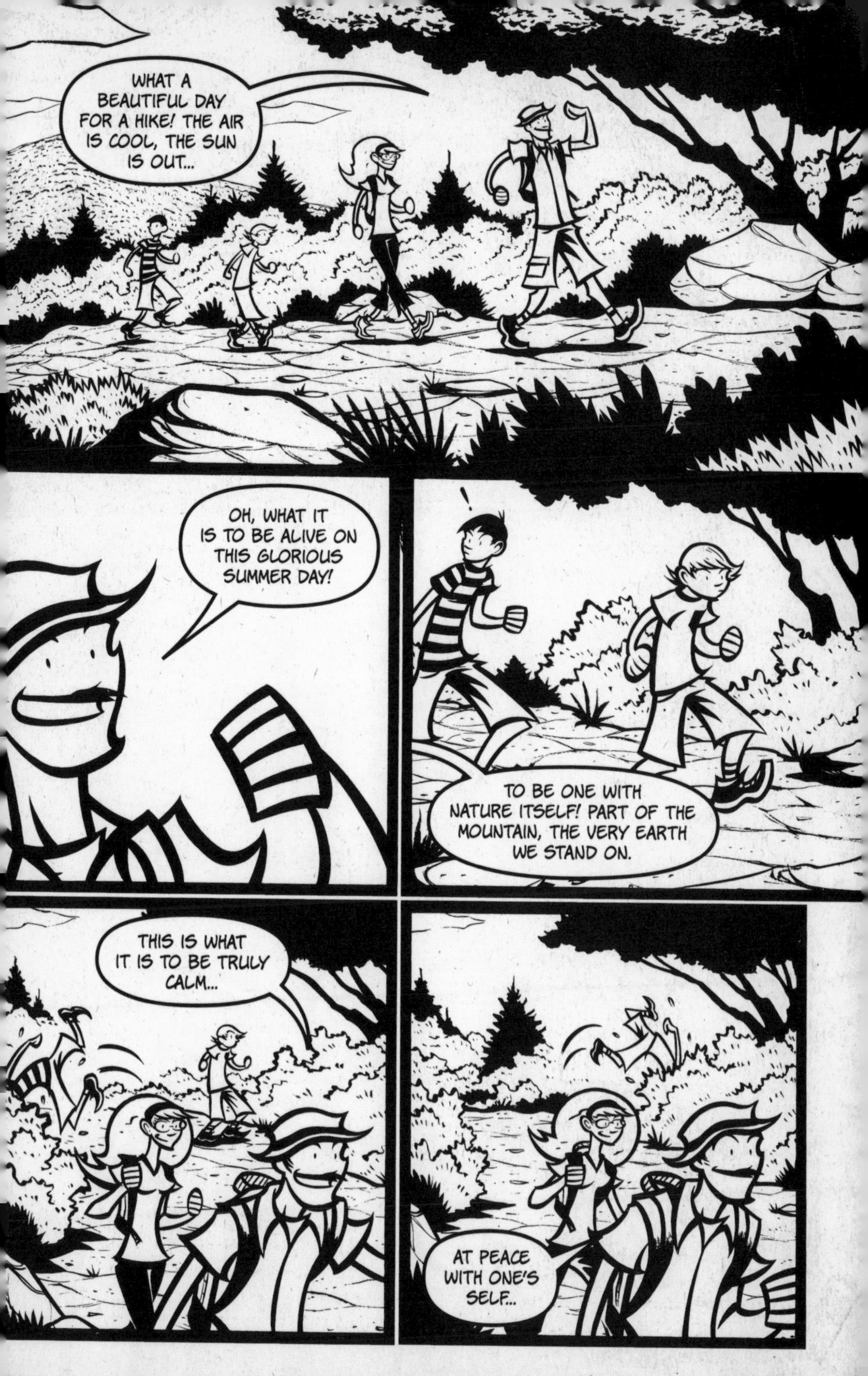
WHAT A BEAUTIFUL DAY FOR A HIKE! THE AIR IS COOL, THE SUN IS OUT...
OH, WHAT IT IS TO BE ALIVE ON THIS GLORIOUS SUMMER DAY!
!
TO BE ONE WITH NATURE ITSELF! PART OF THE MOUNTAIN, THE VERY EARTH WE STAND ON.
THIS IS WHAT IT IS TO BE TRULY CALM...
AT PEACE WITH ONE'S SELF...

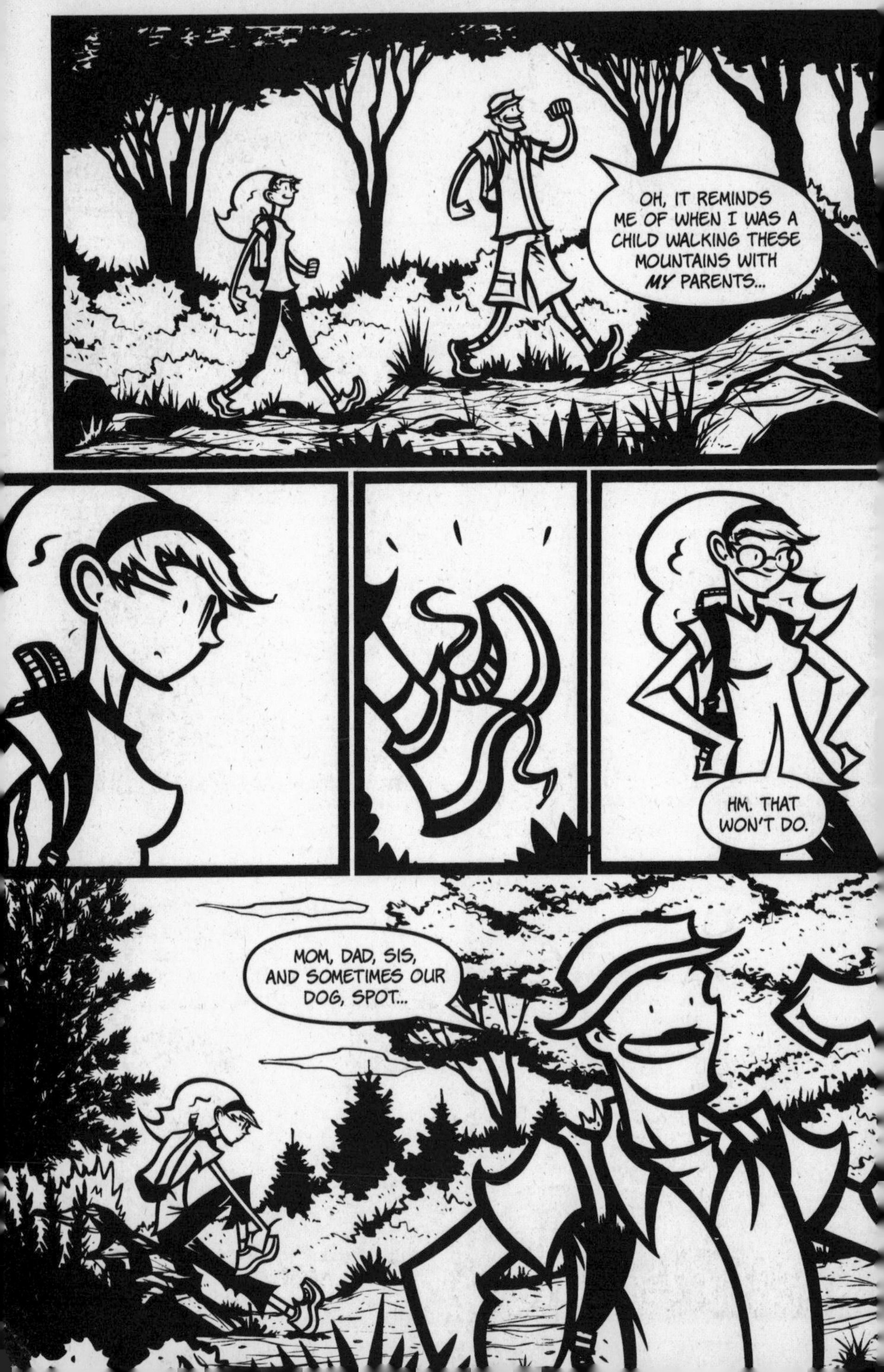
OH, IT REMINDS ME OF WHEN I WAS A CHILD WALKING THESE MOUNTAINS WITH *MY* PARENTS...
HM. THAT WON'T DO.
MOM, DAD, SIS, AND SOMETIMES OUR DOG, SPOT...

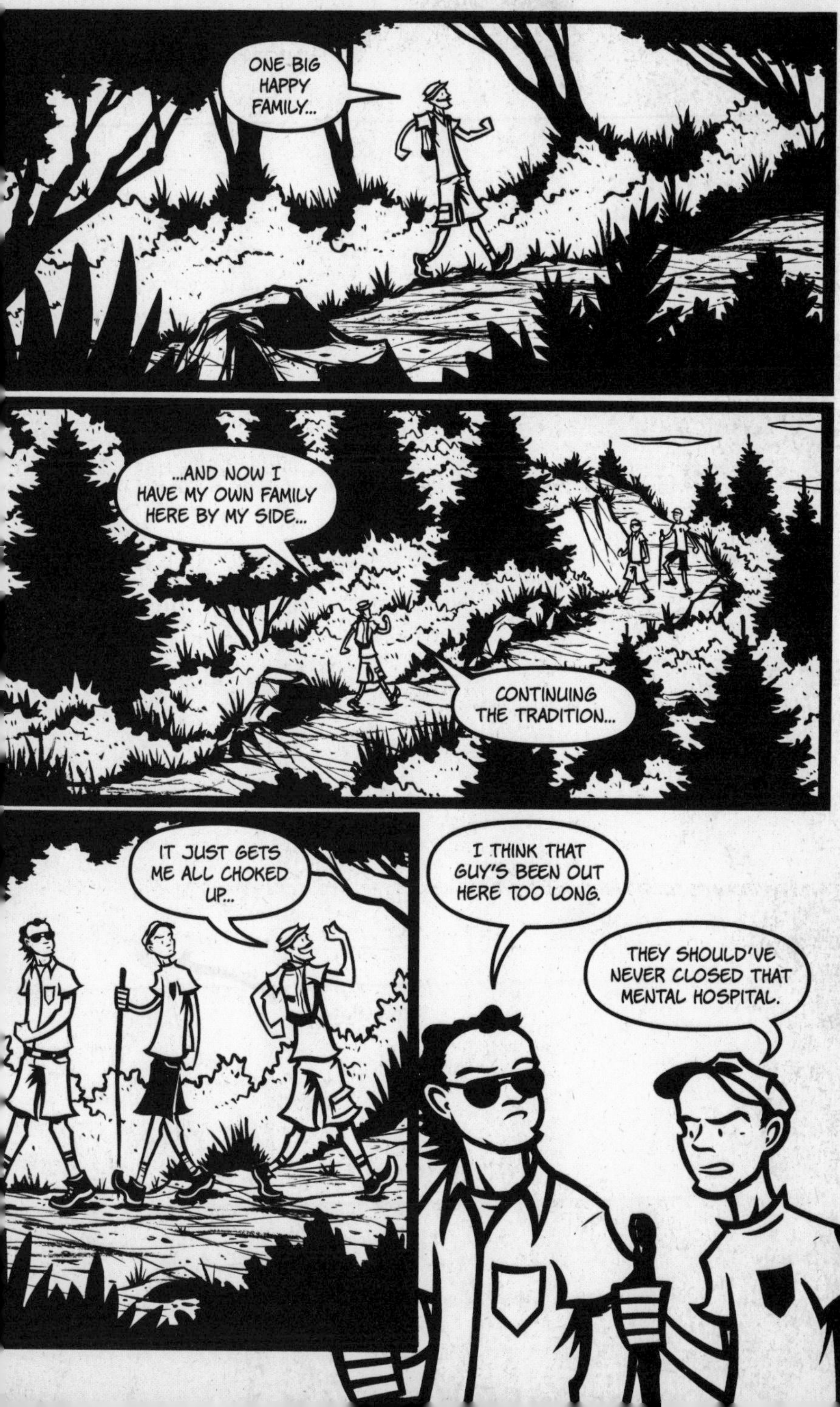
ONE BIG HAPPY FAMILY...
...AND NOW I HAVE MY OWN FAMILY HERE BY MY SIDE...
CONTINUING THE TRADITION...
IT JUST GETS ME ALL CHOKED UP...
I THINK THAT GUY'S BEEN OUT HERE TOO LONG.
THEY SHOULD'VE NEVER CLOSED THAT MENTAL HOSPITAL.

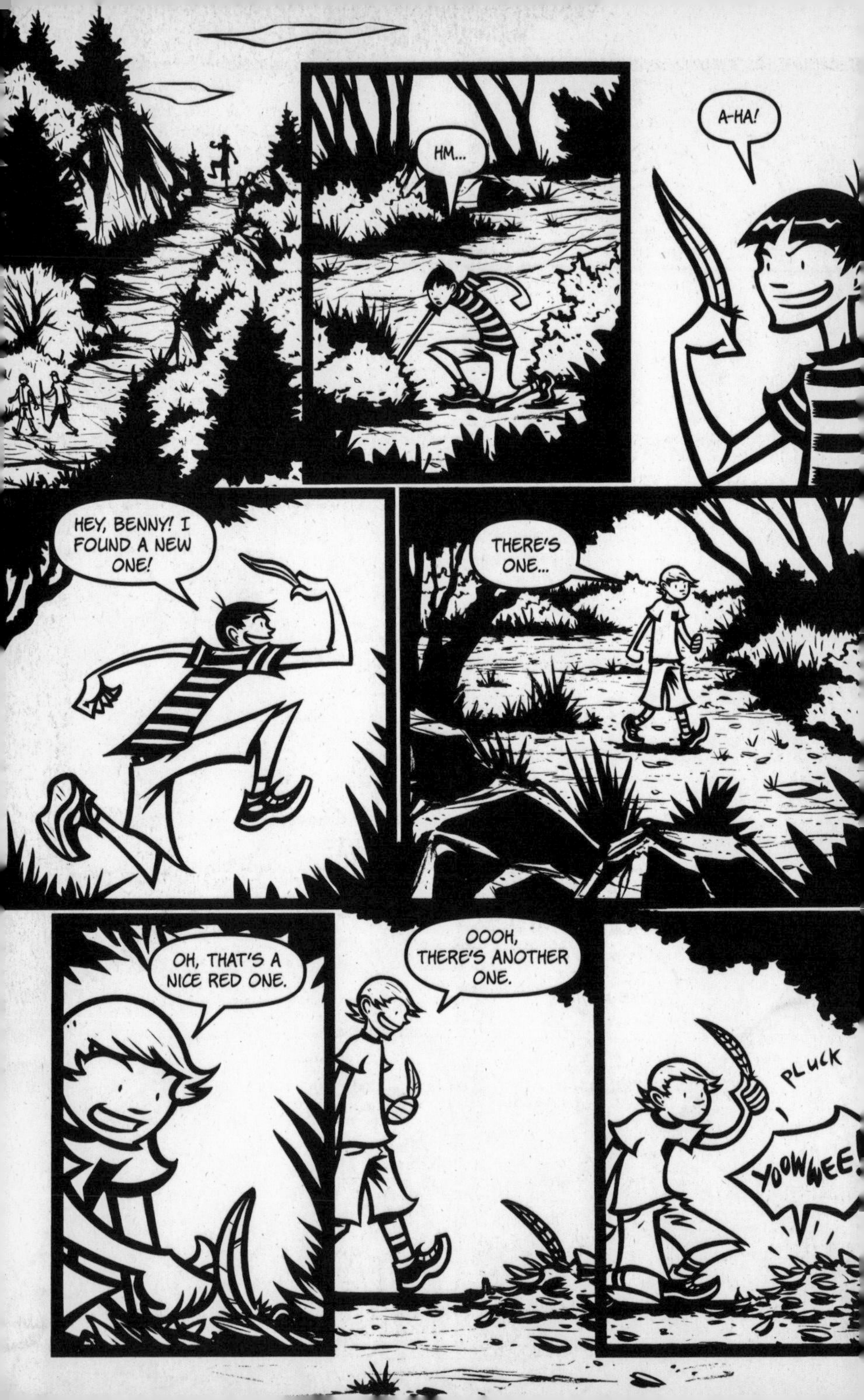
HM...
A-HA!
HEY, BENNY! I FOUND A NEW ONE!
THERE'S ONE...
OH, THAT'S A NICE RED ONE.
OOOH, THERE'S ANOTHER ONE.
PLUCK
YOOWWEE!

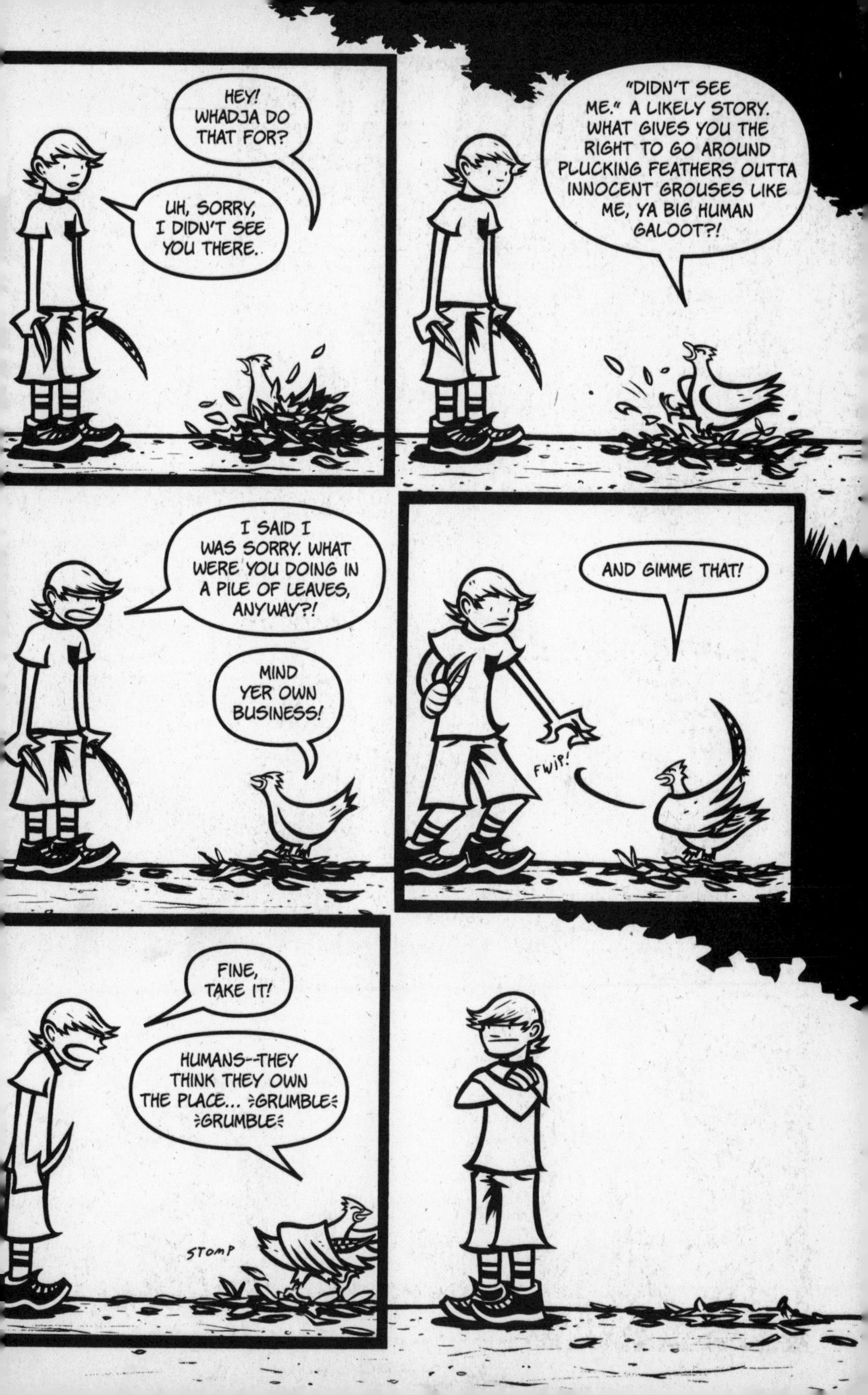
HEY! WHADJA DO THAT FOR?
UH, SORRY, I DIDN'T SEE YOU THERE.
"DIDN'T SEE ME." A LIKELY STORY. WHAT GIVES YOU THE RIGHT TO GO AROUND PLUCKING FEATHERS OUTTA INNOCENT GROUSES LIKE ME, YA BIG HUMAN GALOOT?!
I SAID I WAS SORRY. WHAT WERE YOU DOING IN A PILE OF LEAVES, ANYWAY?!
MIND YER OWN BUSINESS!
AND GIMME THAT!
FWIP!
FINE, TAKE IT!
HUMANS--THEY THINK THEY OWN THE PLACE... ≶GRUMBLE≷ ≶GRUMBLE≷
STOMP

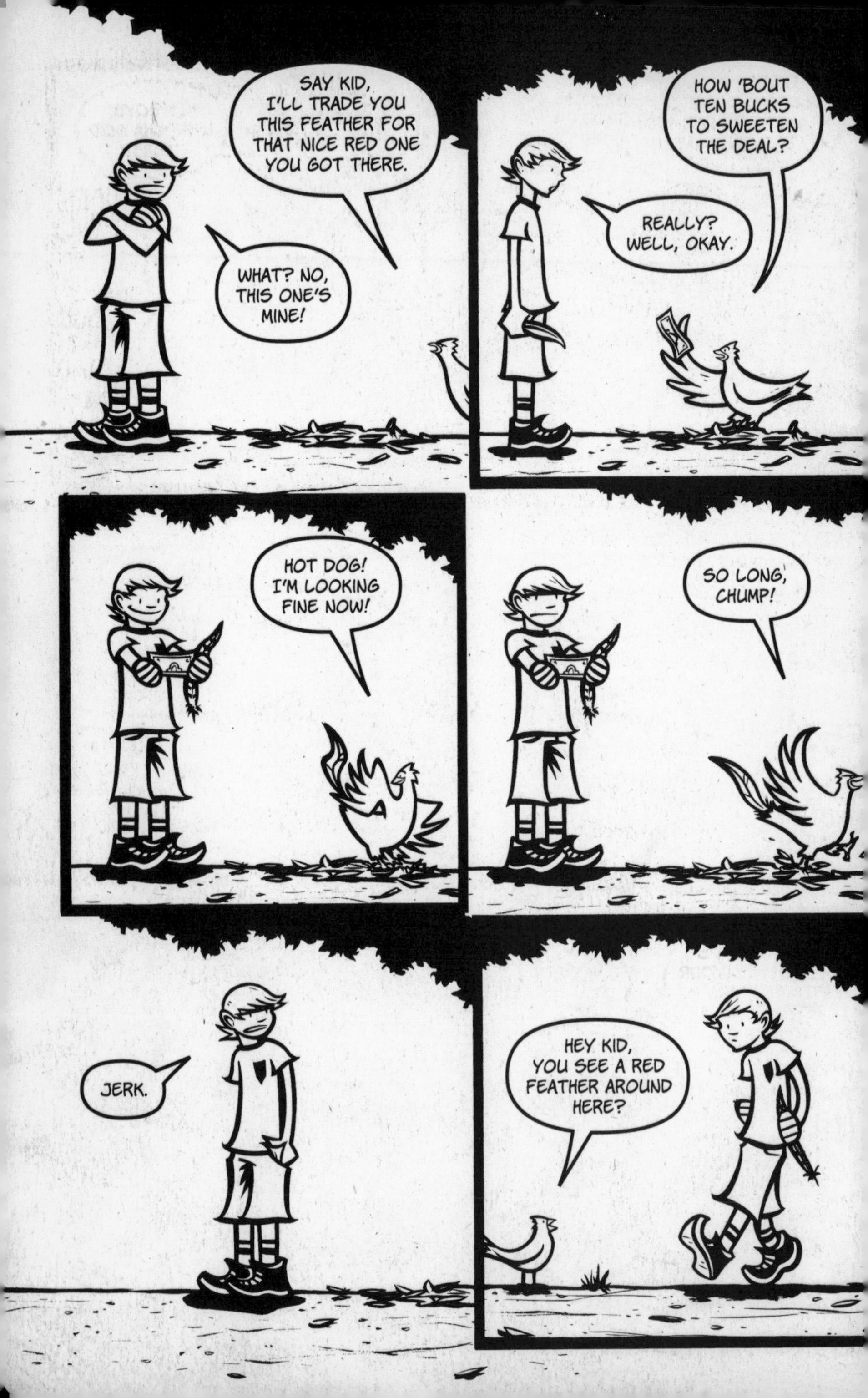
SAY KID, I'LL TRADE YOU THIS FEATHER FOR THAT NICE RED ONE YOU GOT THERE.
WHAT? NO, THIS ONE'S MINE!
HOW 'BOUT TEN BUCKS TO SWEETEN THE DEAL?
REALLY? WELL, OKAY.
HOT DOG! I'M LOOKING FINE NOW!
SO LONG, CHUMP!
JERK.
HEY KID, YOU SEE A RED FEATHER AROUND HERE?

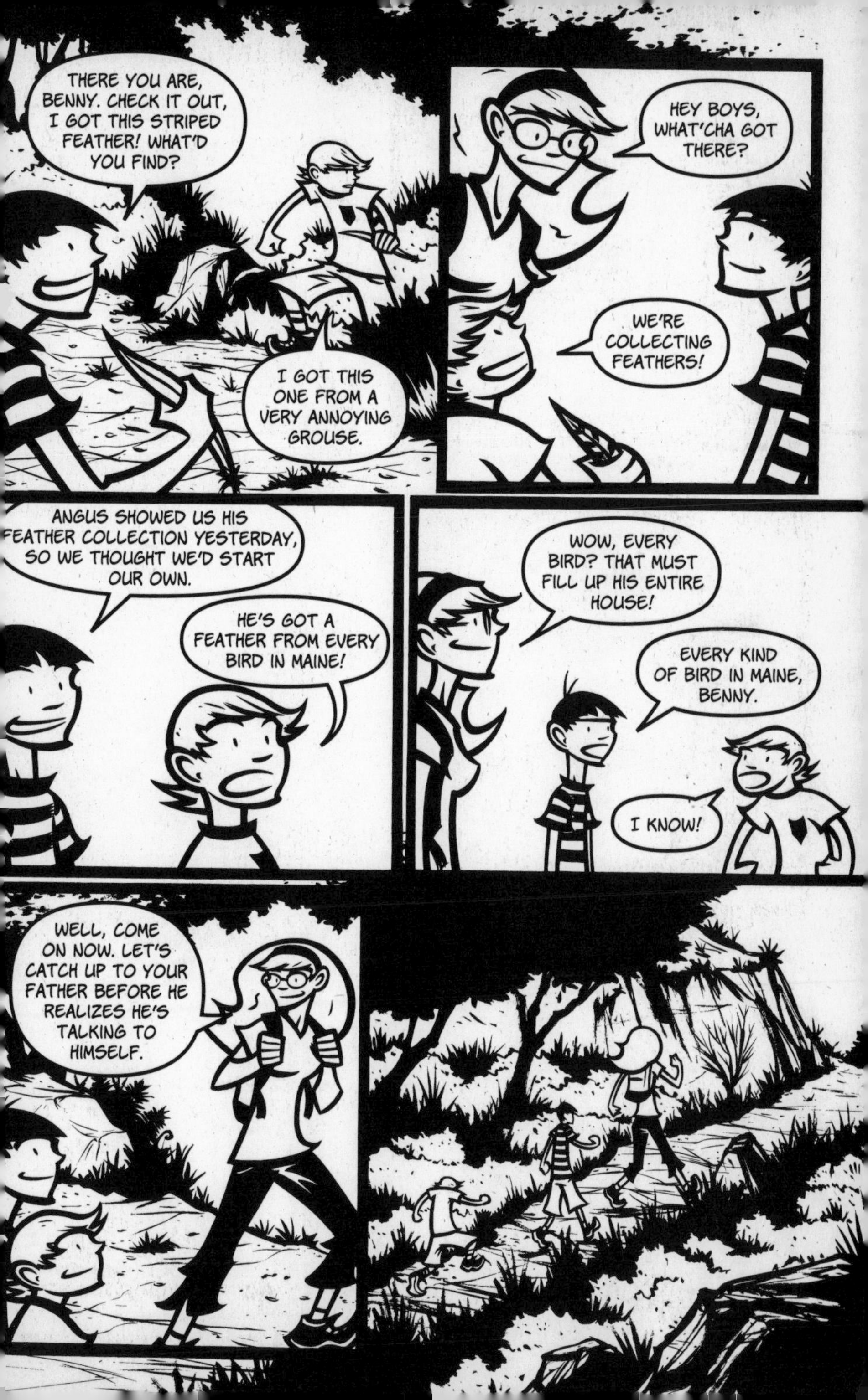
THERE YOU ARE, BENNY. CHECK IT OUT, I GOT THIS STRIPED FEATHER! WHAT'D YOU FIND?
I GOT THIS ONE FROM A VERY ANNOYING GROUSE.
HEY BOYS, WHAT'CHA GOT THERE?
WE'RE COLLECTING FEATHERS!
ANGUS SHOWED US HIS FEATHER COLLECTION YESTERDAY, SO WE THOUGHT WE'D START OUR OWN.
HE'S GOT A FEATHER FROM EVERY BIRD IN MAINE!
WOW, EVERY BIRD? THAT MUST FILL UP HIS ENTIRE HOUSE!
EVERY KIND OF BIRD IN MAINE, BENNY.
I KNOW!
WELL, COME ON NOW. LET'S CATCH UP TO YOUR FATHER BEFORE HE REALIZES HE'S TALKING TO HIMSELF.

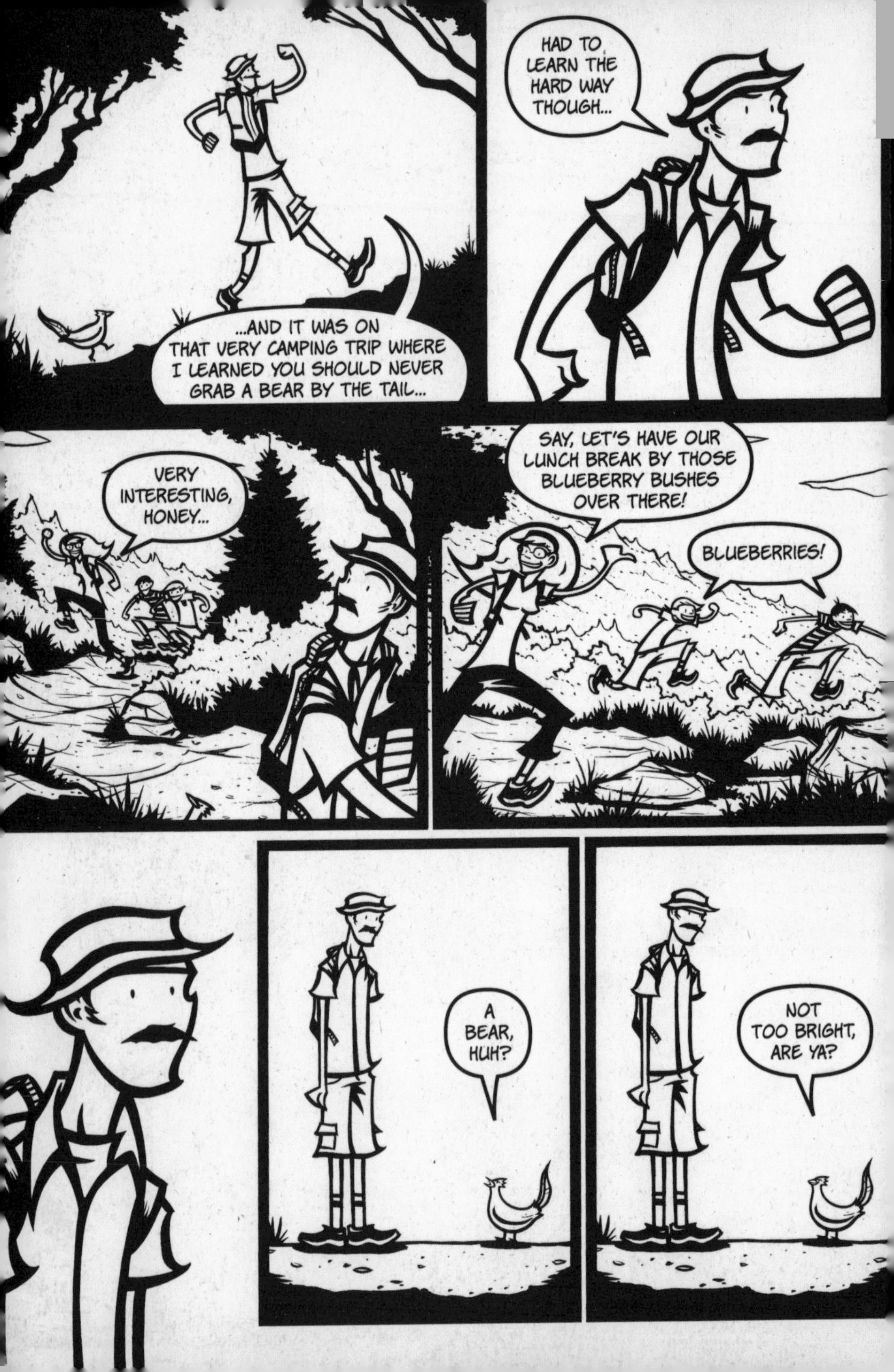
...AND IT WAS ON THAT VERY CAMPING TRIP WHERE I LEARNED YOU SHOULD NEVER GRAB A BEAR BY THE TAIL...
HAD TO LEARN THE HARD WAY THOUGH...
VERY INTERESTING, HONEY...
SAY, LET'S HAVE OUR LUNCH BREAK BY THOSE BLUEBERRY BUSHES OVER THERE!
BLUEBERRIES!
A BEAR, HUH?
NOT TOO BRIGHT, ARE YA?

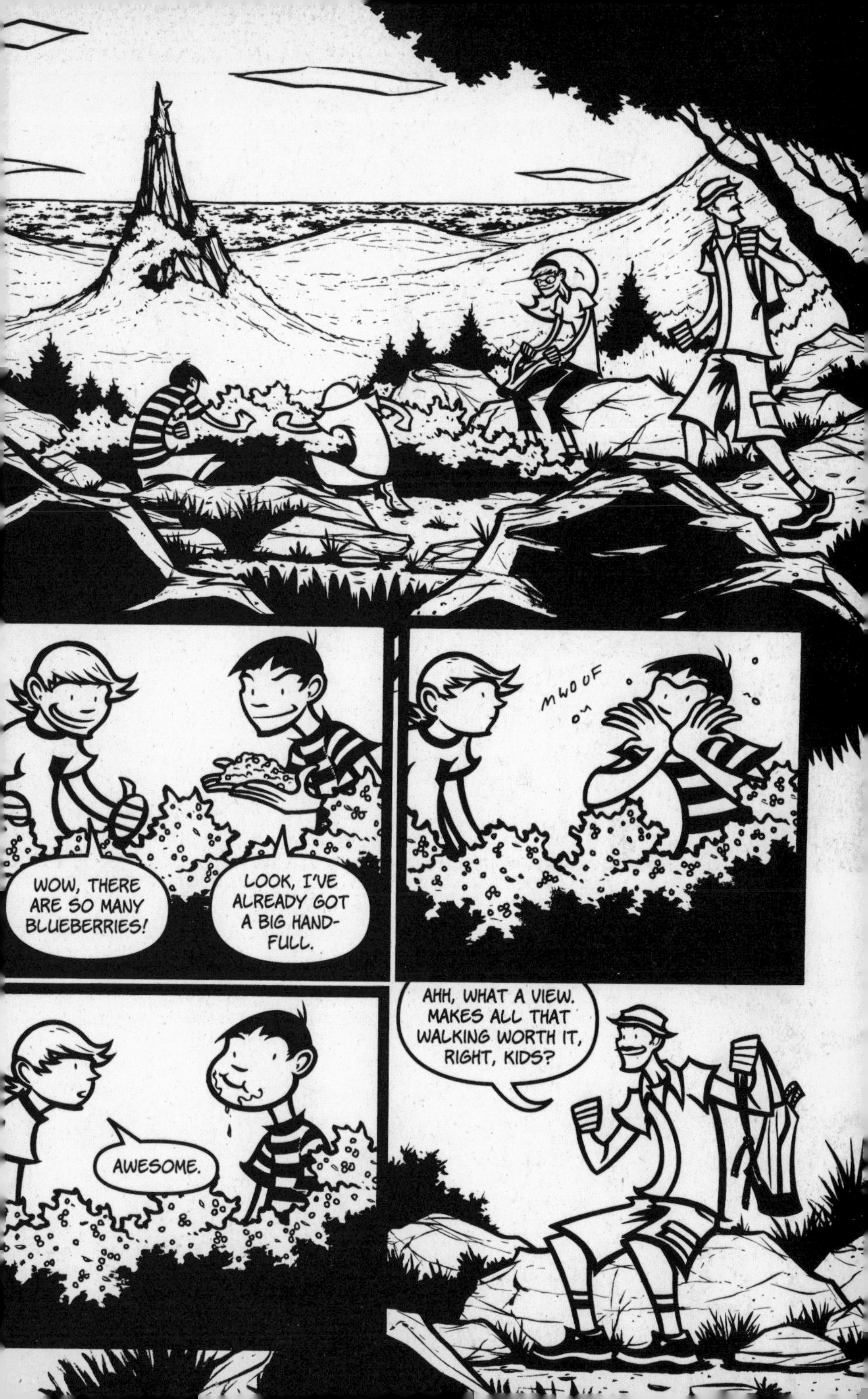
WOW, THERE ARE SO MANY BLUEBERRIES!
LOOK, I'VE ALREADY GOT A BIG HAND-FULL.
MWOOF
AWESOME.
AHH, WHAT A VIEW. MAKES ALL THAT WALKING WORTH IT, RIGHT, KIDS?

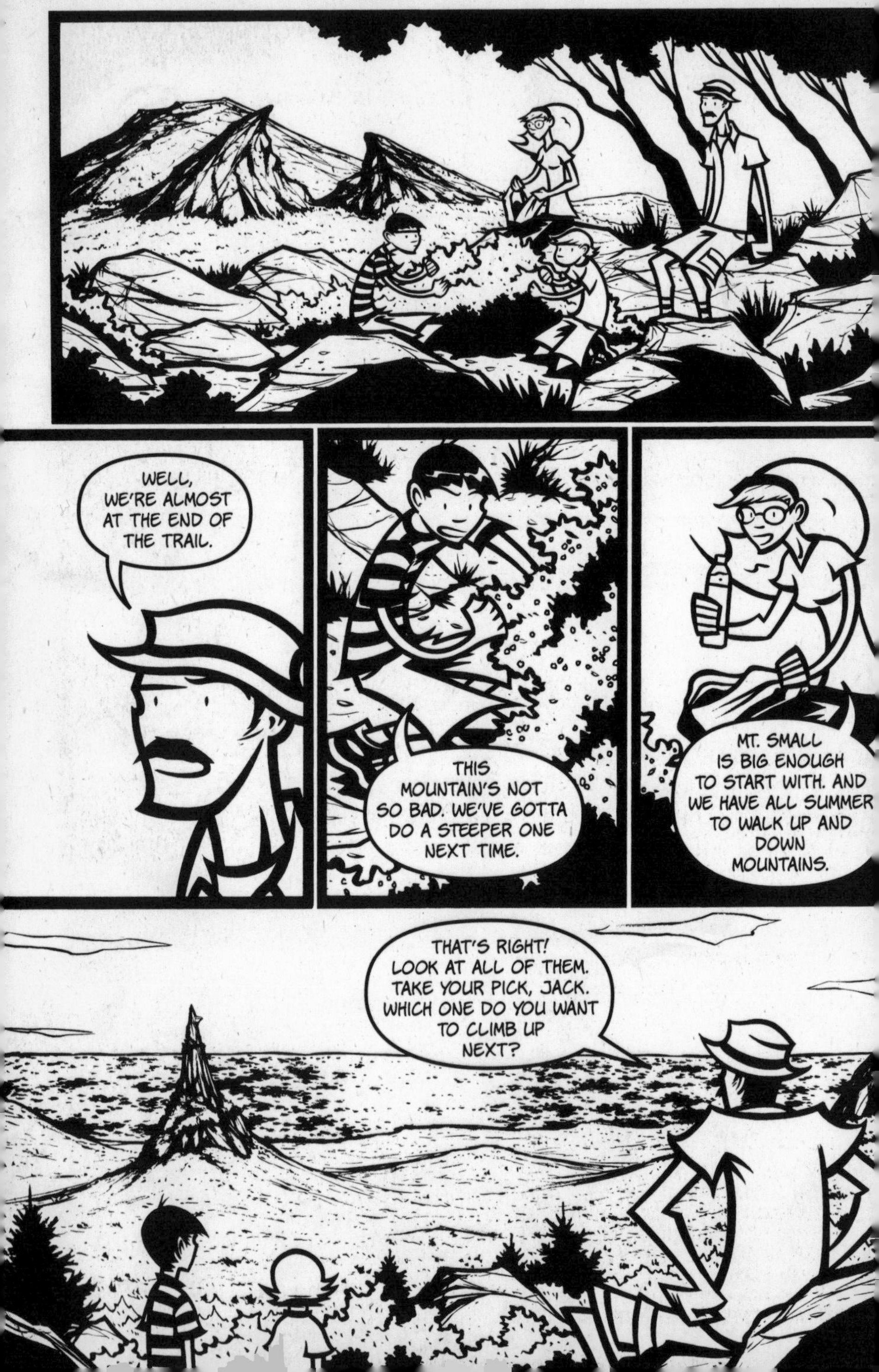

WELL, WE'RE ALMOST AT THE END OF THE TRAIL.
THIS MOUNTAIN'S NOT SO BAD. WE'VE GOTTA DO A STEEPER ONE NEXT TIME.
MT. SMALL IS BIG ENOUGH TO START WITH. AND WE HAVE ALL SUMMER TO WALK UP AND DOWN MOUNTAINS.
THAT'S RIGHT! LOOK AT ALL OF THEM. TAKE YOUR PICK, JACK. WHICH ONE DO YOU WANT TO CLIMB UP NEXT?

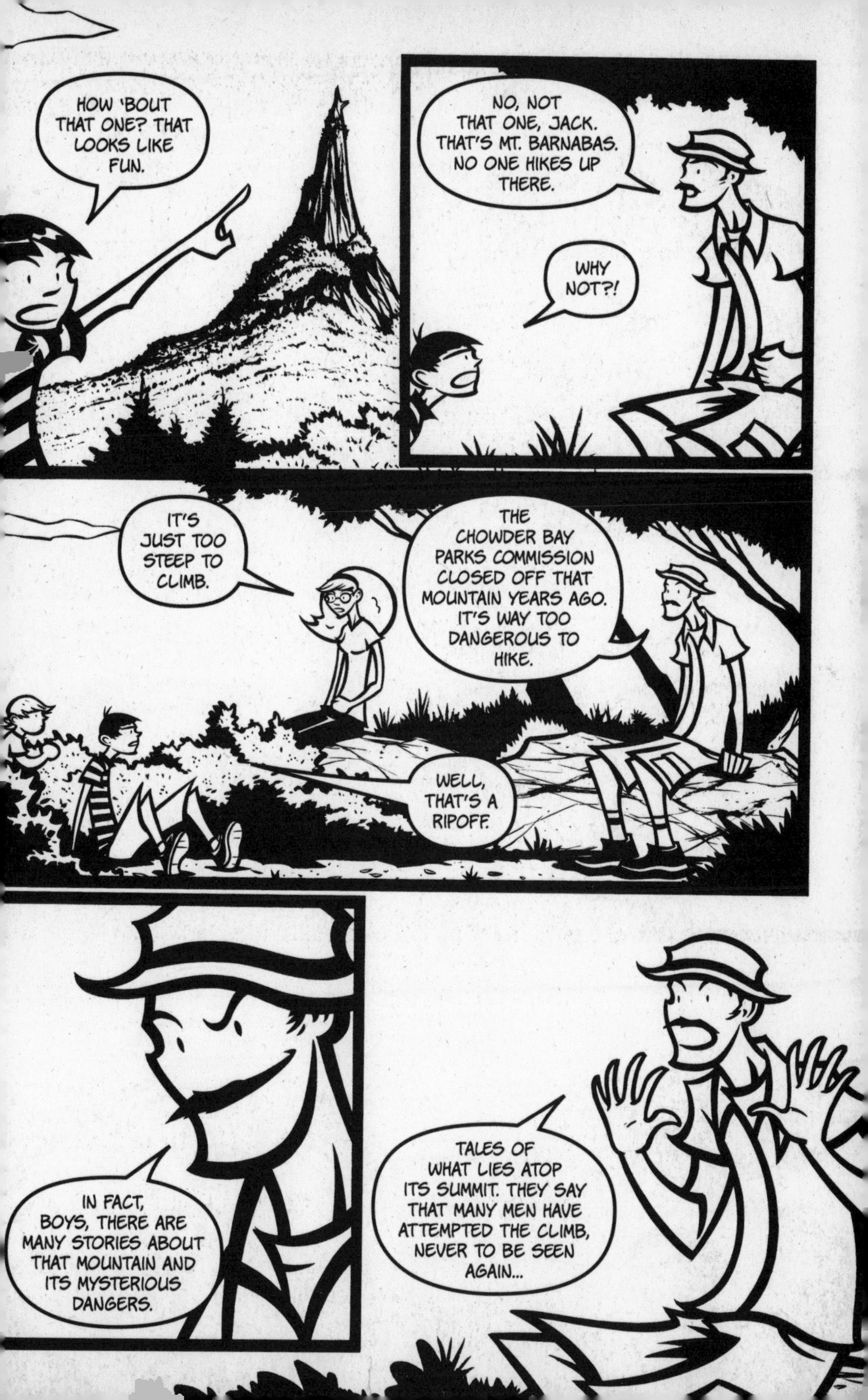
HOW 'BOUT THAT ONE? THAT LOOKS LIKE FUN.
NO, NOT THAT ONE, JACK. THAT'S MT. BARNABAS. NO ONE HIKES UP THERE.
WHY NOT?!
IT'S JUST TOO STEEP TO CLIMB.
THE CHOWDER BAY PARKS COMMISSION CLOSED OFF THAT MOUNTAIN YEARS AGO. IT'S WAY TOO DANGEROUS TO HIKE.
WELL, THAT'S A RIPOFF.
IN FACT, BOYS, THERE ARE MANY STORIES ABOUT THAT MOUNTAIN AND ITS MYSTERIOUS DANGERS.
TALES OF WHAT LIES ATOP ITS SUMMIT. THEY SAY THAT MANY MEN HAVE ATTEMPTED THE CLIMB, NEVER TO BE SEEN AGAIN...

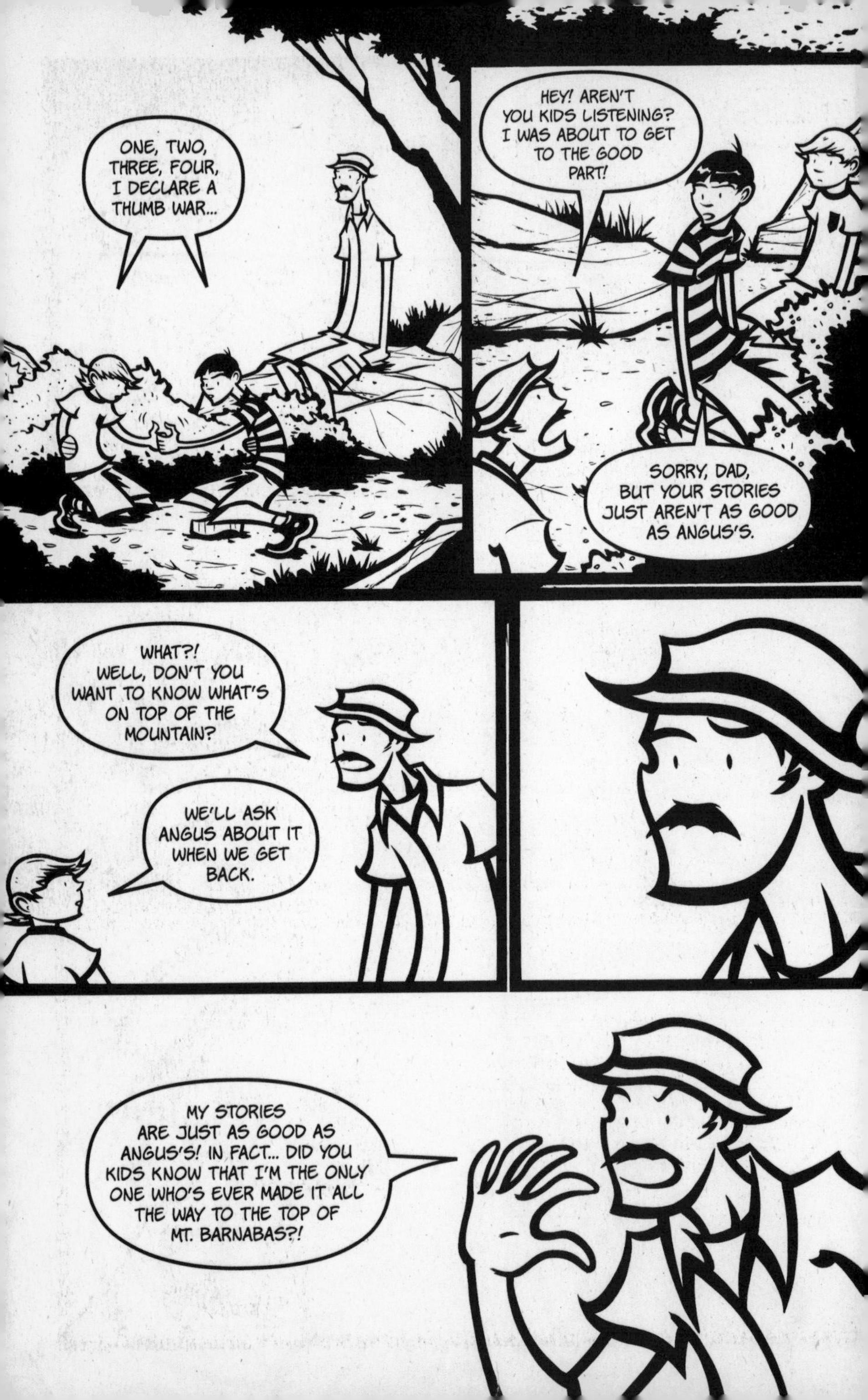
ONE, TWO, THREE, FOUR, I DECLARE A THUMB WAR...
HEY! AREN'T YOU KIDS LISTENING? I WAS ABOUT TO GET TO THE GOOD PART!
SORRY, DAD, BUT YOUR STORIES JUST AREN'T AS GOOD AS ANGUS'S.
WHAT?! WELL, DON'T YOU WANT TO KNOW WHAT'S ON TOP OF THE MOUNTAIN?
WE'LL ASK ANGUS ABOUT IT WHEN WE GET BACK.
MY STORIES ARE JUST AS GOOD AS ANGUS'S! IN FACT... DID YOU KIDS KNOW THAT I'M THE ONLY ONE WHO'S EVER MADE IT ALL THE WAY TO THE TOP OF MT. BARNABAS?!

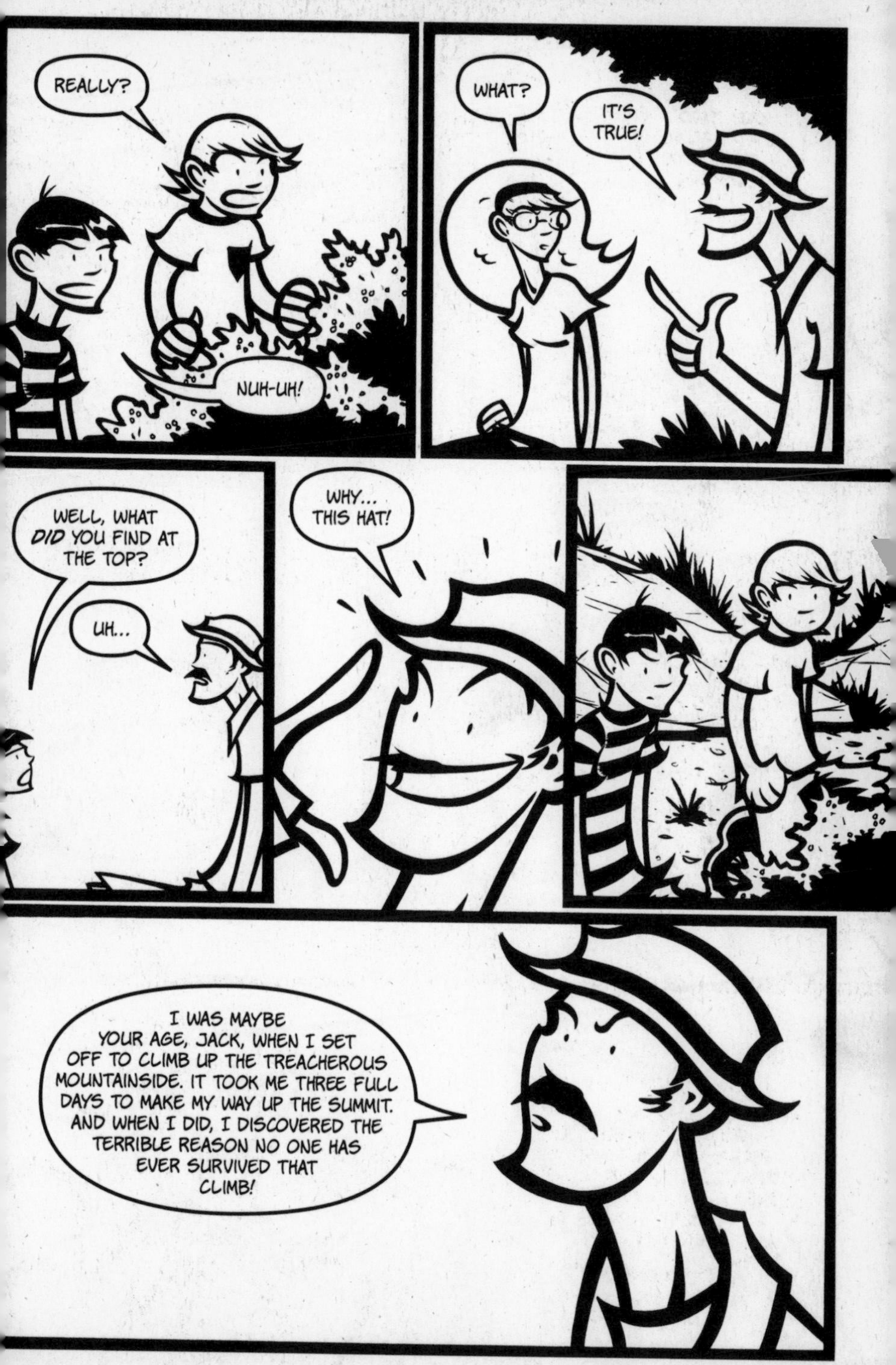
REALLY?
NUH-UH!
WHAT?
IT'S TRUE!
WELL, WHAT *DID* YOU FIND AT THE TOP?
UH...
WHY... THIS HAT!
I WAS MAYBE YOUR AGE, JACK, WHEN I SET OFF TO CLIMB UP THE TREACHEROUS MOUNTAINSIDE. IT TOOK ME THREE FULL DAYS TO MAKE MY WAY UP THE SUMMIT. AND WHEN I DID, I DISCOVERED THE TERRIBLE REASON NO ONE HAS EVER SURVIVED THAT CLIMB!

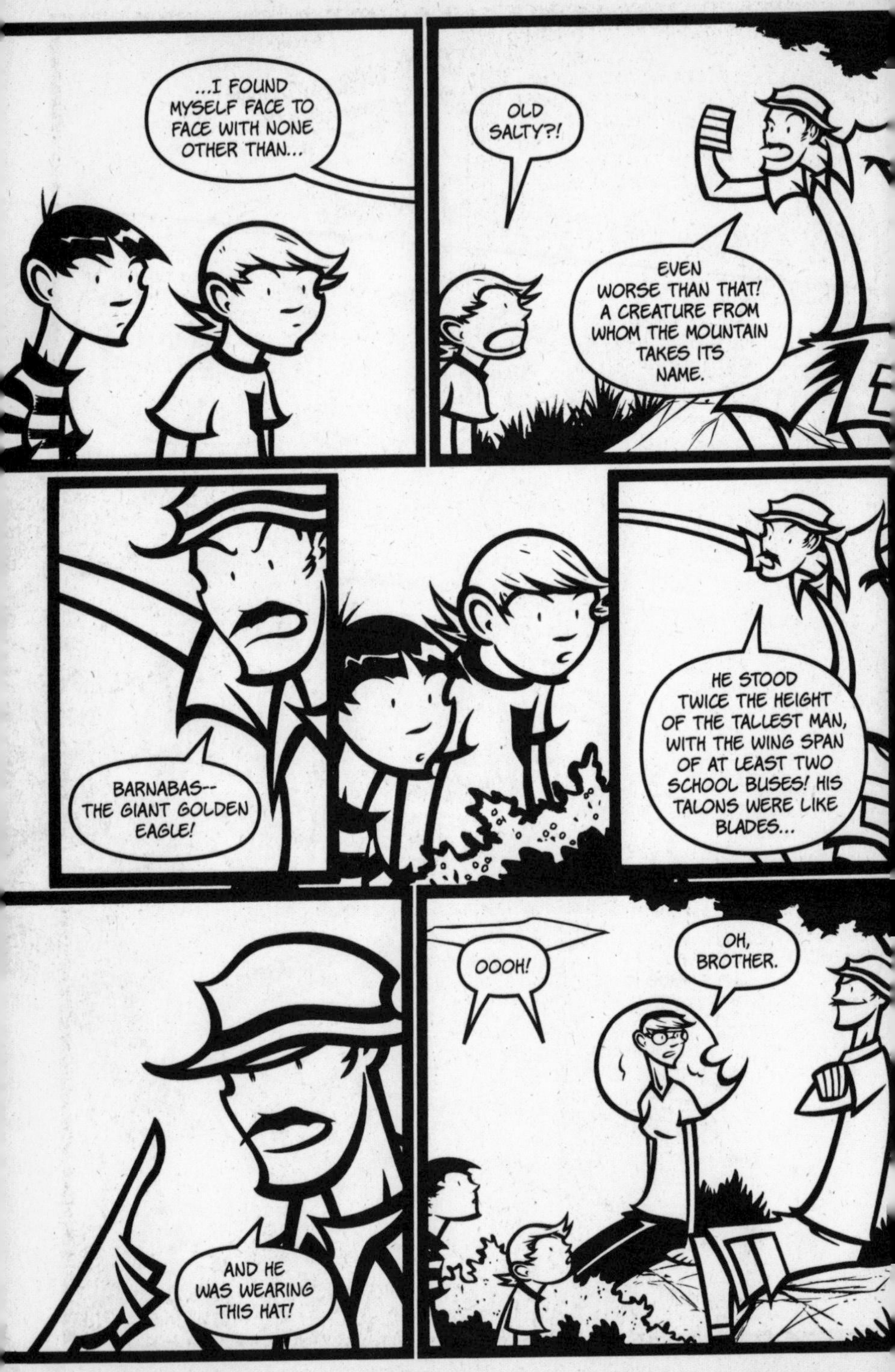
...I FOUND MYSELF FACE TO FACE WITH NONE OTHER THAN...
OLD SALTY?!
EVEN WORSE THAN THAT! A CREATURE FROM WHOM THE MOUNTAIN TAKES ITS NAME.
BARNABAS-- THE GIANT GOLDEN EAGLE!
HE STOOD TWICE THE HEIGHT OF THE TALLEST MAN, WITH THE WING SPAN OF AT LEAST TWO SCHOOL BUSES! HIS TALONS WERE LIKE BLADES...
AND HE WAS WEARING THIS HAT!
OOOH!
OH, BROTHER.

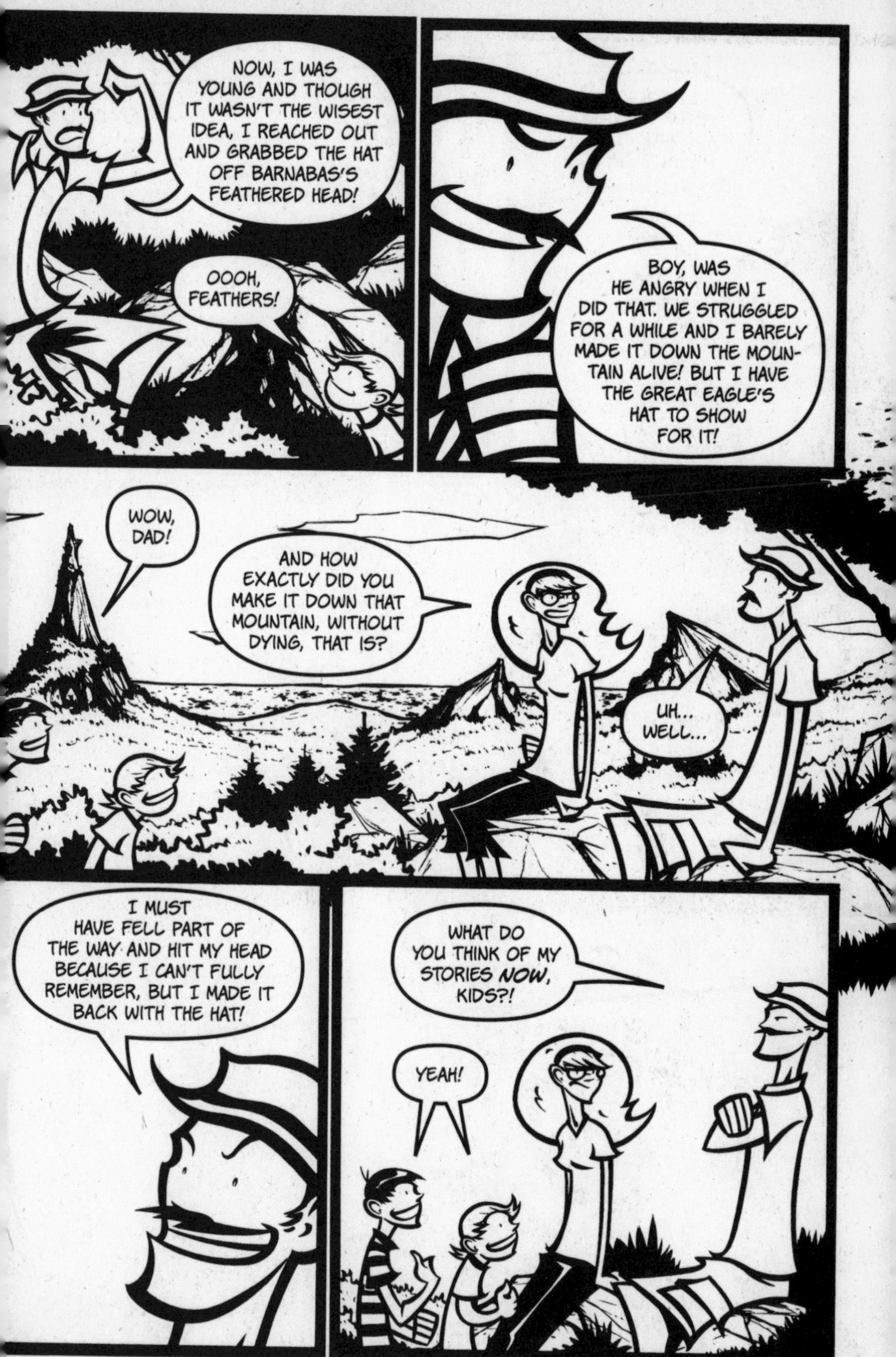
NOW, I WAS YOUNG AND THOUGH IT WASN'T THE WISEST IDEA, I REACHED OUT AND GRABBED THE HAT OFF BARNABAS'S FEATHERED HEAD!
OOOH, FEATHERS!
BOY, WAS HE ANGRY WHEN I DID THAT. WE STRUGGLED FOR A WHILE AND I BARELY MADE IT DOWN THE MOUNTAIN ALIVE! BUT I HAVE THE GREAT EAGLE'S HAT TO SHOW FOR IT!
WOW, DAD!
AND HOW EXACTLY DID YOU MAKE IT DOWN THAT MOUNTAIN, WITHOUT DYING, THAT IS?
UH... WELL...
I MUST HAVE FELL PART OF THE WAY AND HIT MY HEAD BECAUSE I CAN'T FULLY REMEMBER, BUT I MADE IT BACK WITH THE HAT!
WHAT DO YOU THINK OF MY STORIES *NOW*, KIDS?!
YEAH!

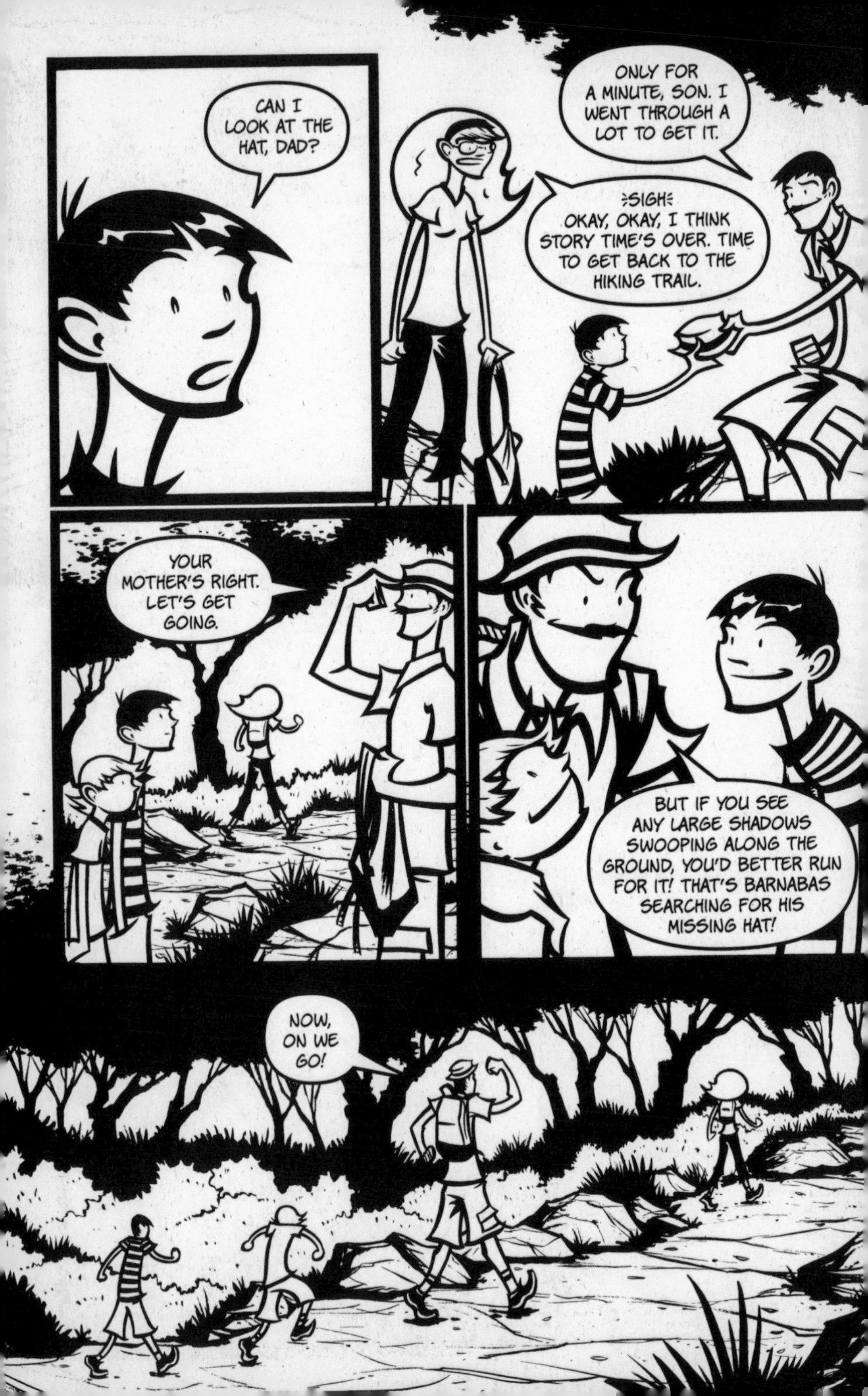
CAN I LOOK AT THE HAT, DAD?
ONLY FOR A MINUTE, SON. I WENT THROUGH A LOT TO GET IT.
SIGH
OKAY, OKAY, I THINK STORY TIME'S OVER. TIME TO GET BACK TO THE HIKING TRAIL.
YOUR MOTHER'S RIGHT. LET'S GET GOING.
BUT IF YOU SEE ANY LARGE SHADOWS SWOOPING ALONG THE GROUND, YOU'D BETTER RUN FOR IT! THAT'S BARNABAS SEARCHING FOR HIS MISSING HAT!
NOW, ON WE GO!

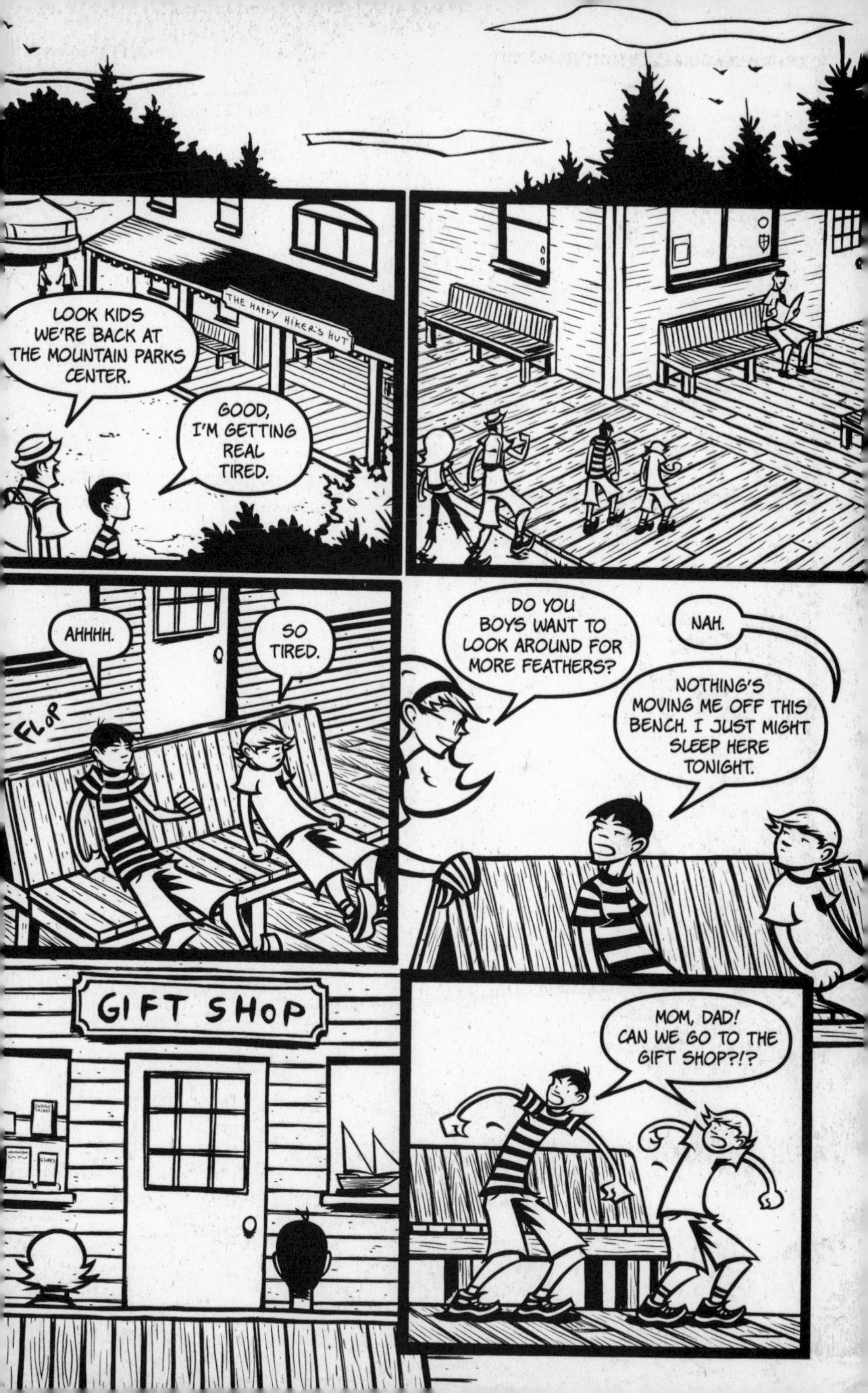
LOOK KIDS WE'RE BACK AT THE MOUNTAIN PARKS CENTER.
THE HAPPY HIKER'S HUT
GOOD, I'M GETTING REAL TIRED.
FLOP
AHHHH.
SO TIRED.
DO YOU BOYS WANT TO LOOK AROUND FOR MORE FEATHERS?
NAH.
NOTHING'S MOVING ME OFF THIS BENCH. I JUST MIGHT SLEEP HERE TONIGHT.
GIFT SHOP
MOM, DAD! CAN WE GO TO THE GIFT SHOP?!?

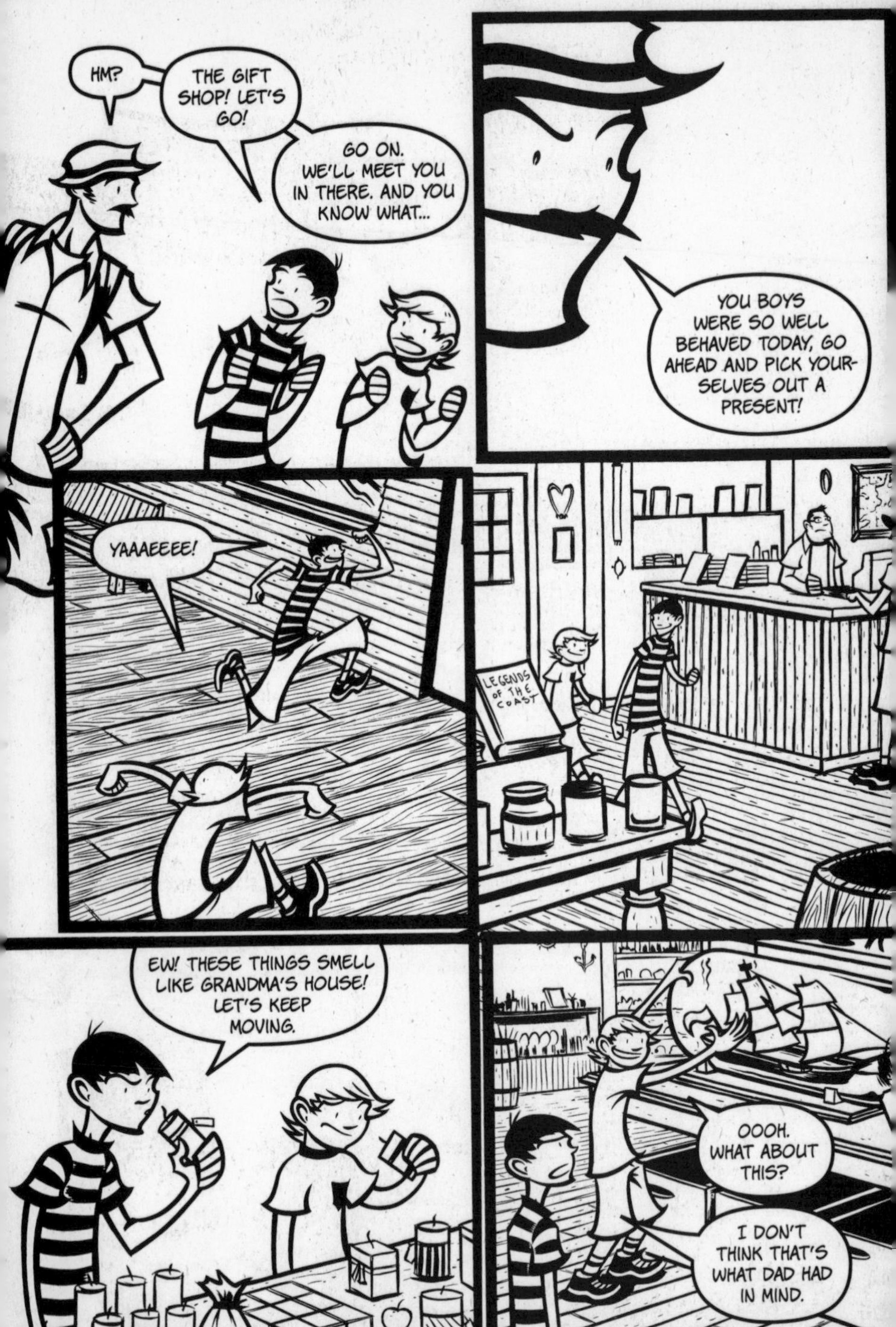
HM?
THE GIFT SHOP! LET'S GO!
GO ON. WE'LL MEET YOU IN THERE. AND YOU KNOW WHAT...
YOU BOYS WERE SO WELL BEHAVED TODAY, GO AHEAD AND PICK YOURSELVES OUT A PRESENT!
YAAAEEEE!
LEGENDS OF THE COAST
EW! THESE THINGS SMELL LIKE GRANDMA'S HOUSE! LET'S KEEP MOVING.
OOOH. WHAT ABOUT THIS?
I DON'T THINK THAT'S WHAT DAD HAD IN MIND.

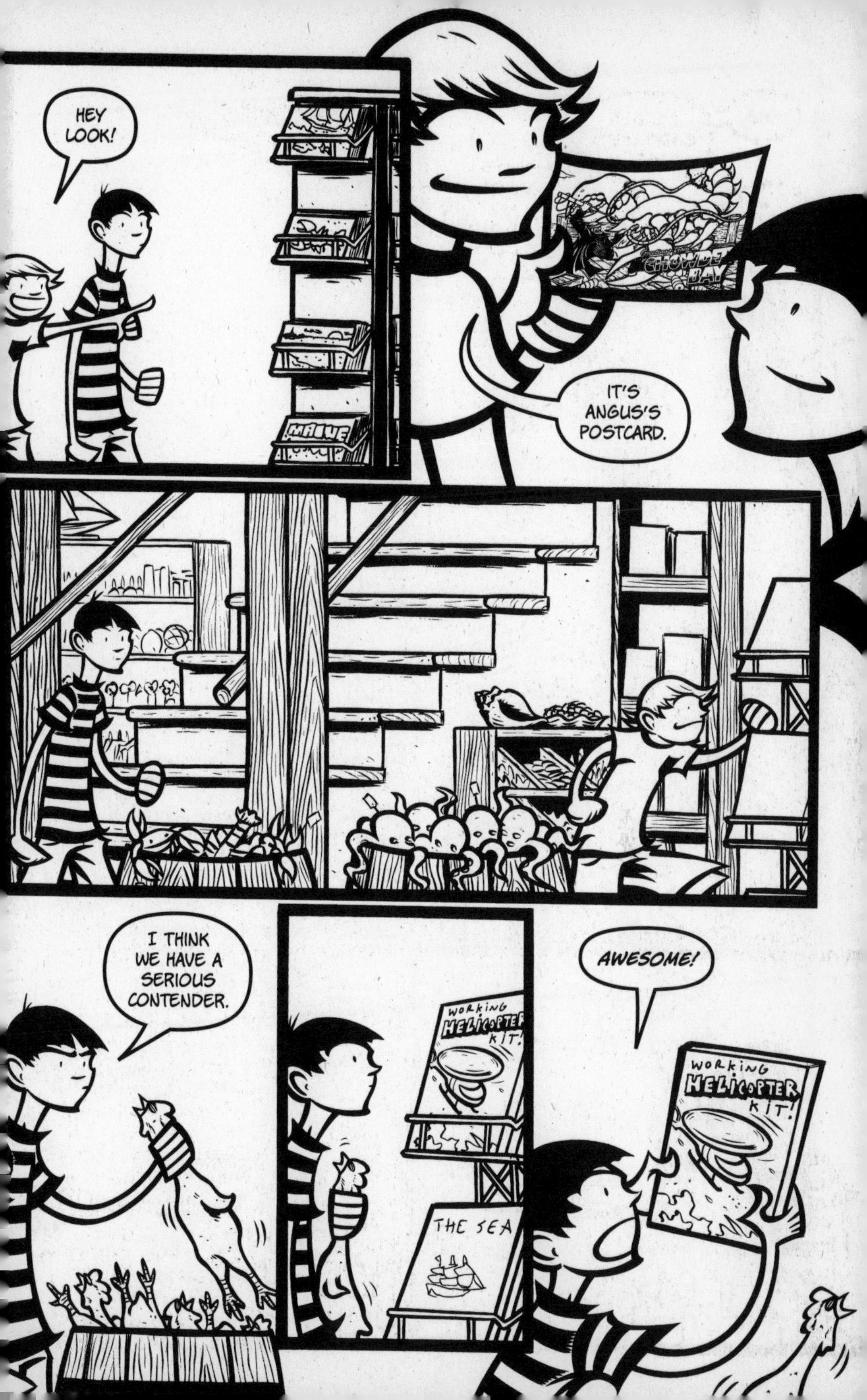
HEY LOOK!
BAY
IT'S ANGUS'S POSTCARD.
I THINK WE HAVE A SERIOUS CONTENDER.
WORKING HELICOPTER KIT!
THE SEA
AWESOME!
WORKING HELICOPTER KIT!

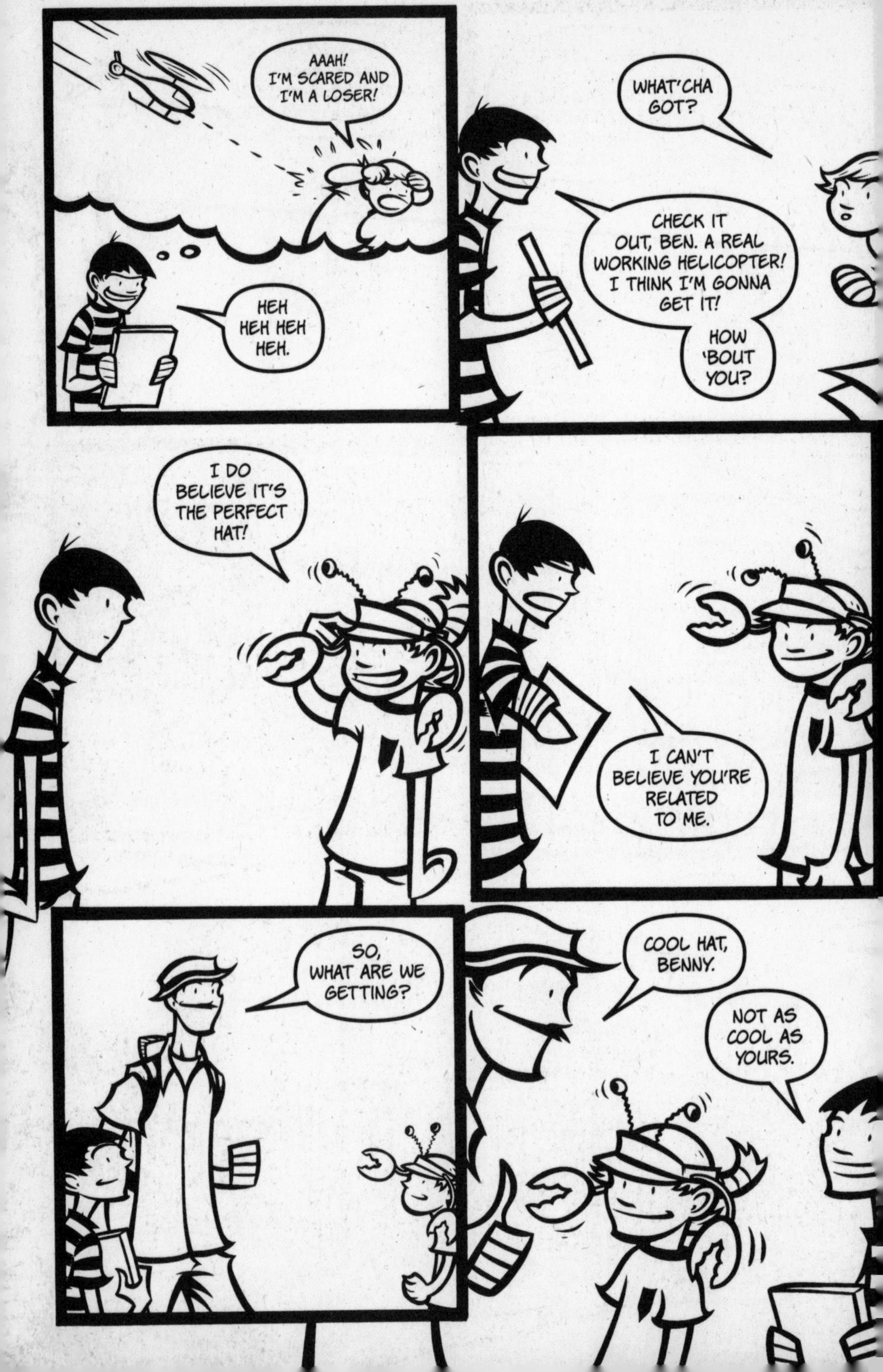
AAAH! I'M SCARED AND I'M A LOSER!
HEH HEH HEH HEH.
WHAT'CHA GOT?
CHECK IT OUT, BEN. A REAL WORKING HELICOPTER! I THINK I'M GONNA GET IT!
HOW 'BOUT YOU?
I DO BELIEVE IT'S THE PERFECT HAT!
I CAN'T BELIEVE YOU'RE RELATED TO ME.
SO, WHAT ARE WE GETTING?
COOL HAT, BENNY.
NOT AS COOL AS YOURS.

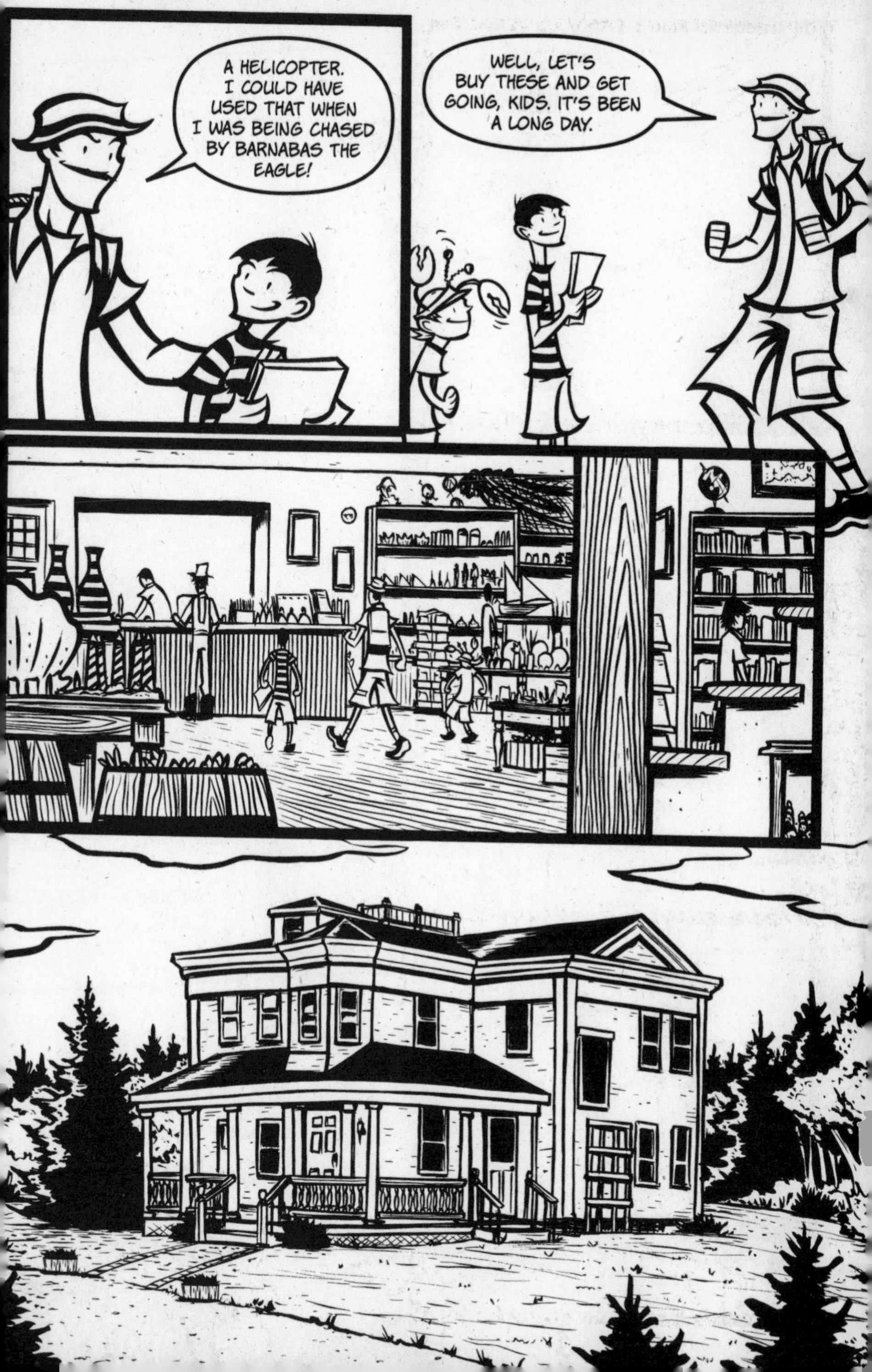
A HELICOPTER. I COULD HAVE USED THAT WHEN I WAS BEING CHASED BY BARNABAS THE EAGLE!
WELL, LET'S BUY THESE AND GET GOING, KIDS. IT'S BEEN A LONG DAY.

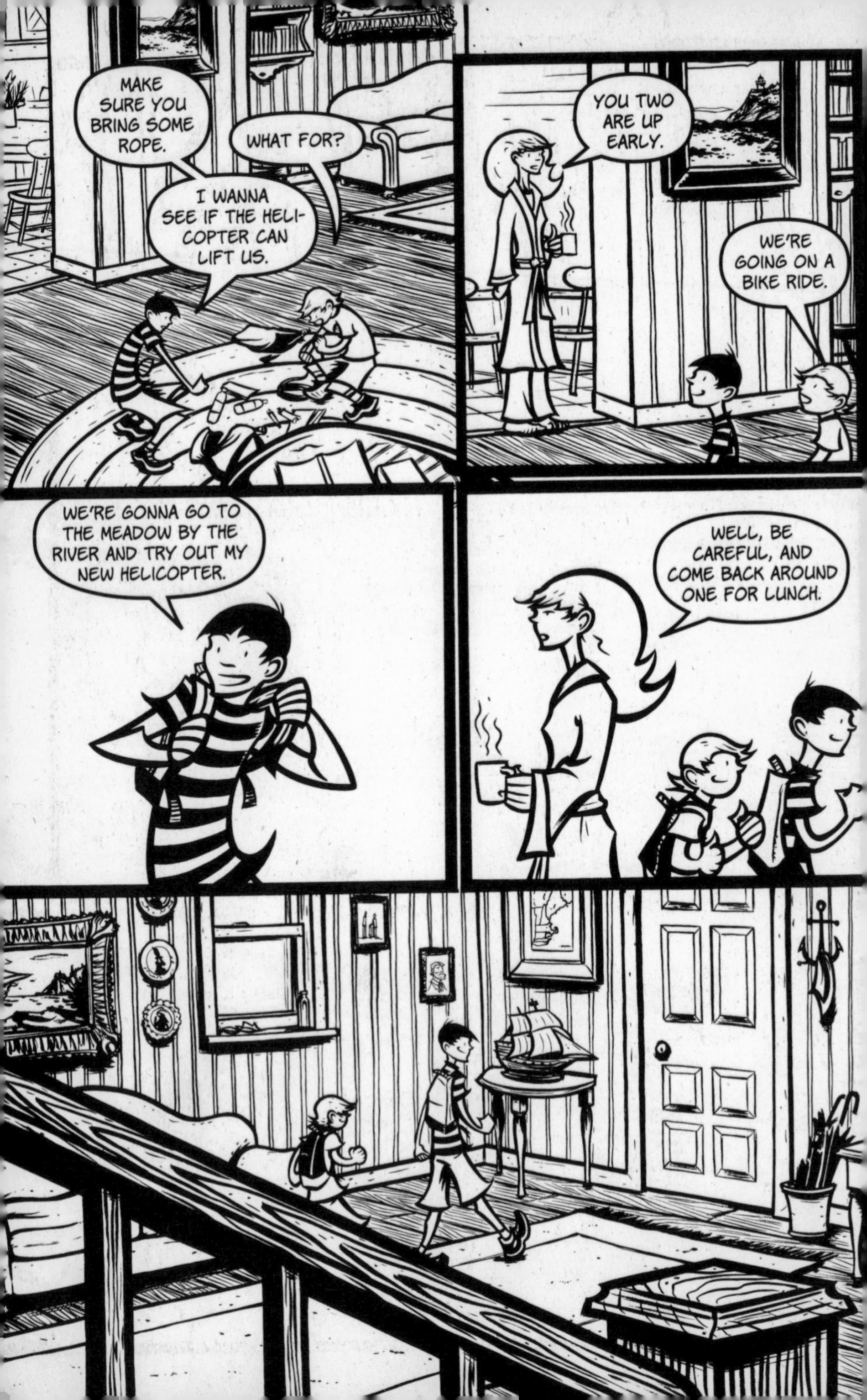
MAKE SURE YOU BRING SOME ROPE.
WHAT FOR?
I WANNA SEE IF THE HELI-COPTER CAN LIFT US.
YOU TWO ARE UP EARLY.
WE'RE GOING ON A BIKE RIDE.
WE'RE GONNA GO TO THE MEADOW BY THE RIVER AND TRY OUT MY NEW HELICOPTER.
WELL, BE CAREFUL, AND COME BACK AROUND ONE FOR LUNCH.

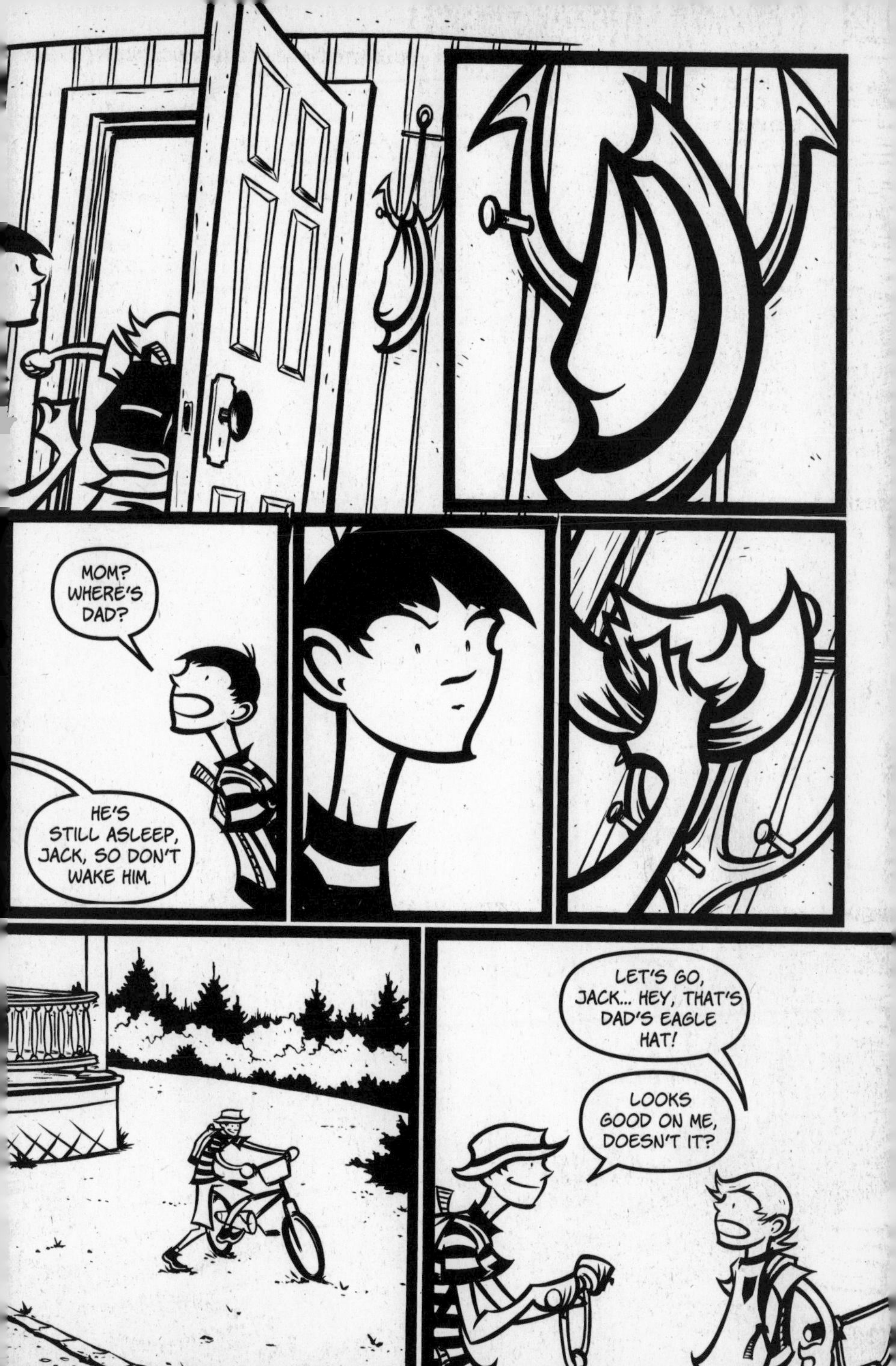
MOM? WHERE'S DAD?
HE'S STILL ASLEEP, JACK, SO DON'T WAKE HIM.
LET'S GO, JACK... HEY, THAT'S DAD'S EAGLE HAT!
LOOKS GOOD ON ME, DOESN'T IT?

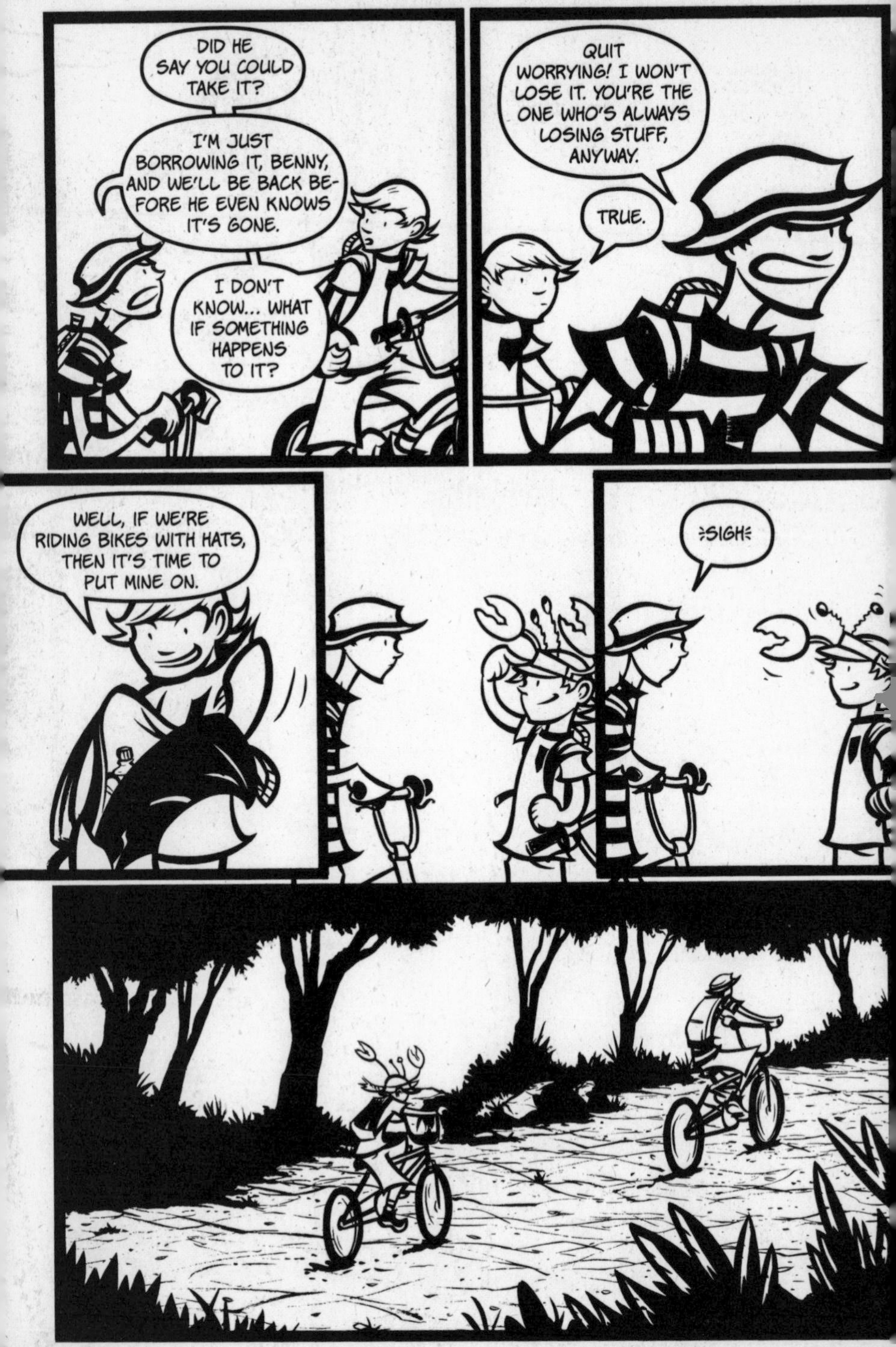

DID HE SAY YOU COULD TAKE IT?
I'M JUST BORROWING IT, BENNY, AND WE'LL BE BACK BE- FORE HE EVEN KNOWS IT'S GONE.
I DON'T KNOW... WHAT IF SOMETHING HAPPENS TO IT?
QUIT WORRYING! I WON'T LOSE IT. YOU'RE THE ONE WHO'S ALWAYS LOSING STUFF, ANYWAY.
TRUE.
WELL, IF WE'RE RIDING BIKES WITH HATS, THEN IT'S TIME TO PUT MINE ON.
SIGH

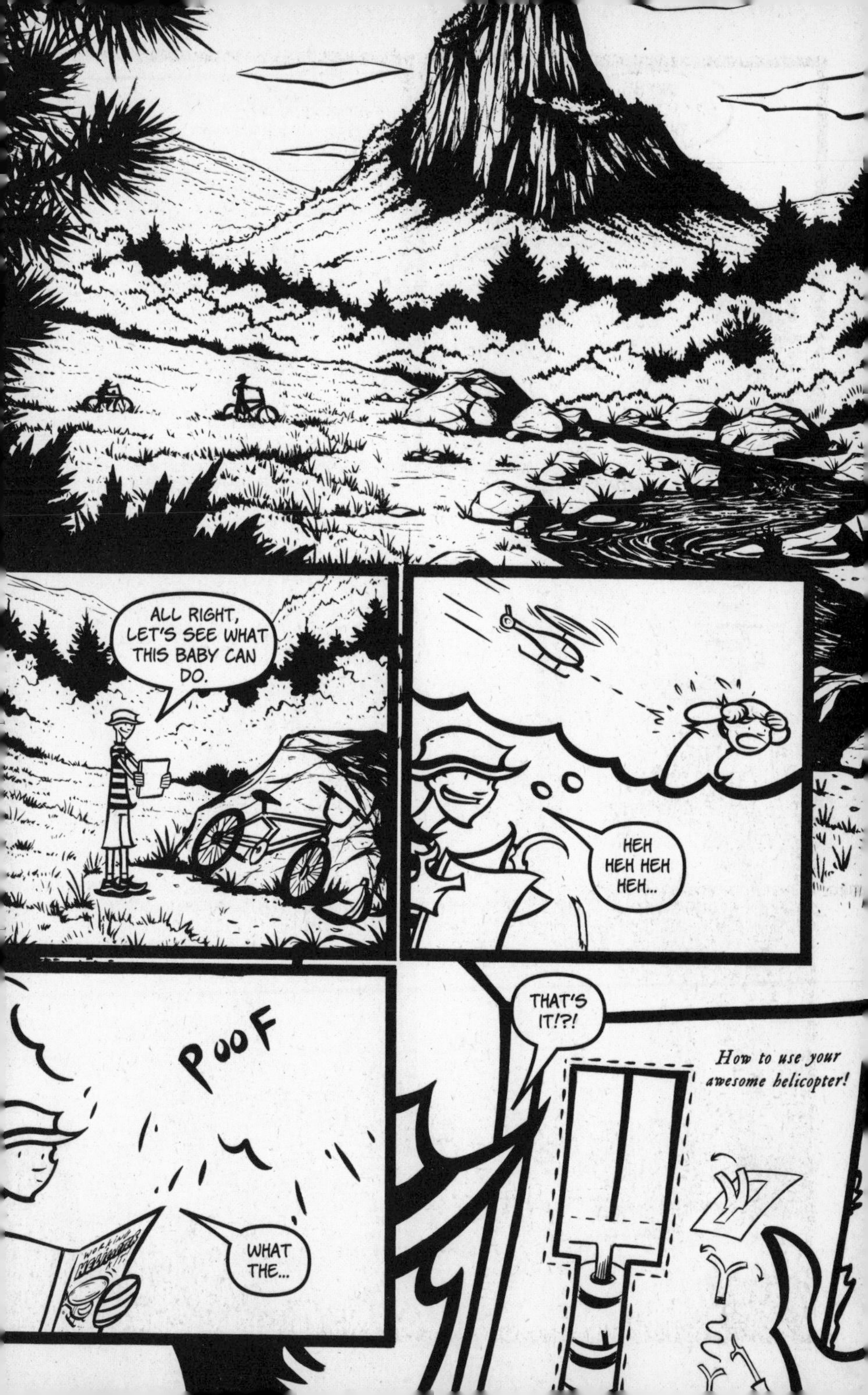
ALL RIGHT, LET'S SEE WHAT THIS BABY CAN DO.
HEH HEH HEH HEH...
POOF
WHAT THE...
THAT'S IT!?!
How to use your awesome helicopter!

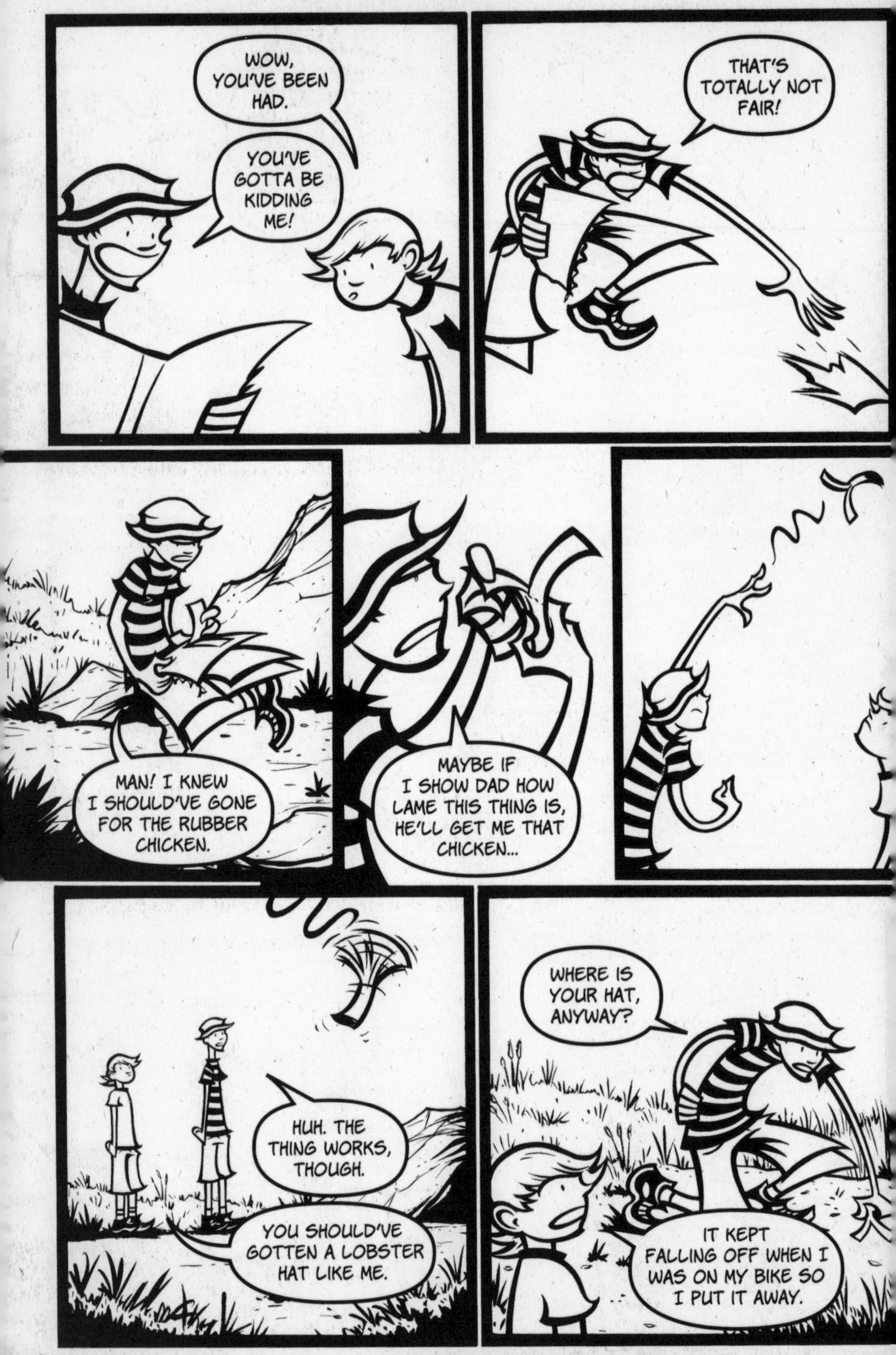
WOW, YOU'VE BEEN HAD.
YOU'VE GOTTA BE KIDDING ME!
THAT'S TOTALLY NOT FAIR!
MAN! I KNEW I SHOULD'VE GONE FOR THE RUBBER CHICKEN.
MAYBE IF I SHOW DAD HOW LAME THIS THING IS, HE'LL GET ME THAT CHICKEN...
HUH. THE THING WORKS, THOUGH.
YOU SHOULD'VE GOTTEN A LOBSTER HAT LIKE ME.
WHERE IS YOUR HAT, ANYWAY?
IT KEPT FALLING OFF WHEN I WAS ON MY BIKE SO I PUT IT AWAY.

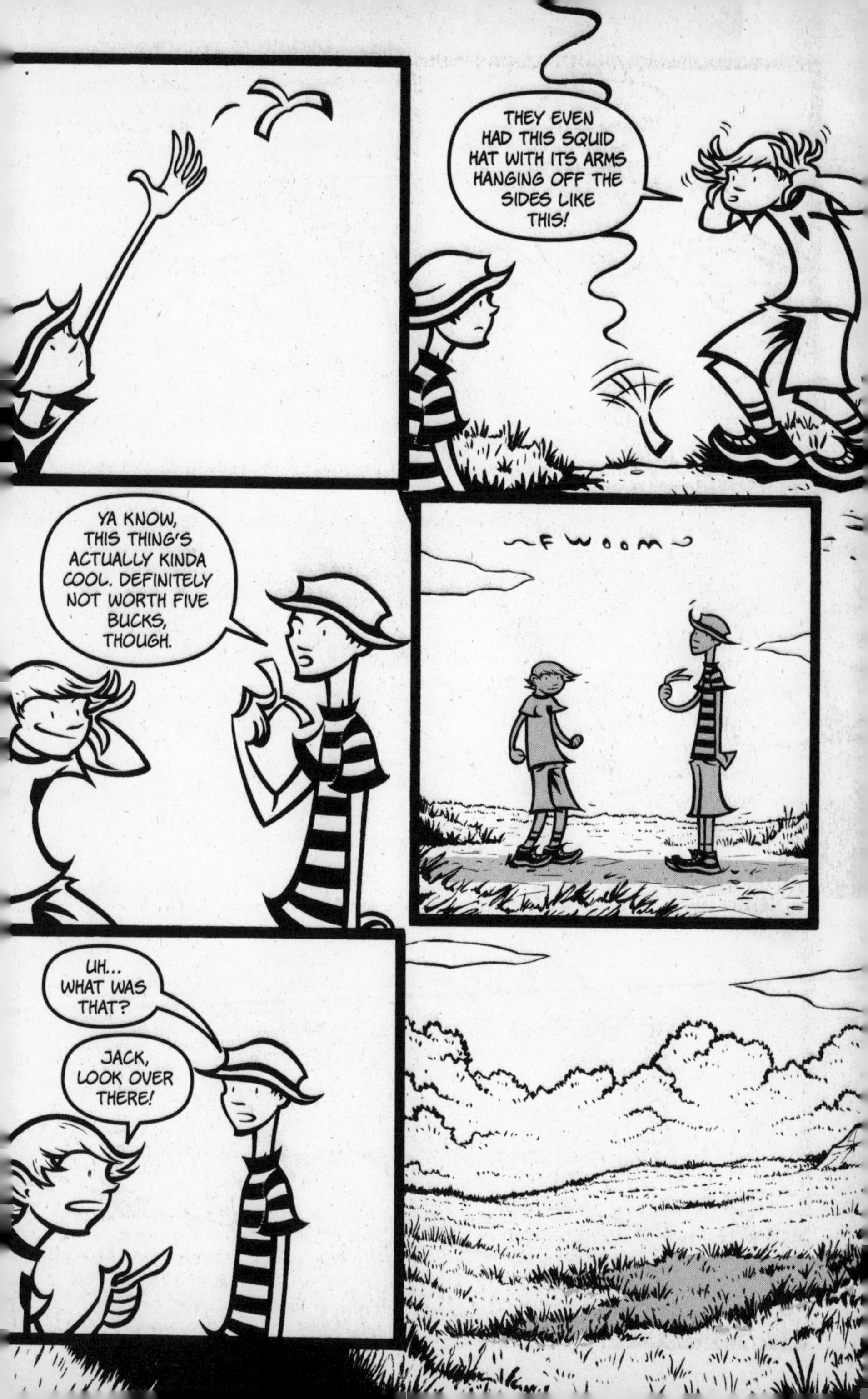
THEY EVEN HAD THIS SQUID HAT WITH ITS ARMS HANGING OFF THE SIDES LIKE THIS!
YA KNOW, THIS THING'S ACTUALLY KINDA COOL. DEFINITELY NOT WORTH FIVE BUCKS, THOUGH.
~FWOOM~
UH... WHAT WAS THAT?
JACK, LOOK OVER THERE!

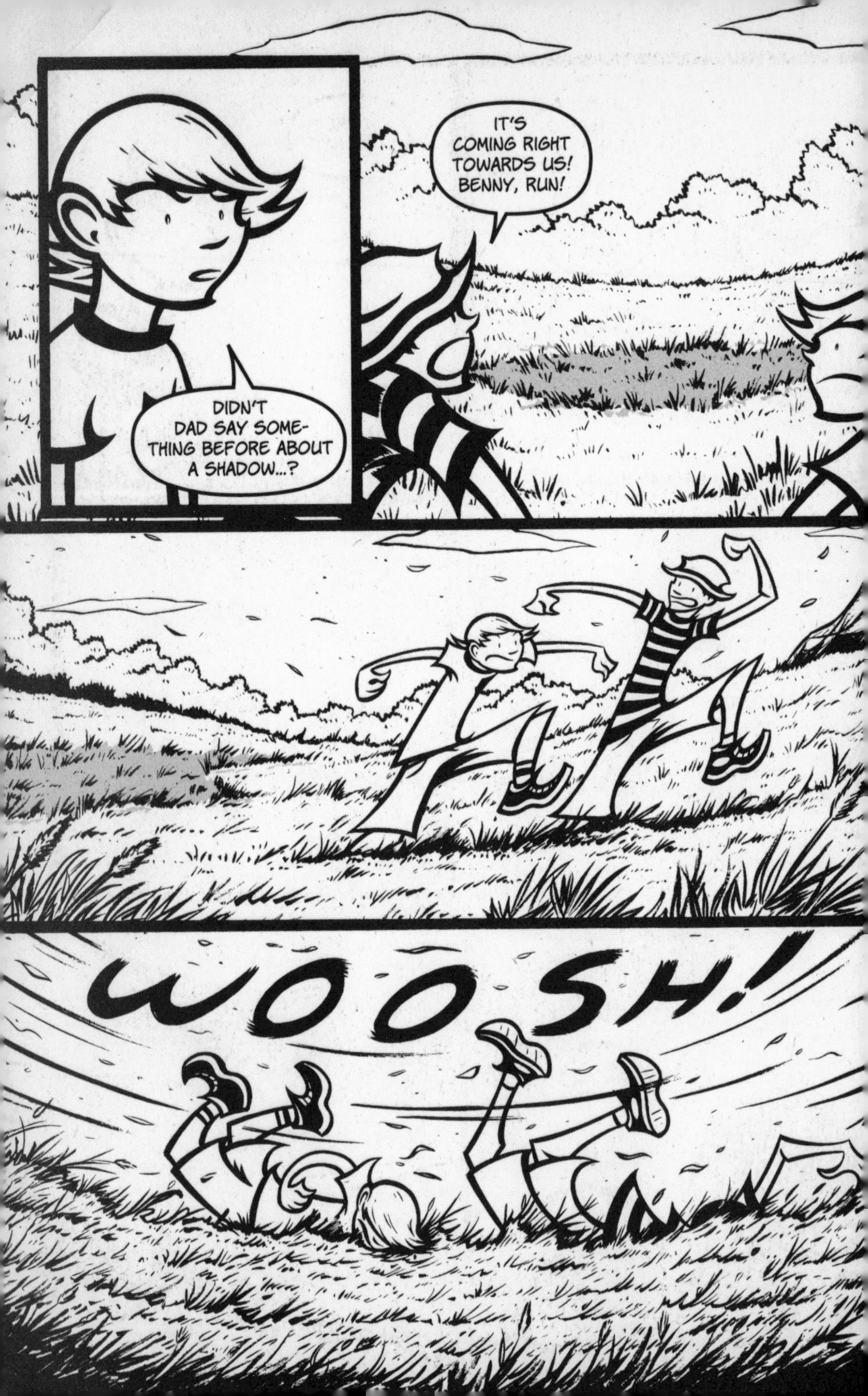
DIDN'T DAD SAY SOME-THING BEFORE ABOUT A SHADOW...?
IT'S COMING RIGHT TOWARDS US! BENNY, RUN!
WOOSH!

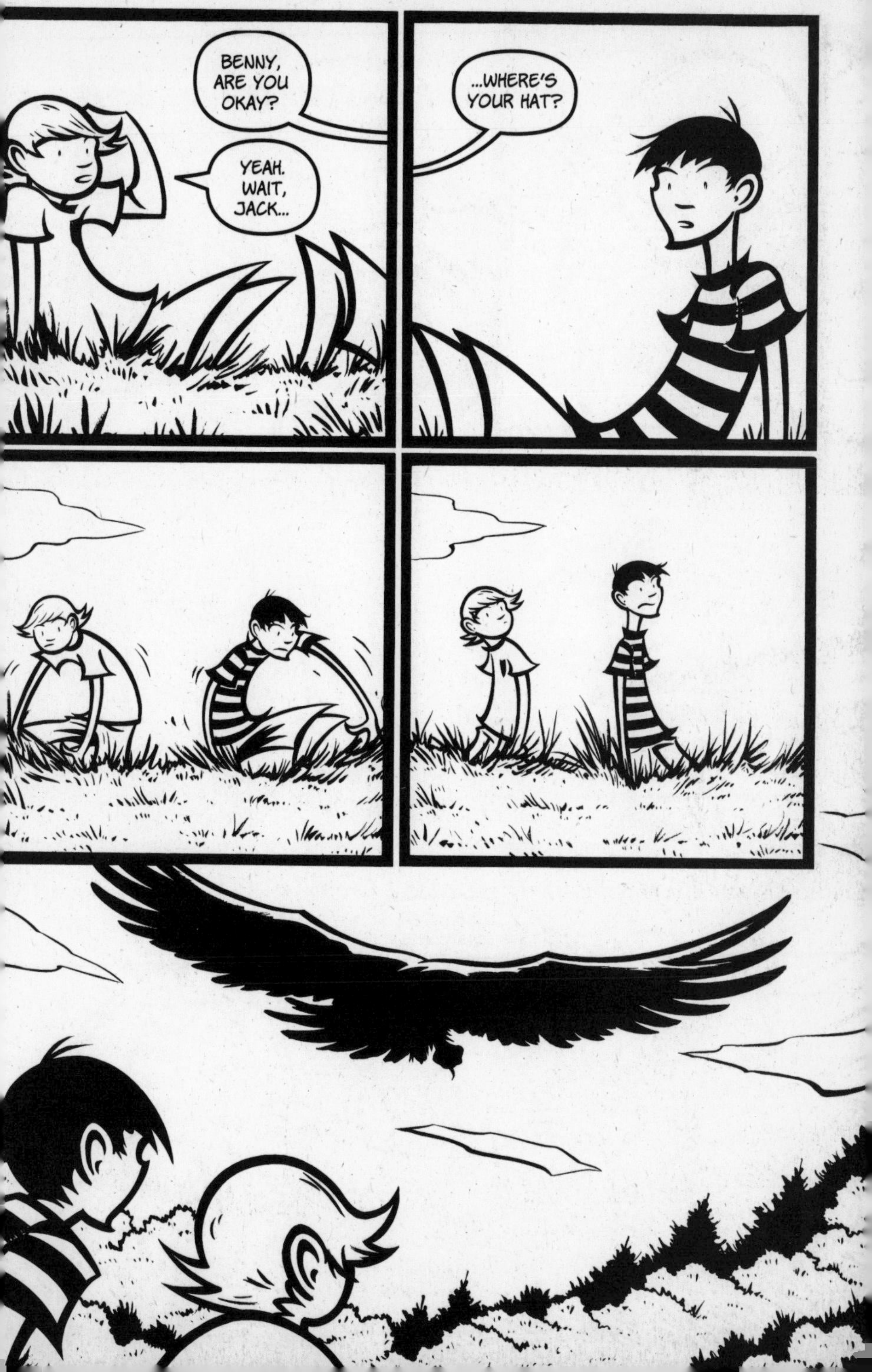
BENNY, ARE YOU OKAY?
YEAH. WAIT, JACK...
...WHERE'S YOUR HAT?

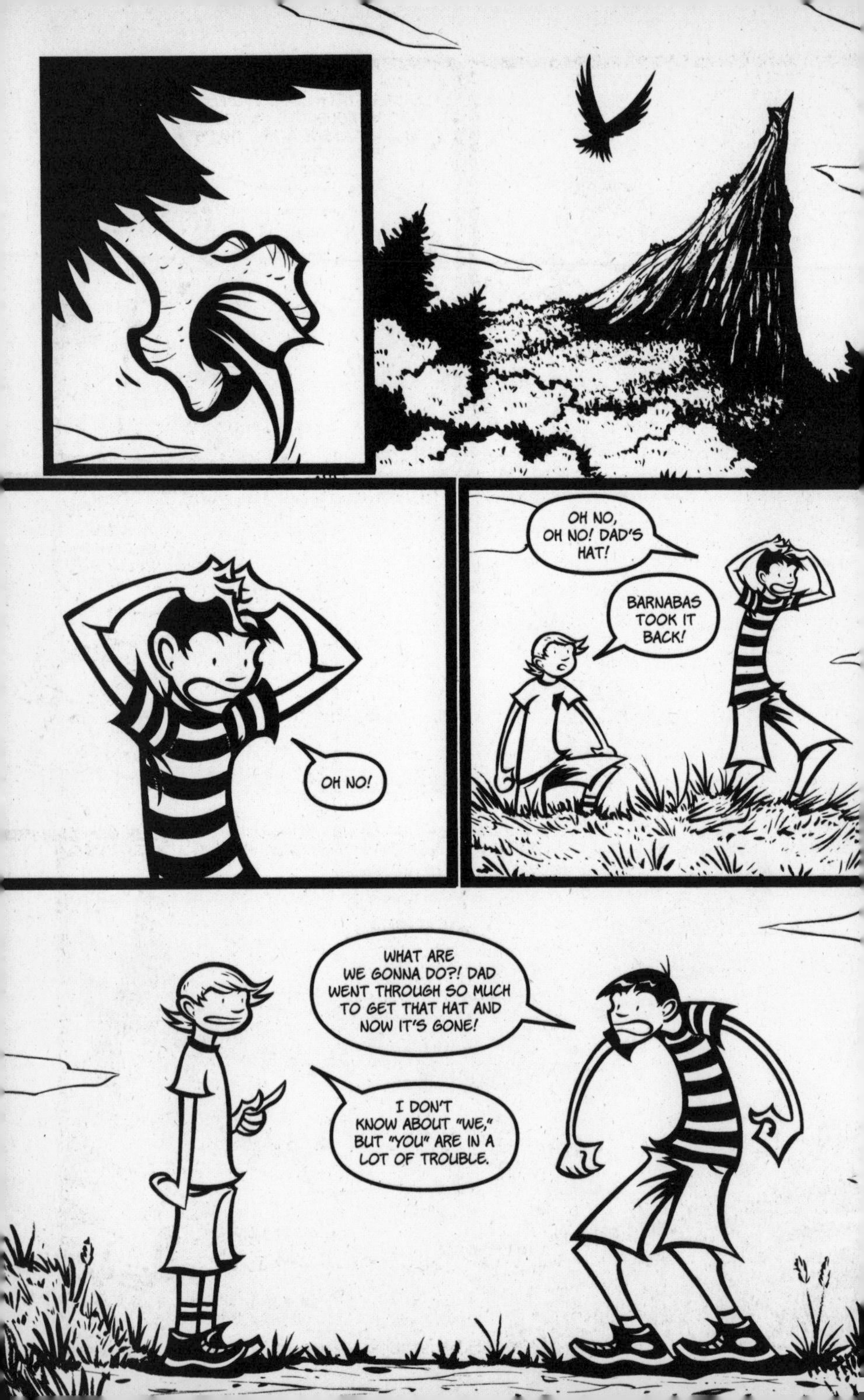
OH NO!
OH NO, OH NO! DAD'S HAT!
BARNABAS TOOK IT BACK!
WHAT ARE WE GONNA DO?! DAD WENT THROUGH SO MUCH TO GET THAT HAT AND NOW IT'S GONE!
I DON'T KNOW ABOUT "WE," BUT "YOU" ARE IN A LOT OF TROUBLE.

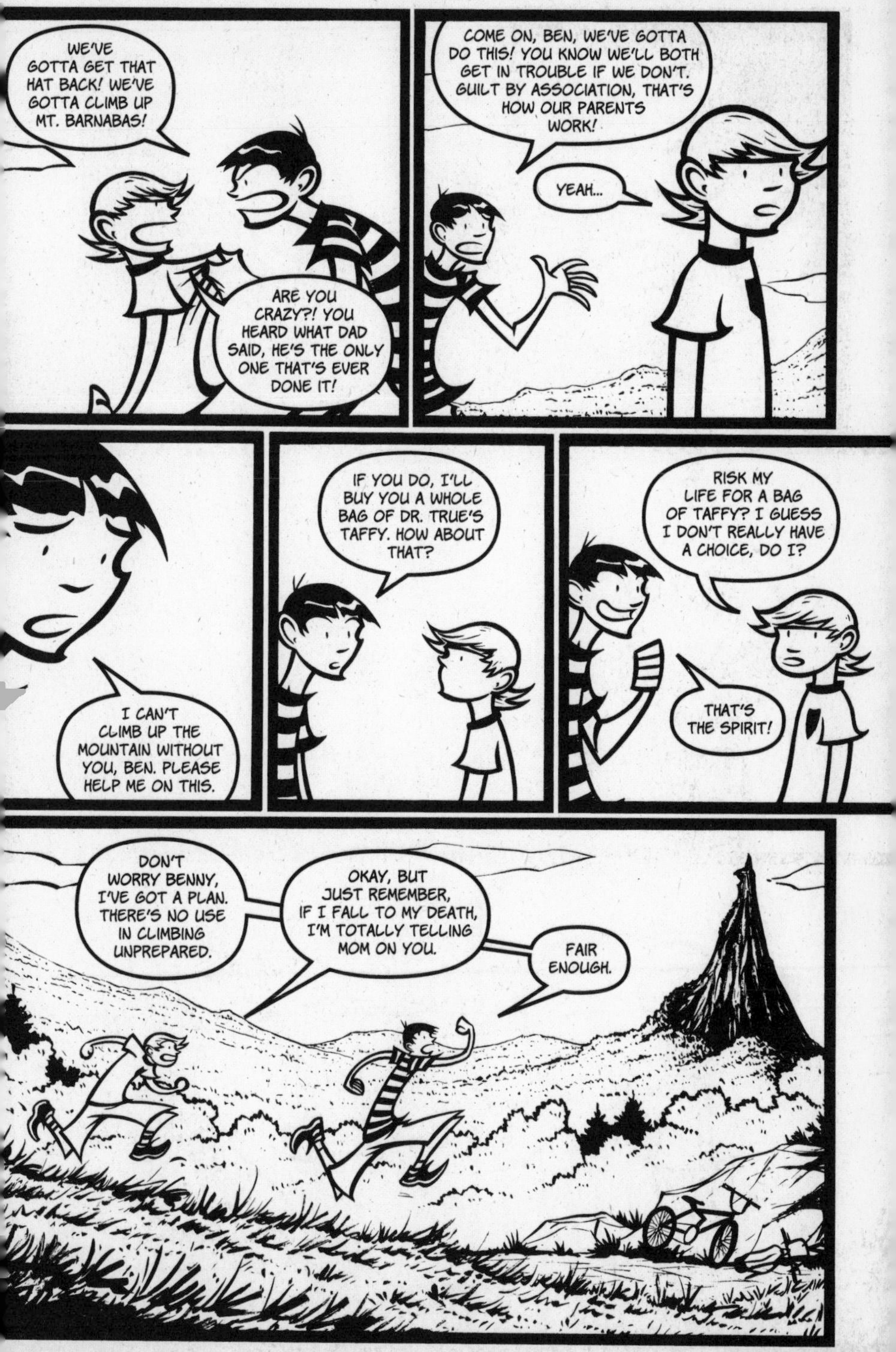
WE'VE GOTTA GET THAT HAT BACK! WE'VE GOTTA CLIMB UP MT. BARNABAS!
ARE YOU CRAZY?! YOU HEARD WHAT DAD SAID, HE'S THE ONLY ONE THAT'S EVER DONE IT!
COME ON, BEN, WE'VE GOTTA DO THIS! YOU KNOW WE'LL BOTH GET IN TROUBLE IF WE DON'T. GUILT BY ASSOCIATION, THAT'S HOW OUR PARENTS WORK!
YEAH...
I CAN'T CLIMB UP THE MOUNTAIN WITHOUT YOU, BEN. PLEASE HELP ME ON THIS.
IF YOU DO, I'LL BUY YOU A WHOLE BAG OF DR. TRUE'S TAFFY. HOW ABOUT THAT?
RISK MY LIFE FOR A BAG OF TAFFY? I GUESS I DON'T REALLY HAVE A CHOICE, DO I?
THAT'S THE SPIRIT!
DON'T WORRY BENNY, I'VE GOT A PLAN. THERE'S NO USE IN CLIMBING UNPREPARED.
OKAY, BUT JUST REMEMBER, IF I FALL TO MY DEATH, I'M TOTALLY TELLING MOM ON YOU.
FAIR ENOUGH.

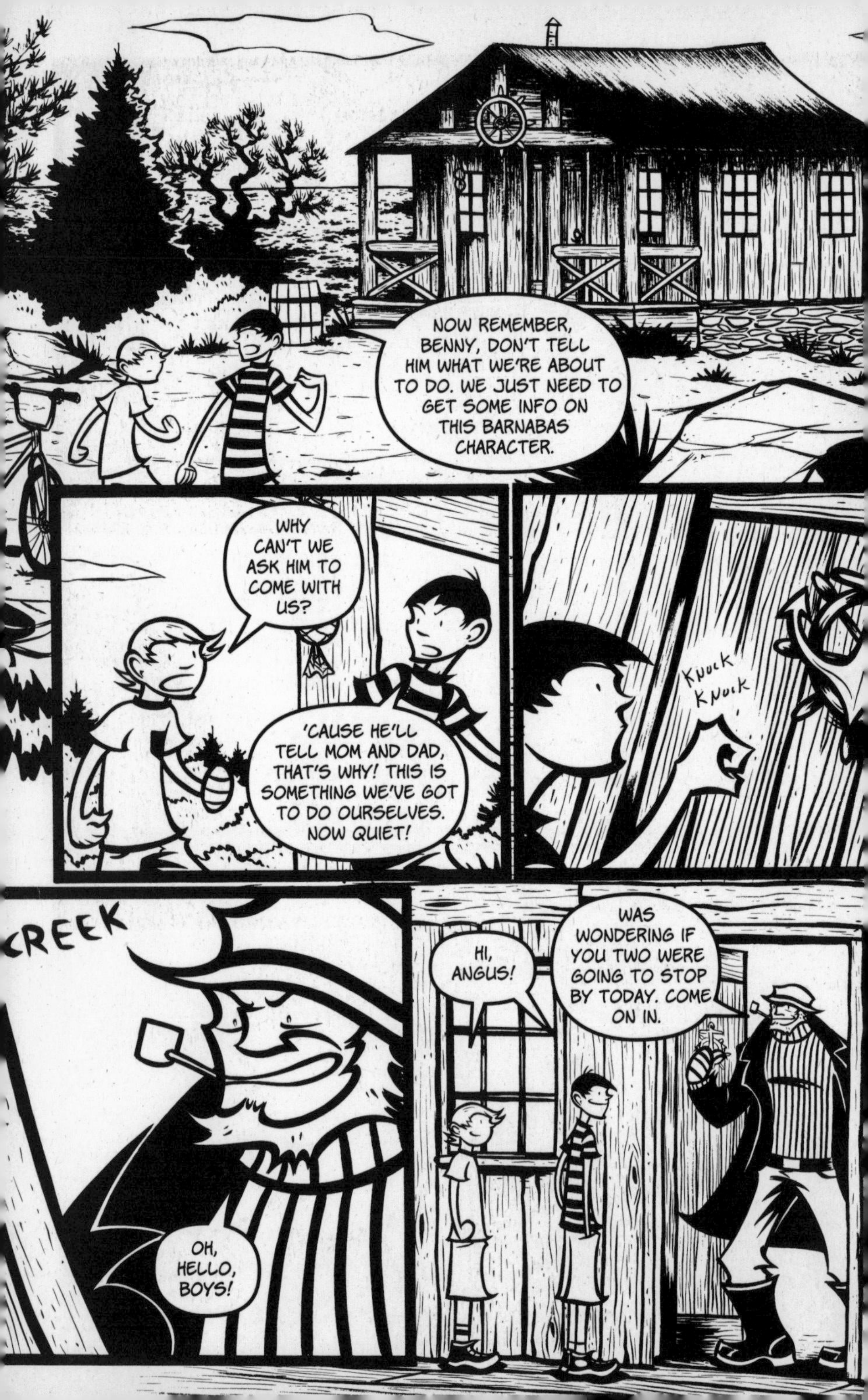

NOW REMEMBER, BENNY, DON'T TELL HIM WHAT WE'RE ABOUT TO DO. WE JUST NEED TO GET SOME INFO ON THIS BARNABAS CHARACTER.
WHY CAN'T WE ASK HIM TO COME WITH US?
'CAUSE HE'LL TELL MOM AND DAD, THAT'S WHY! THIS IS SOMETHING WE'VE GOT TO DO OURSELVES. NOW QUIET!
KNUCK KNUCK
CREEK
OH, HELLO, BOYS!
HI, ANGUS!
WAS WONDERING IF YOU TWO WERE GOING TO STOP BY TODAY. COME ON IN.

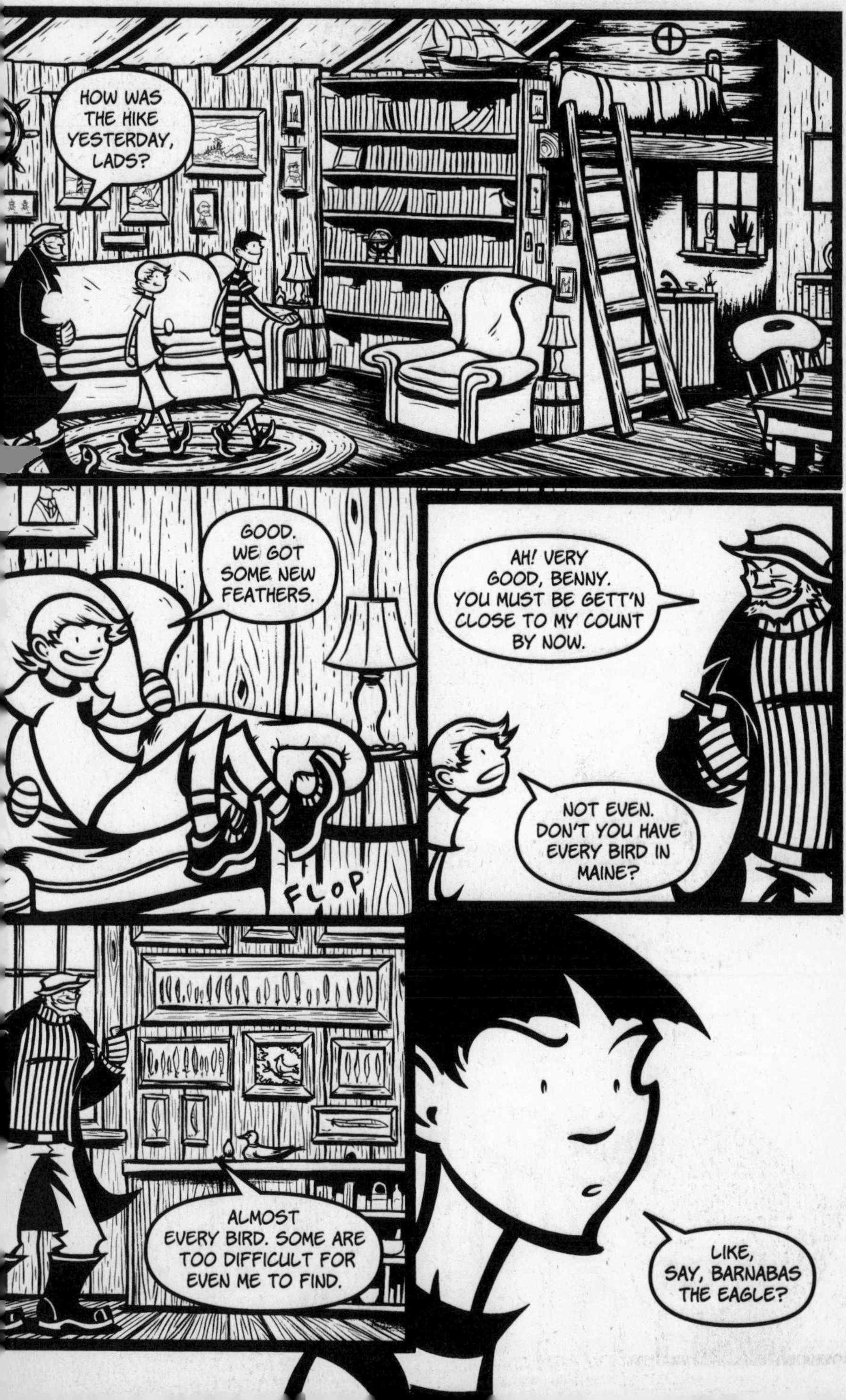
HOW WAS THE HIKE YESTERDAY, LADS?
GOOD. WE GOT SOME NEW FEATHERS.
FLOP
AH! VERY GOOD, BENNY. YOU MUST BE GETT'N CLOSE TO MY COUNT BY NOW.
NOT EVEN. DON'T YOU HAVE EVERY BIRD IN MAINE?
ALMOST EVERY BIRD. SOME ARE TOO DIFFICULT FOR EVEN ME TO FIND.
LIKE, SAY, BARNABAS THE EAGLE?

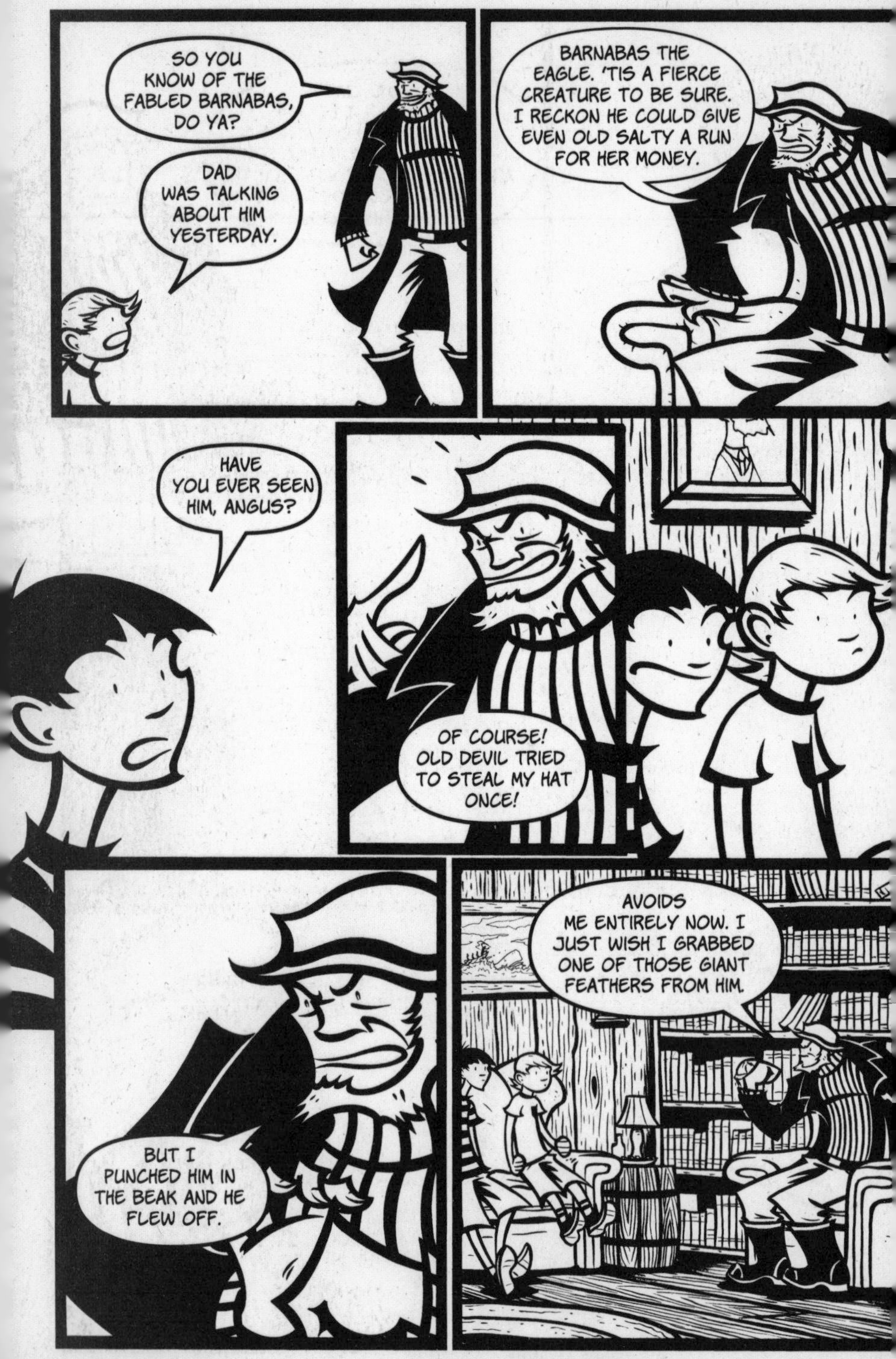
SO YOU KNOW OF THE FABLED BARNABAS, DO YA?
DAD WAS TALKING ABOUT HIM YESTERDAY.
BARNABAS THE EAGLE. 'TIS A FIERCE CREATURE TO BE SURE. I RECKON HE COULD GIVE EVEN OLD SALTY A RUN FOR HER MONEY.
HAVE YOU EVER SEEN HIM, ANGUS?
OF COURSE! OLD DEVIL TRIED TO STEAL MY HAT ONCE!
BUT I PUNCHED HIM IN THE BEAK AND HE FLEW OFF.
AVOIDS ME ENTIRELY NOW. I JUST WISH I GRABBED ONE OF THOSE GIANT FEATHERS FROM HIM.

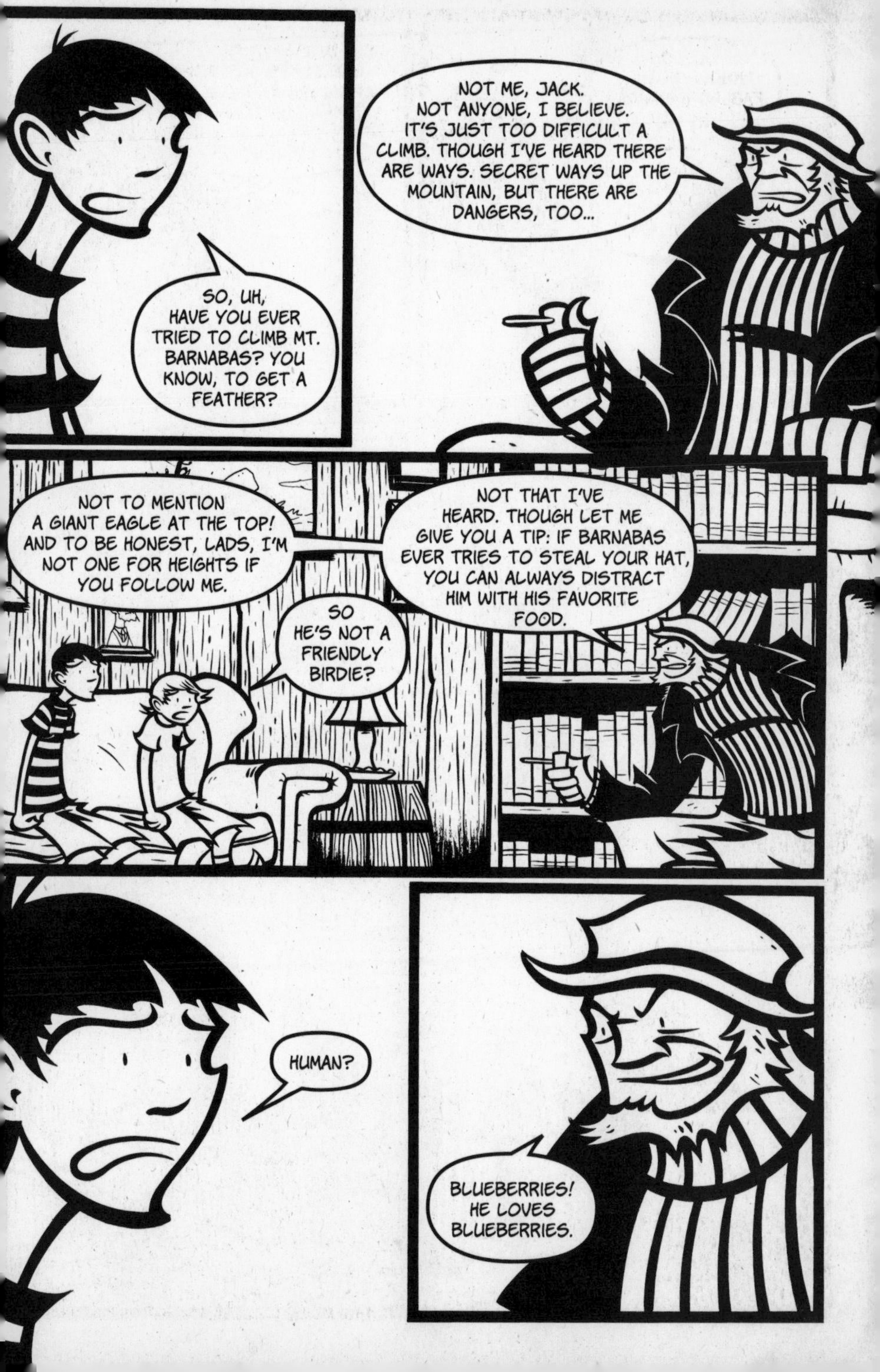
SO, UH, HAVE YOU EVER TRIED TO CLIMB MT. BARNABAS? YOU KNOW, TO GET A FEATHER?
NOT ME, JACK. NOT ANYONE, I BELIEVE. IT'S JUST TOO DIFFICULT A CLIMB. THOUGH I'VE HEARD THERE ARE WAYS. SECRET WAYS UP THE MOUNTAIN, BUT THERE ARE DANGERS, TOO...
NOT TO MENTION A GIANT EAGLE AT THE TOP! AND TO BE HONEST, LADS, I'M NOT ONE FOR HEIGHTS IF YOU FOLLOW ME.
SO HE'S NOT A FRIENDLY BIRDIE?
NOT THAT I'VE HEARD. THOUGH LET ME GIVE YOU A TIP: IF BARNABAS EVER TRIES TO STEAL YOUR HAT, YOU CAN ALWAYS DISTRACT HIM WITH HIS FAVORITE FOOD.
HUMAN?
BLUEBERRIES! HE LOVES BLUEBERRIES.

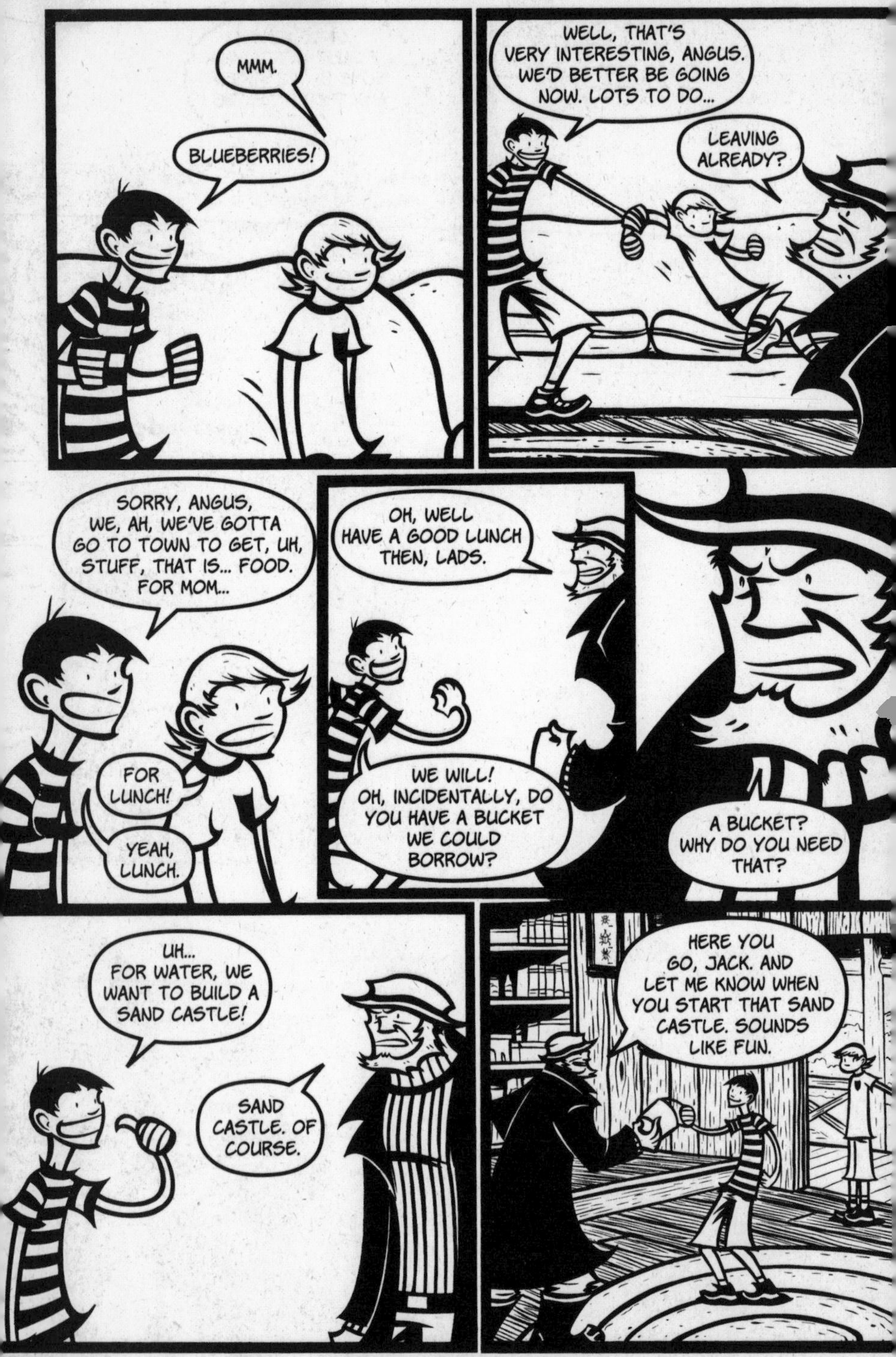
MMM.
BLUEBERRIES!
WELL, THAT'S VERY INTERESTING, ANGUS. WE'D BETTER BE GOING NOW. LOTS TO DO...
LEAVING ALREADY?
SORRY, ANGUS, WE, AH, WE'VE GOTTA GO TO TOWN TO GET, UH, STUFF, THAT IS... FOOD. FOR MOM...
FOR LUNCH!
YEAH, LUNCH.
OH, WELL HAVE A GOOD LUNCH THEN, LADS.
WE WILL! OH, INCIDENTALLY, DO YOU HAVE A BUCKET WE COULD BORROW?
A BUCKET? WHY DO YOU NEED THAT?
UH... FOR WATER, WE WANT TO BUILD A SAND CASTLE!
SAND CASTLE. OF COURSE.
HERE YOU GO, JACK. AND LET ME KNOW WHEN YOU START THAT SAND CASTLE. SOUNDS LIKE FUN.

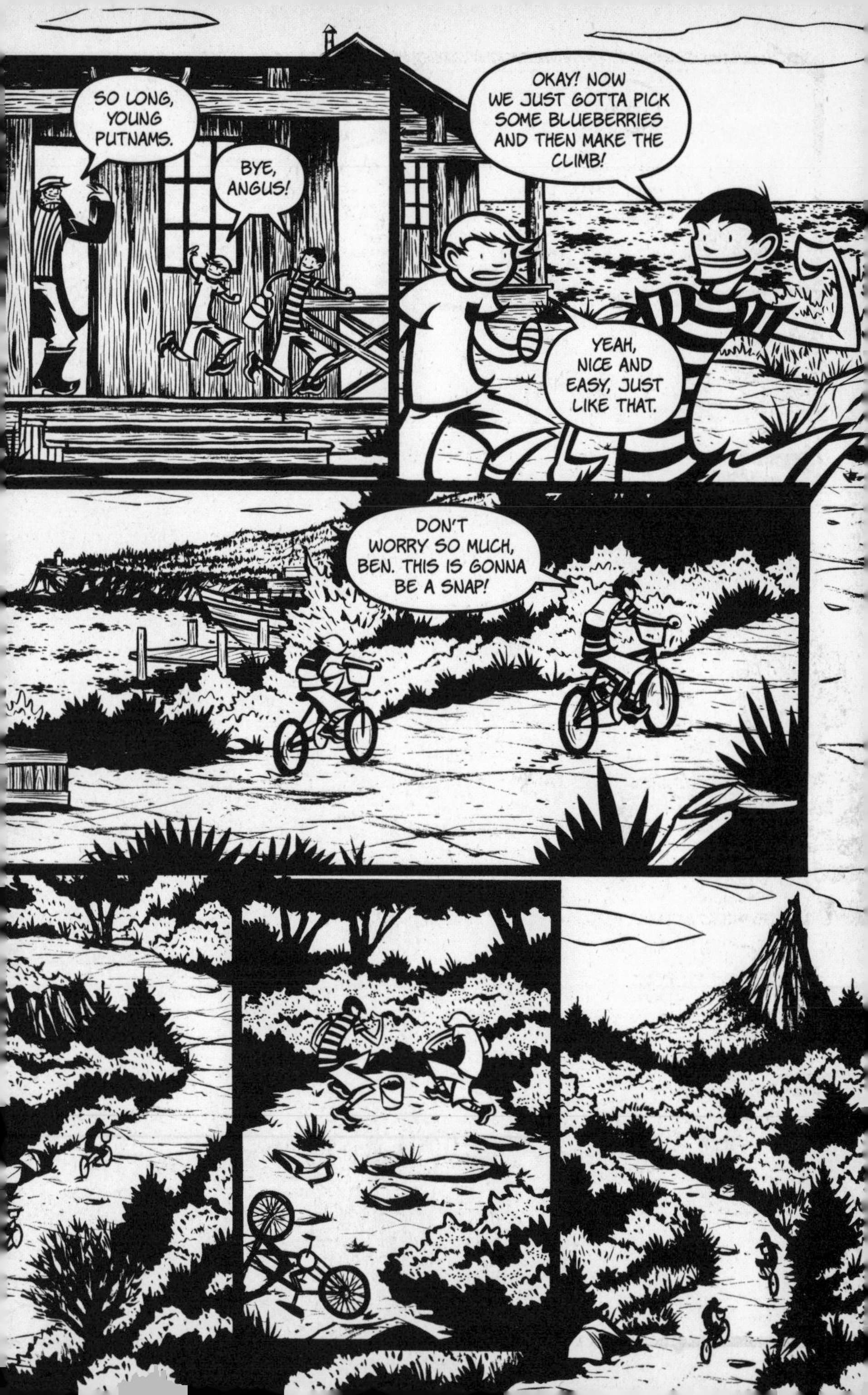
SO LONG, YOUNG PUTNAMS.
BYE, ANGUS!
OKAY! NOW WE JUST GOTTA PICK SOME BLUEBERRIES AND THEN MAKE THE CLIMB!
YEAH, NICE AND EASY, JUST LIKE THAT.
DON'T WORRY SO MUCH, BEN. THIS IS GONNA BE A SNAP!

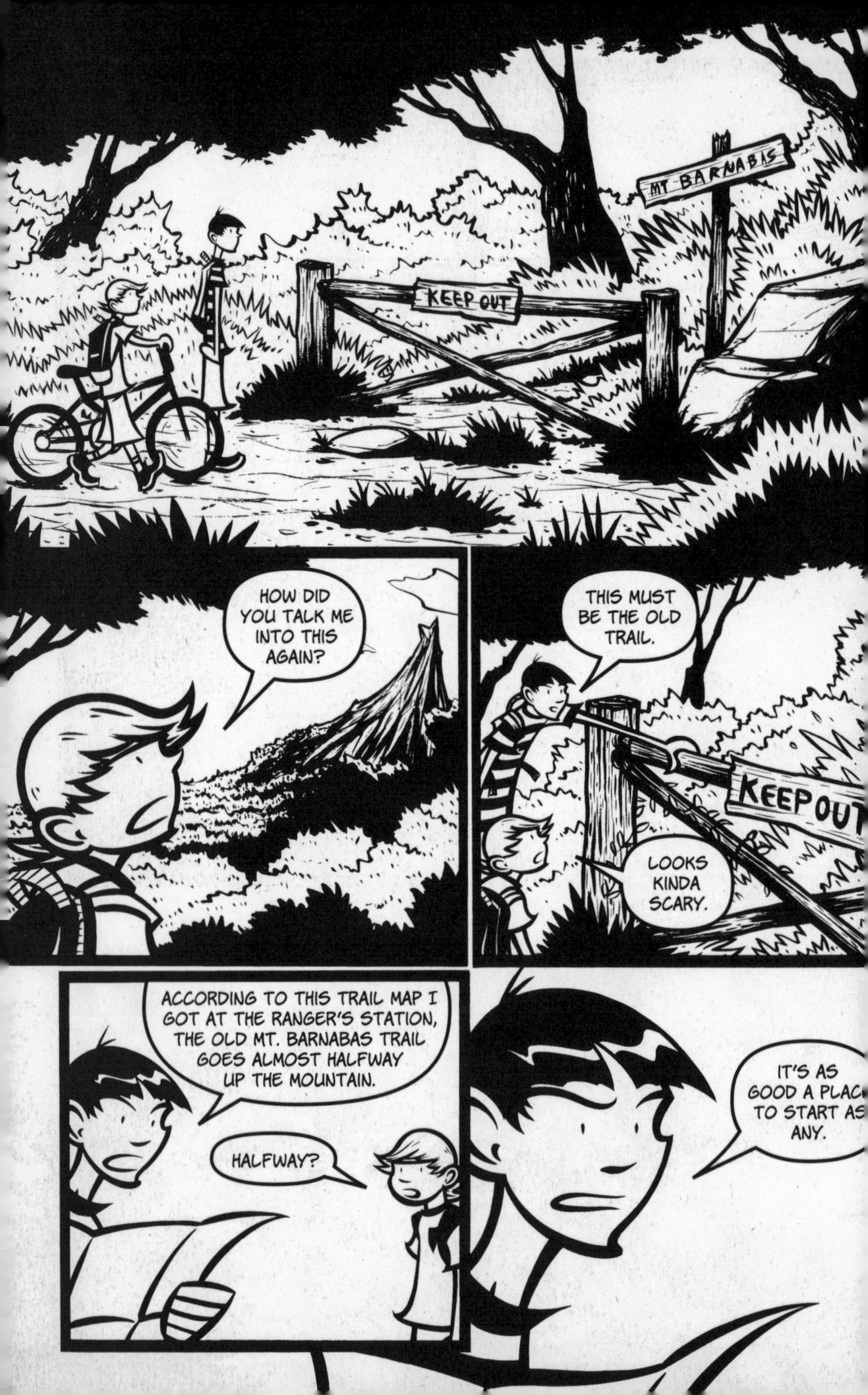
MT BARNABAS
KEEP OUT
HOW DID YOU TALK ME INTO THIS AGAIN?
THIS MUST BE THE OLD TRAIL.
KEEP OUT
LOOKS KINDA SCARY.
ACCORDING TO THIS TRAIL MAP I GOT AT THE RANGER'S STATION, THE OLD MT. BARNABAS TRAIL GOES ALMOST HALFWAY UP THE MOUNTAIN.
HALFWAY?
IT'S AS GOOD A PLAC TO START AS ANY.

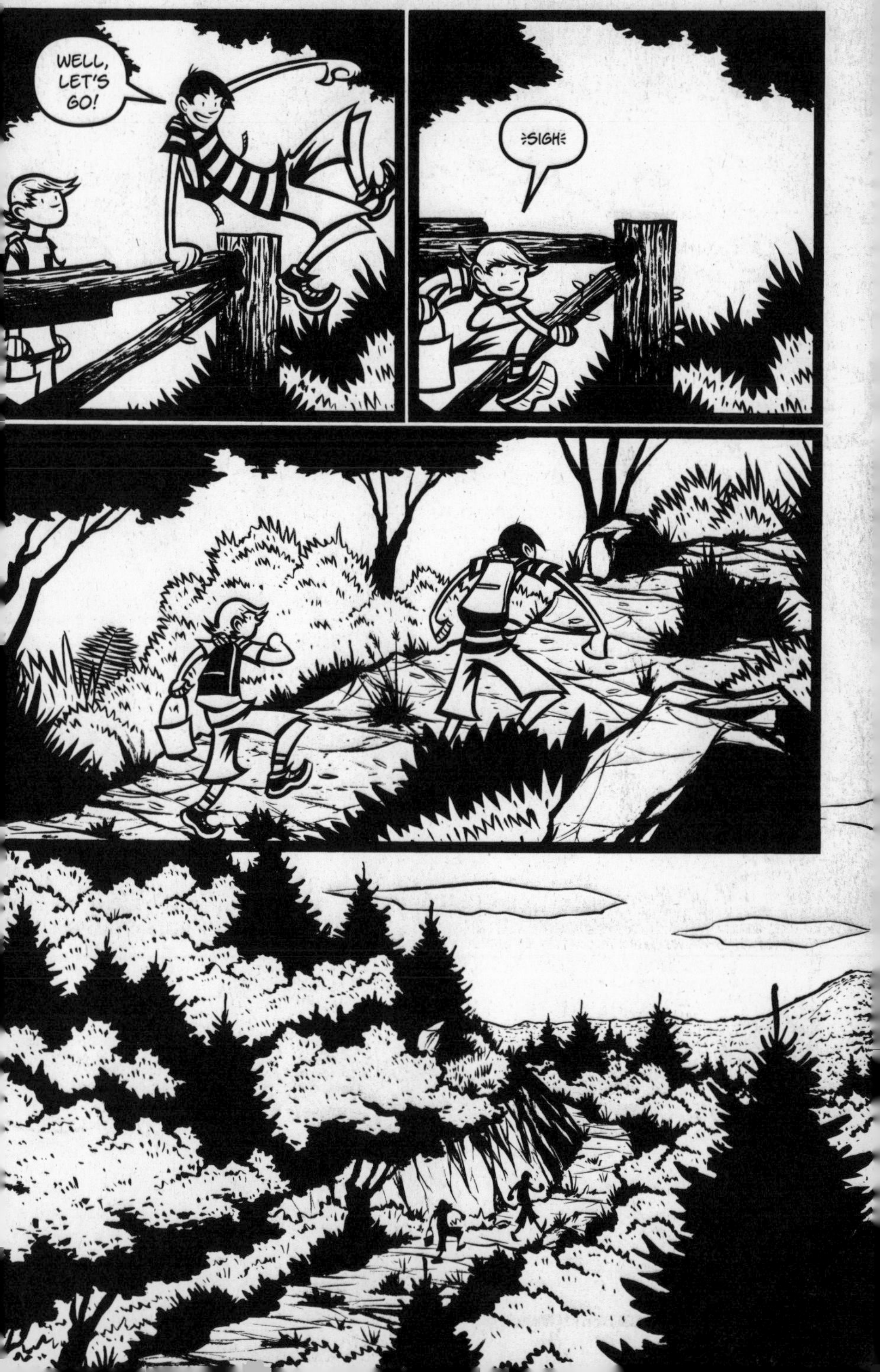
WELL, LET'S GO!
SIGH

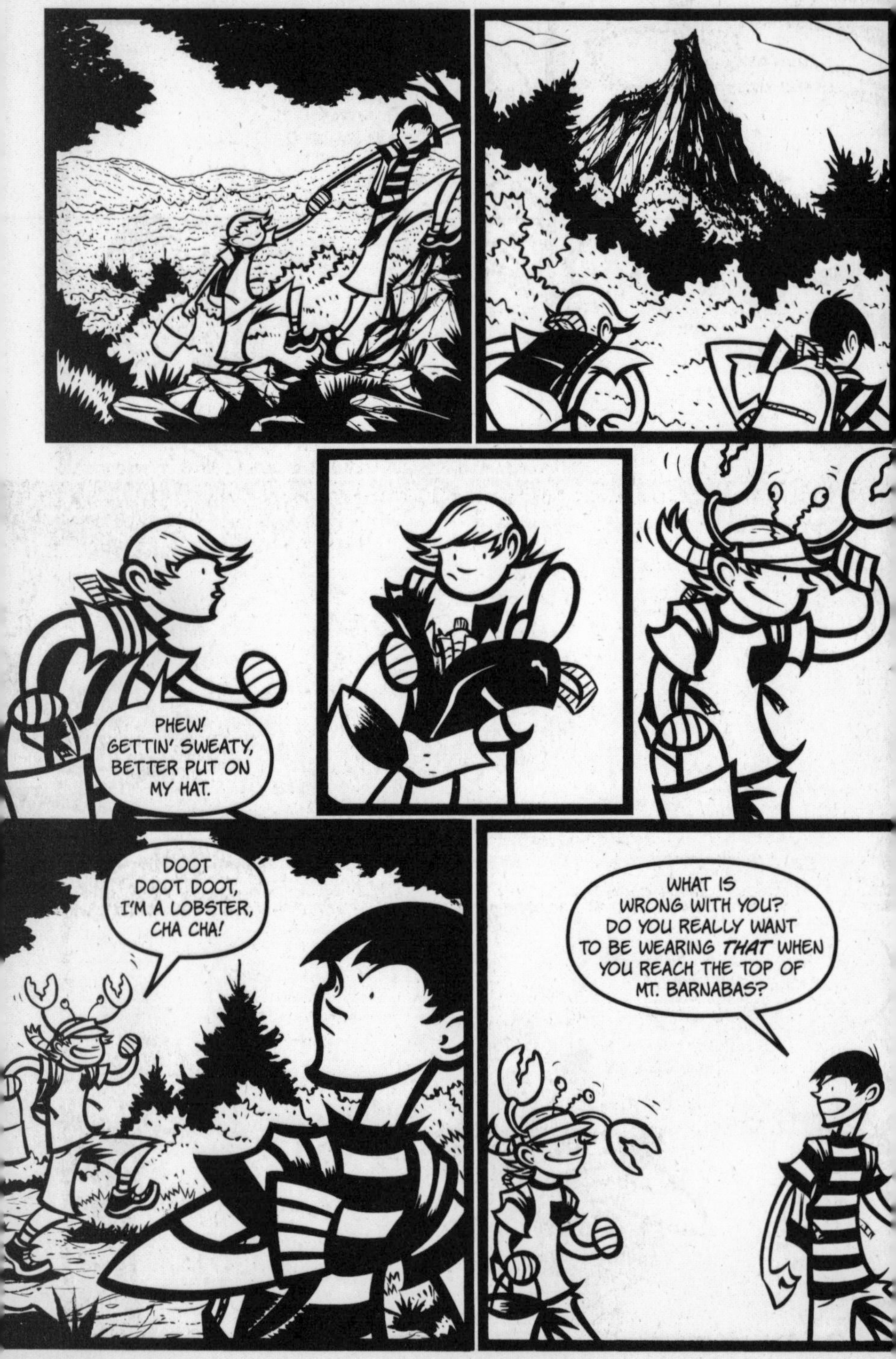
PHEW! GETTIN' SWEATY, BETTER PUT ON MY HAT.
DOOT DOOT DOOT, I'M A LOBSTER, CHA CHA!
WHAT IS WRONG WITH YOU? DO YOU REALLY WANT TO BE WEARING *THAT* WHEN YOU REACH THE TOP OF MT. BARNABAS?

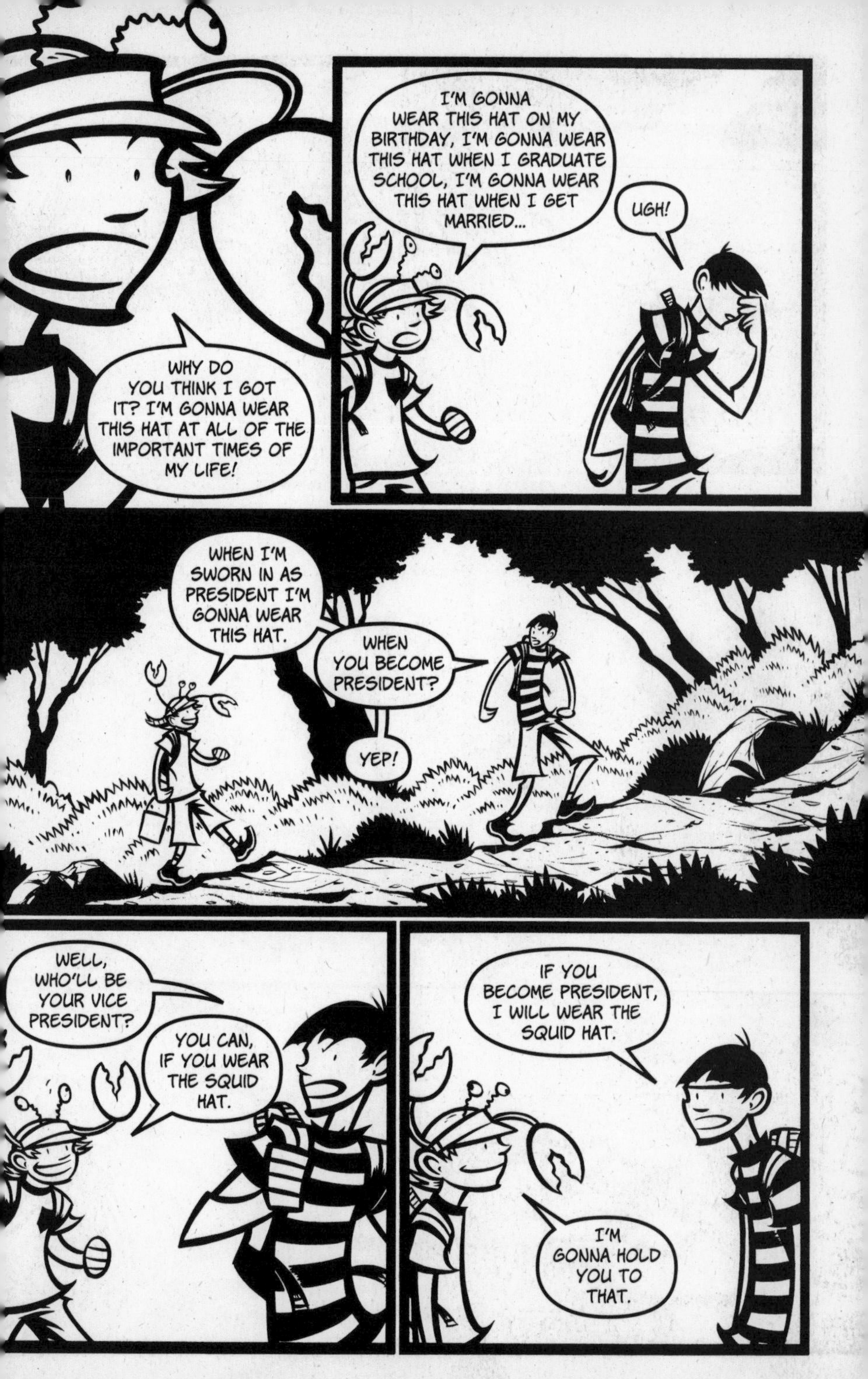
WHY DO YOU THINK I GOT IT? I'M GONNA WEAR THIS HAT AT ALL OF THE IMPORTANT TIMES OF MY LIFE!
I'M GONNA WEAR THIS HAT ON MY BIRTHDAY, I'M GONNA WEAR THIS HAT WHEN I GRADUATE SCHOOL, I'M GONNA WEAR THIS HAT WHEN I GET MARRIED...
UGH!
WHEN I'M SWORN IN AS PRESIDENT I'M GONNA WEAR THIS HAT.
WHEN YOU BECOME PRESIDENT?
YEP!
WELL, WHO'LL BE YOUR VICE PRESIDENT?
YOU CAN, IF YOU WEAR THE SQUID HAT.
IF YOU BECOME PRESIDENT, I WILL WEAR THE SQUID HAT.
I'M GONNA HOLD YOU TO THAT.

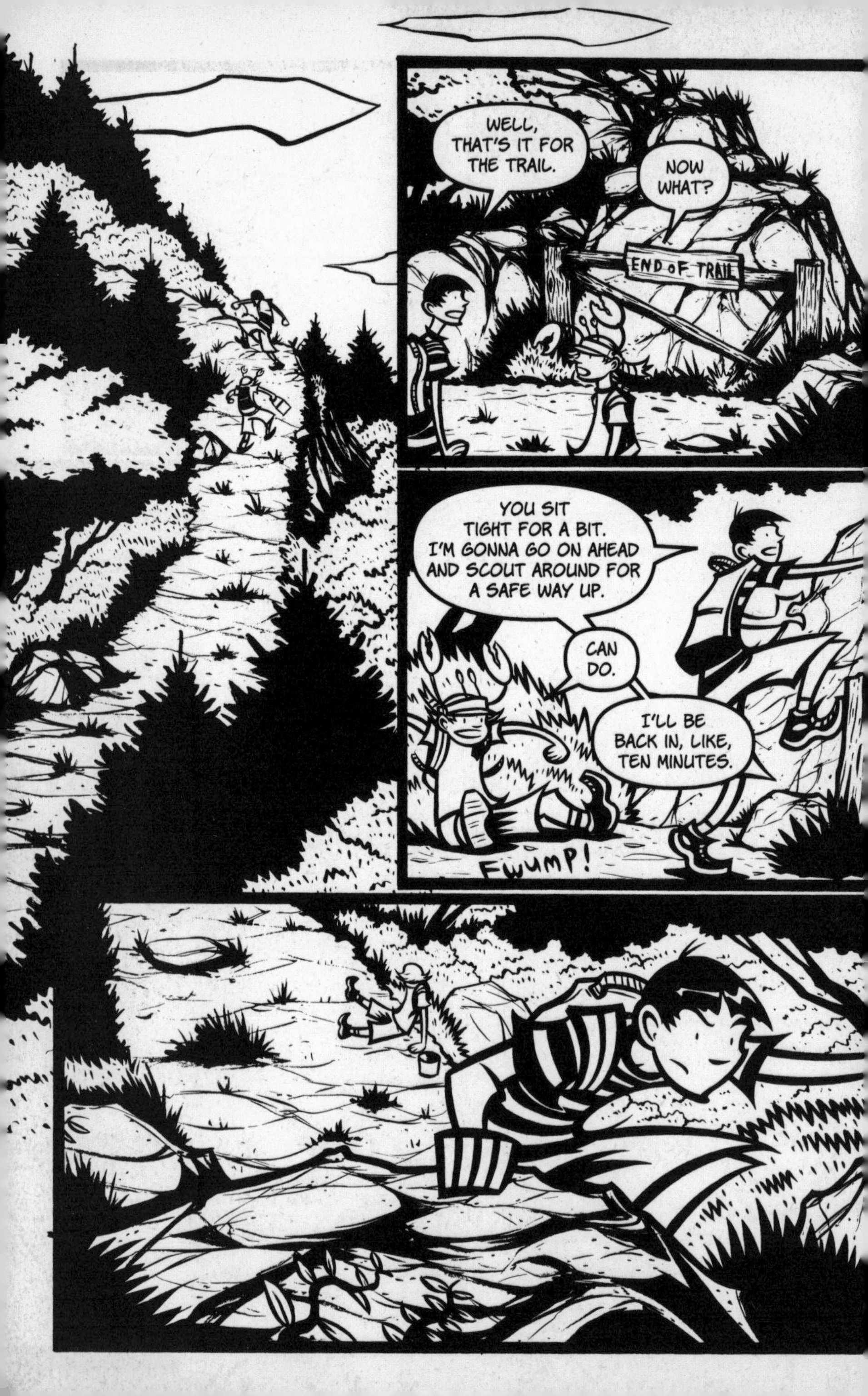
WELL, THAT'S IT FOR THE TRAIL.
NOW WHAT?
END OF TRAIL
YOU SIT TIGHT FOR A BIT. I'M GONNA GO ON AHEAD AND SCOUT AROUND FOR A SAFE WAY UP.
CAN DO.
I'LL BE BACK IN, LIKE, TEN MINUTES.
FWUMP!

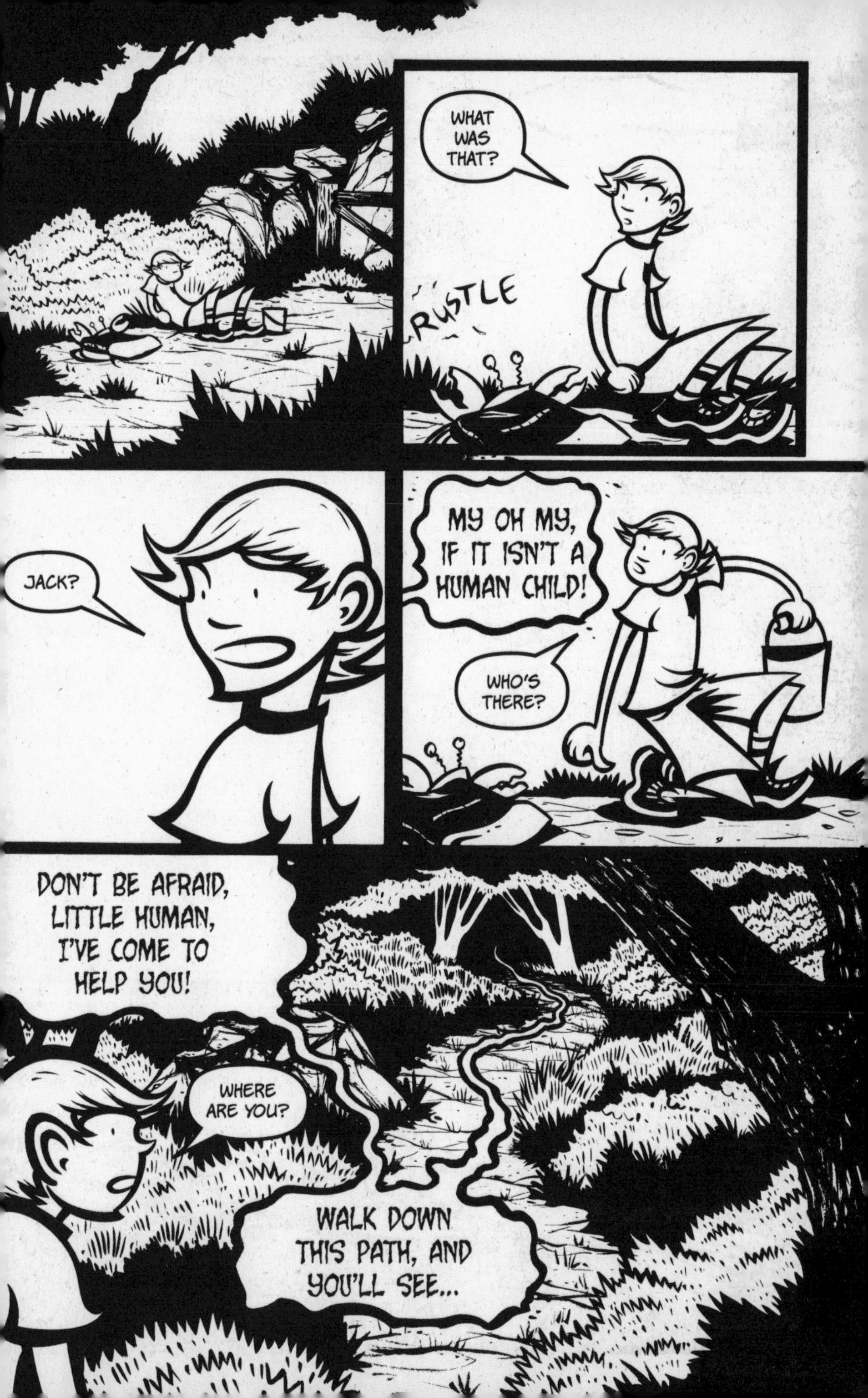
WHAT WAS THAT?
RUSTLE
JACK?
MY OH MY, IF IT ISN'T A HUMAN CHILD!
WHO'S THERE?
DON'T BE AFRAID, LITTLE HUMAN, I'VE COME TO HELP YOU!
WHERE ARE YOU?
WALK DOWN THIS PATH, AND YOU'LL SEE...

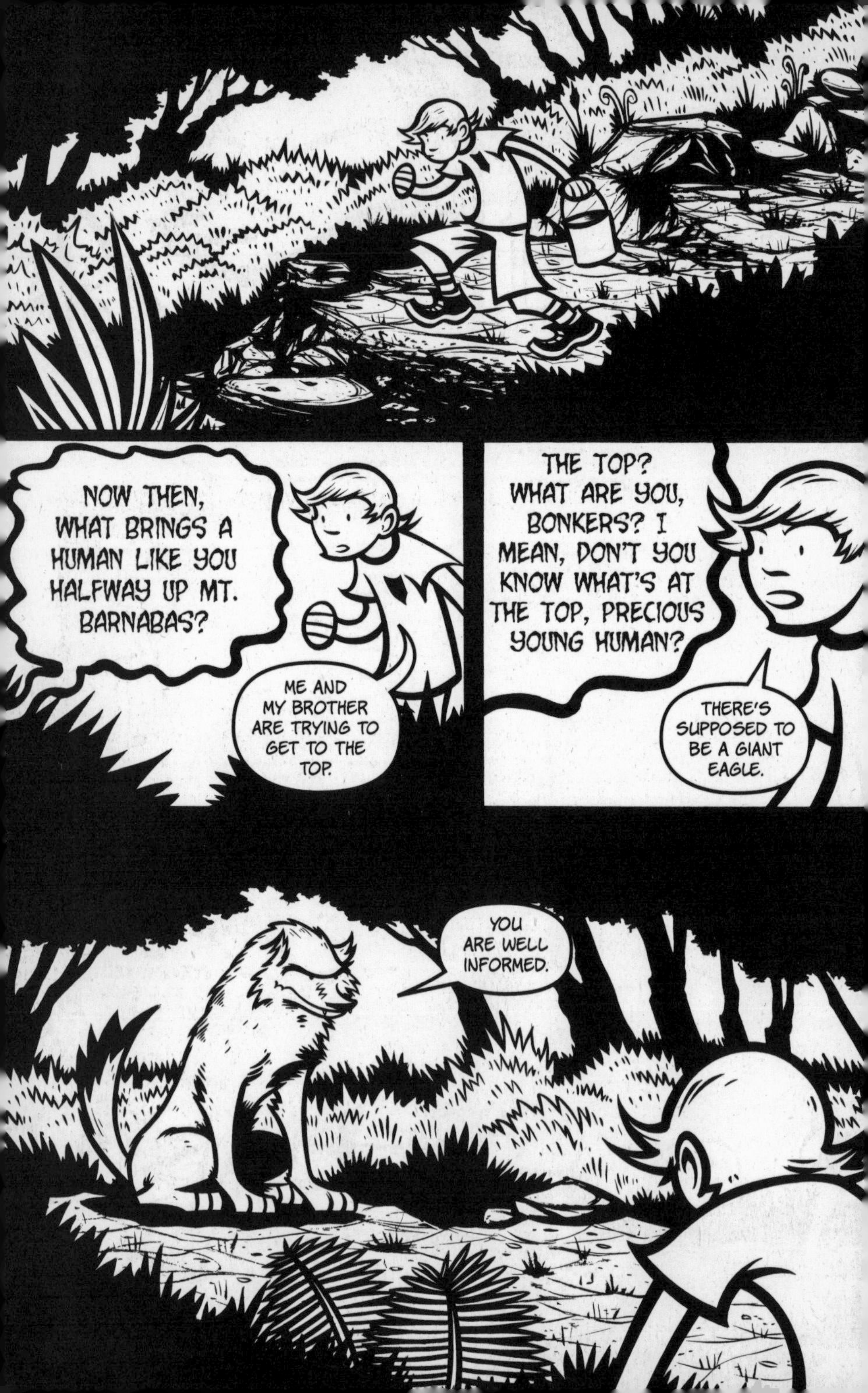
NOW THEN, WHAT BRINGS A HUMAN LIKE YOU HALFWAY UP MT. BARNABAS?
ME AND MY BROTHER ARE TRYING TO GET TO THE TOP.
THE TOP? WHAT ARE YOU, BONKERS? I MEAN, DON'T YOU KNOW WHAT'S AT THE TOP, PRECIOUS YOUNG HUMAN?
THERE'S SUPPOSED TO BE A GIANT EAGLE.
YOU ARE WELL INFORMED.

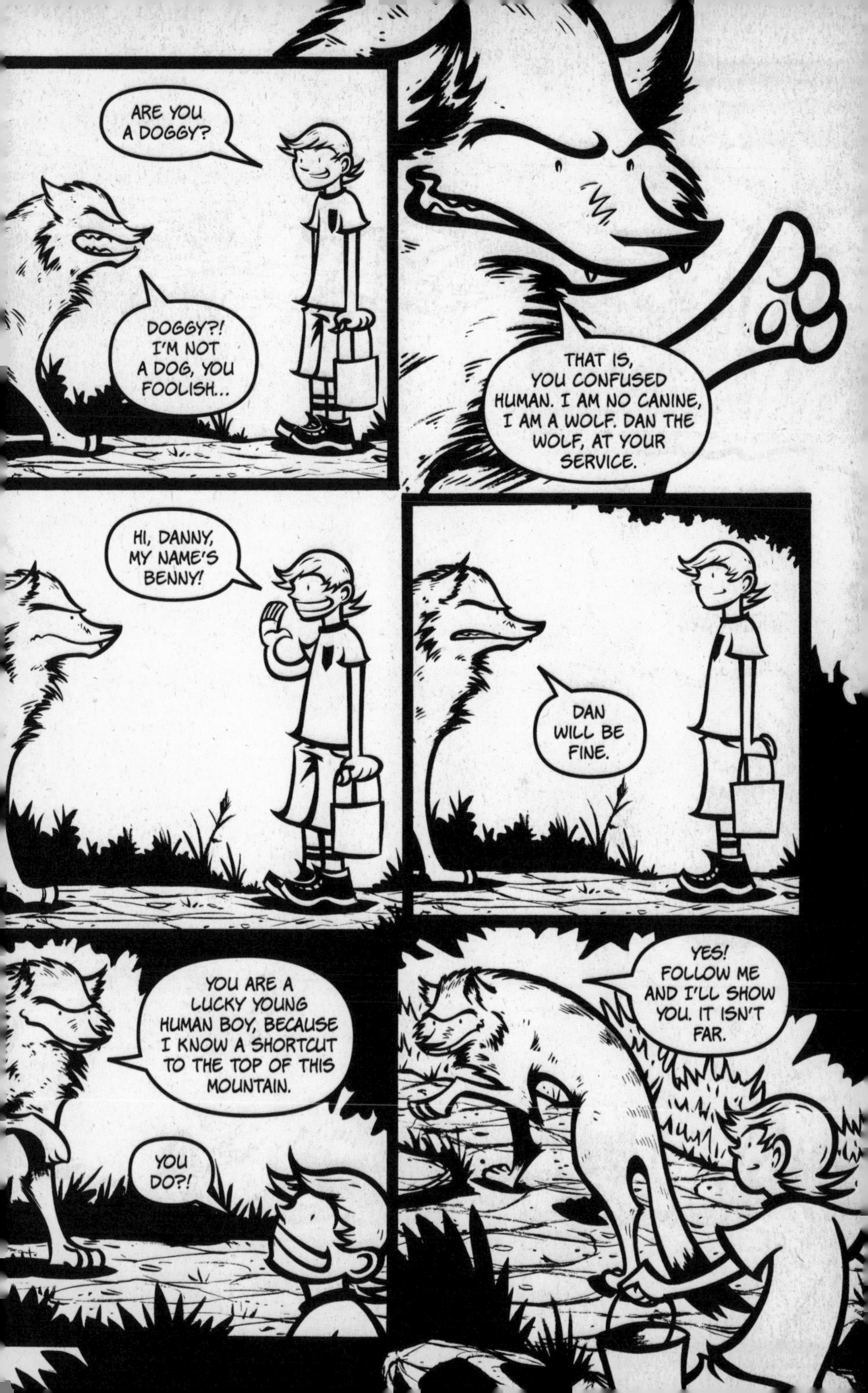
ARE YOU A DOGGY?
DOGGY?! I'M NOT A DOG, YOU FOOLISH...
THAT IS, YOU CONFUSED HUMAN. I AM NO CANINE, I AM A WOLF. DAN THE WOLF, AT YOUR SERVICE.
HI, DANNY, MY NAME'S BENNY!
DAN WILL BE FINE.
YOU ARE A LUCKY YOUNG HUMAN BOY, BECAUSE I KNOW A SHORTCUT TO THE TOP OF THIS MOUNTAIN.
YOU DO?!
YES! FOLLOW ME AND I'LL SHOW YOU. IT ISN'T FAR.

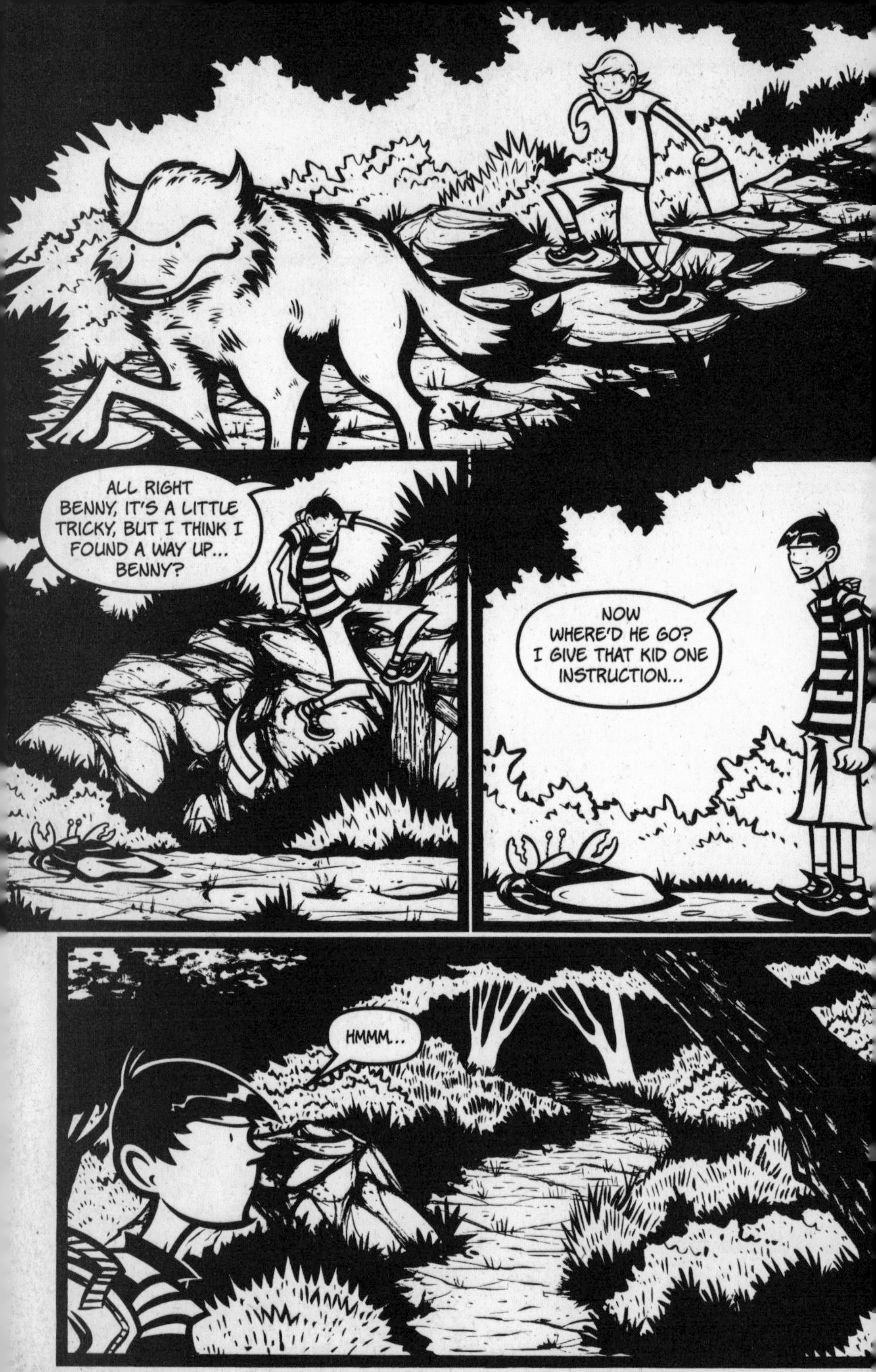
ALL RIGHT BENNY, IT'S A LITTLE TRICKY, BUT I THINK I FOUND A WAY UP... BENNY?
NOW WHERE'D HE GO? I GIVE THAT KID ONE INSTRUCTION...
HMMM...

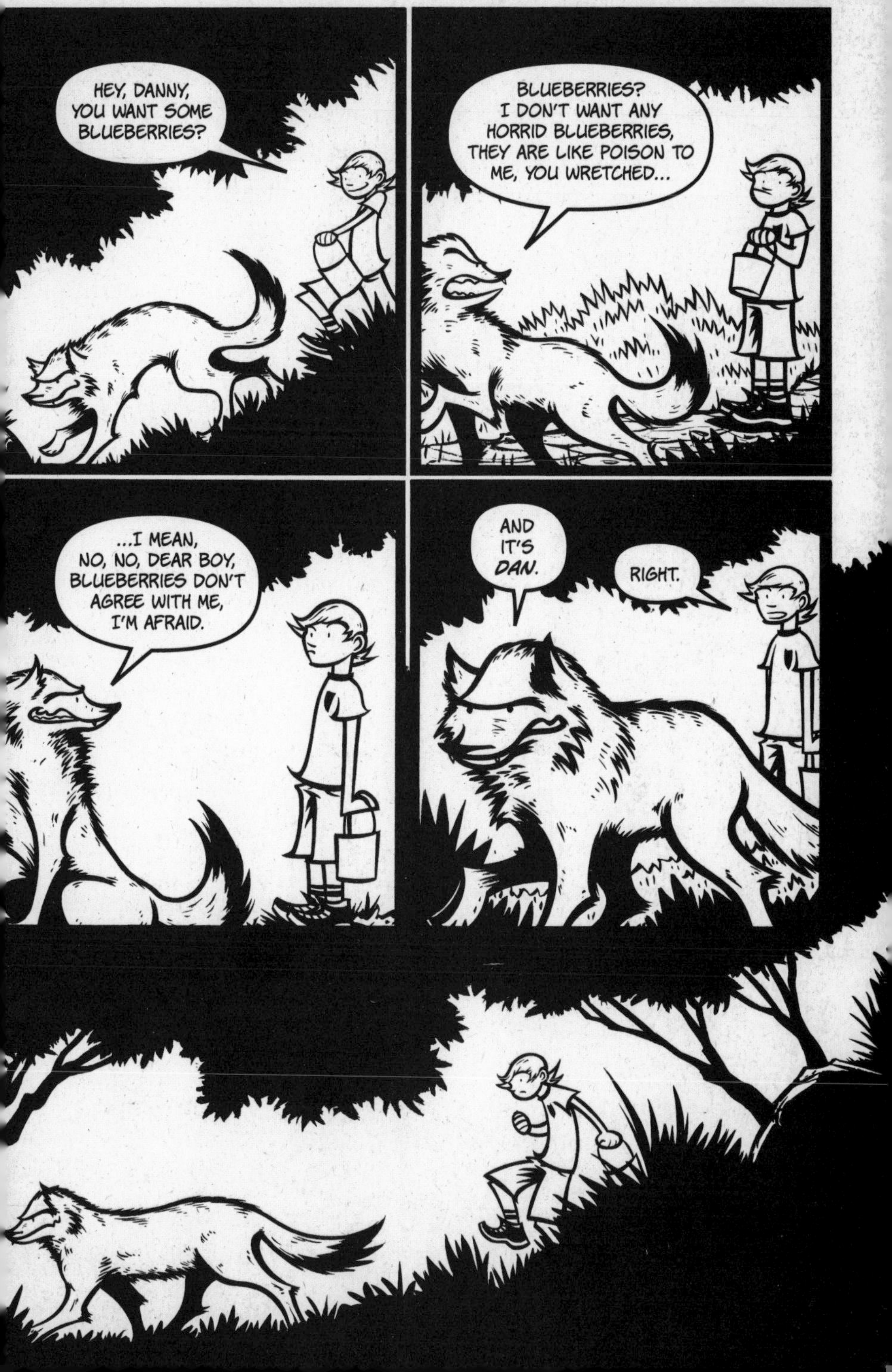
HEY, DANNY, YOU WANT SOME BLUEBERRIES?
BLUEBERRIES? I DON'T WANT ANY HORRID BLUEBERRIES, THEY ARE LIKE POISON TO ME, YOU WRETCHED...
...I MEAN, NO, NO, DEAR BOY, BLUEBERRIES DON'T AGREE WITH ME, I'M AFRAID.
AND IT'S *DAN*.
RIGHT.

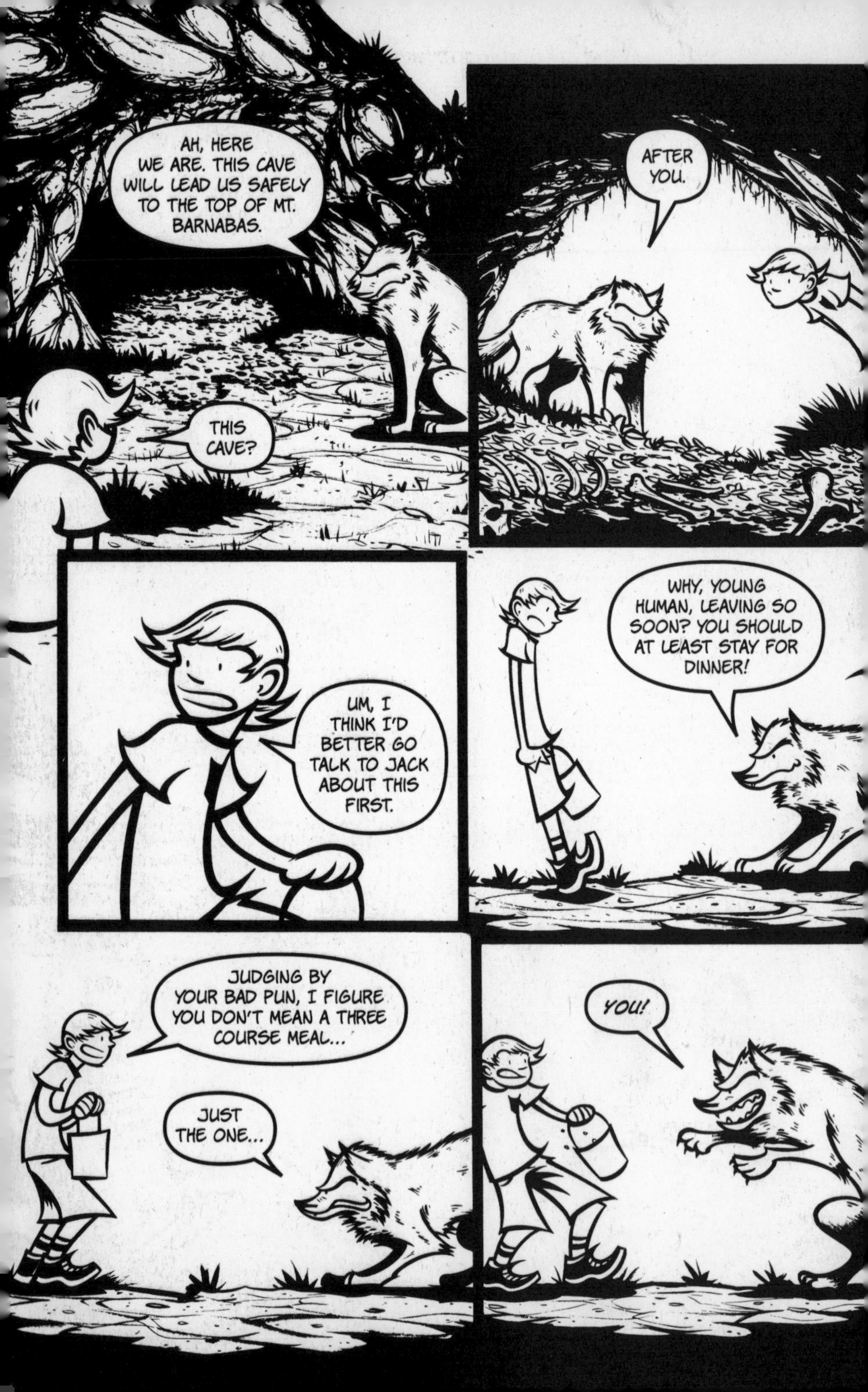
AH, HERE WE ARE. THIS CAVE WILL LEAD US SAFELY TO THE TOP OF MT. BARNABAS.
THIS CAVE?
AFTER YOU.
UM, I THINK I'D BETTER GO TALK TO JACK ABOUT THIS FIRST.
WHY, YOUNG HUMAN, LEAVING SO SOON? YOU SHOULD AT LEAST STAY FOR DINNER!
JUDGING BY YOUR BAD PUN, I FIGURE YOU DON'T MEAN A THREE COURSE MEAL...
JUST THE ONE...
YOU!

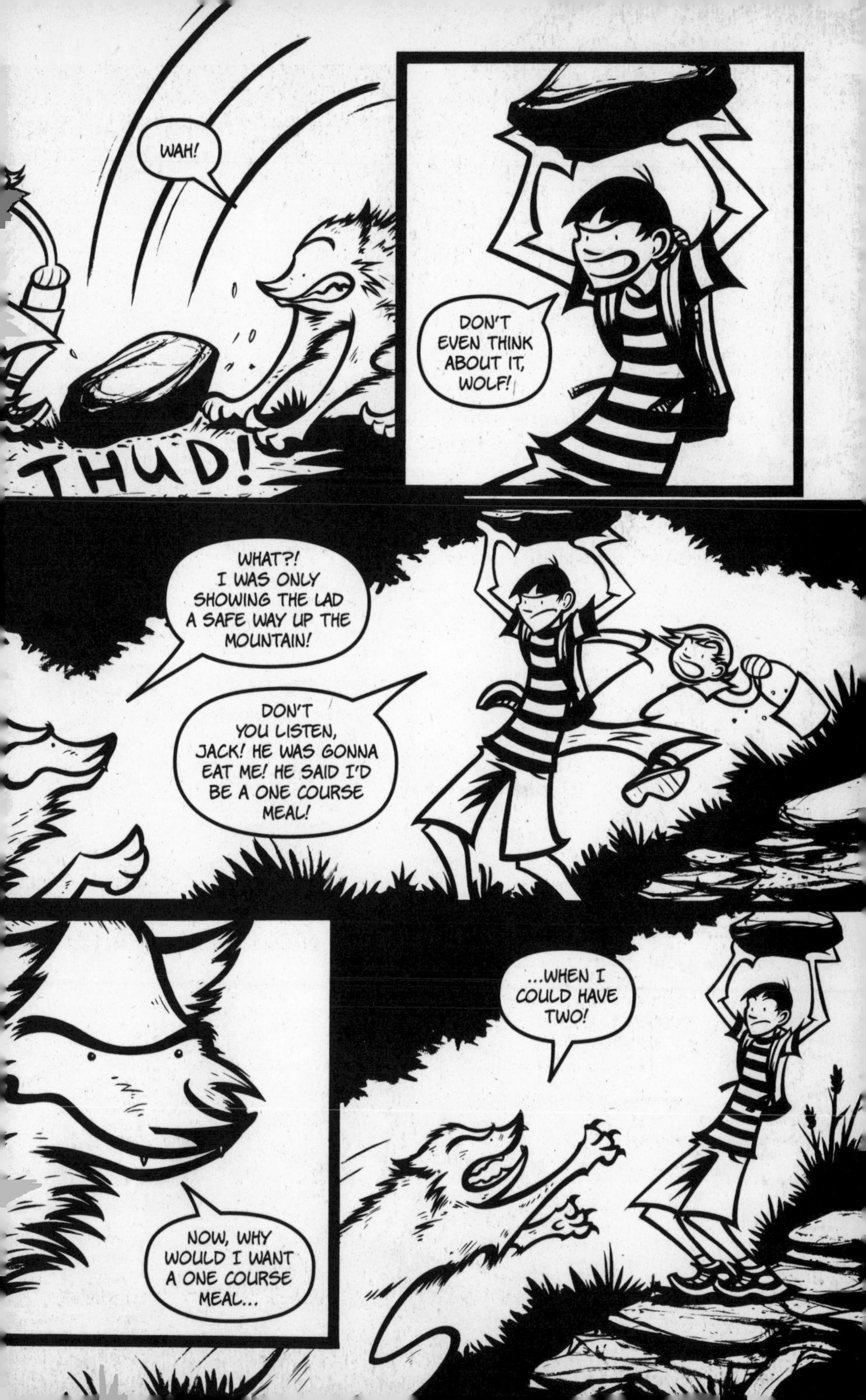
WAH!
THUD!
DON'T EVEN THINK ABOUT IT, WOLF!
WHAT?! I WAS ONLY SHOWING THE LAD A SAFE WAY UP THE MOUNTAIN!
DON'T YOU LISTEN, JACK! HE WAS GONNA EAT ME! HE SAID I'D BE A ONE COURSE MEAL!
NOW, WHY WOULD I WANT A ONE COURSE MEAL...
...WHEN I COULD HAVE TWO!

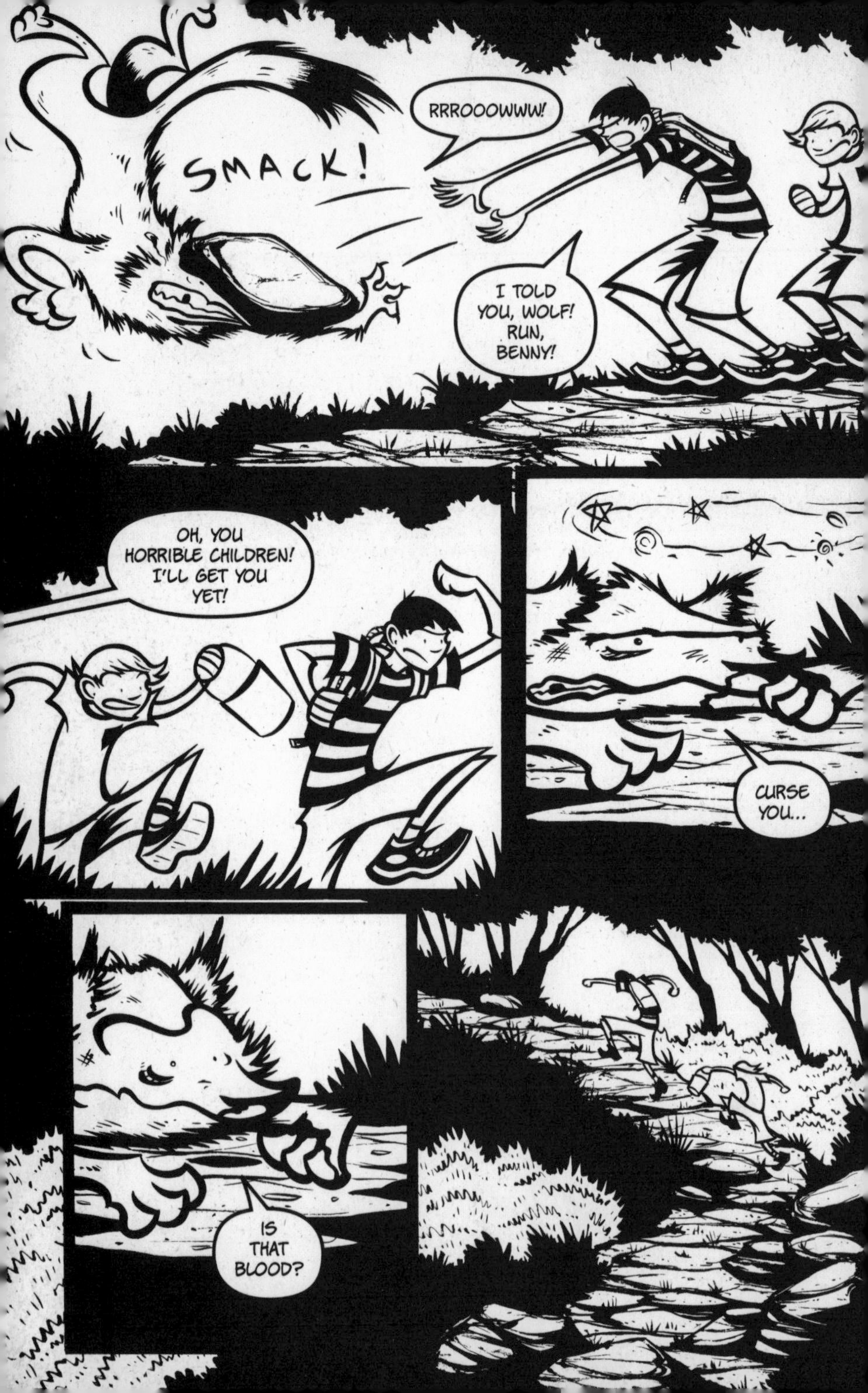
SMACK!
RRROOOWWW!
I TOLD YOU, WOLF! RUN, BENNY!
OH, YOU HORRIBLE CHILDREN! I'LL GET YOU YET!
CURSE YOU...
IS THAT BLOOD?

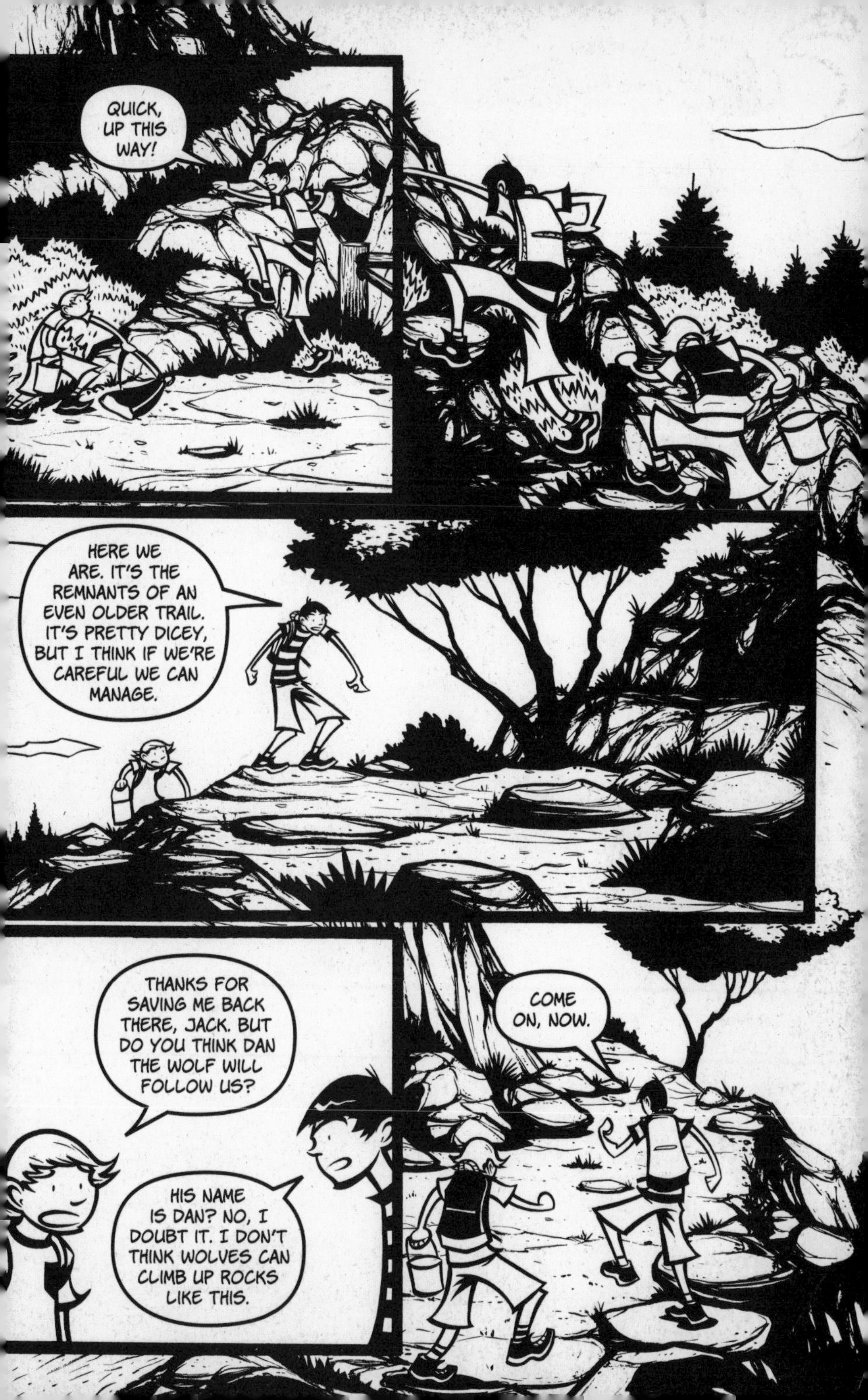

QUICK, UP THIS WAY!
HERE WE ARE. IT'S THE REMNANTS OF AN EVEN OLDER TRAIL. IT'S PRETTY DICEY, BUT I THINK IF WE'RE CAREFUL WE CAN MANAGE.
THANKS FOR SAVING ME BACK THERE, JACK. BUT DO YOU THINK DAN THE WOLF WILL FOLLOW US?
HIS NAME IS DAN? NO, I DOUBT IT. I DON'T THINK WOLVES CAN CLIMB UP ROCKS LIKE THIS.
COME ON, NOW.

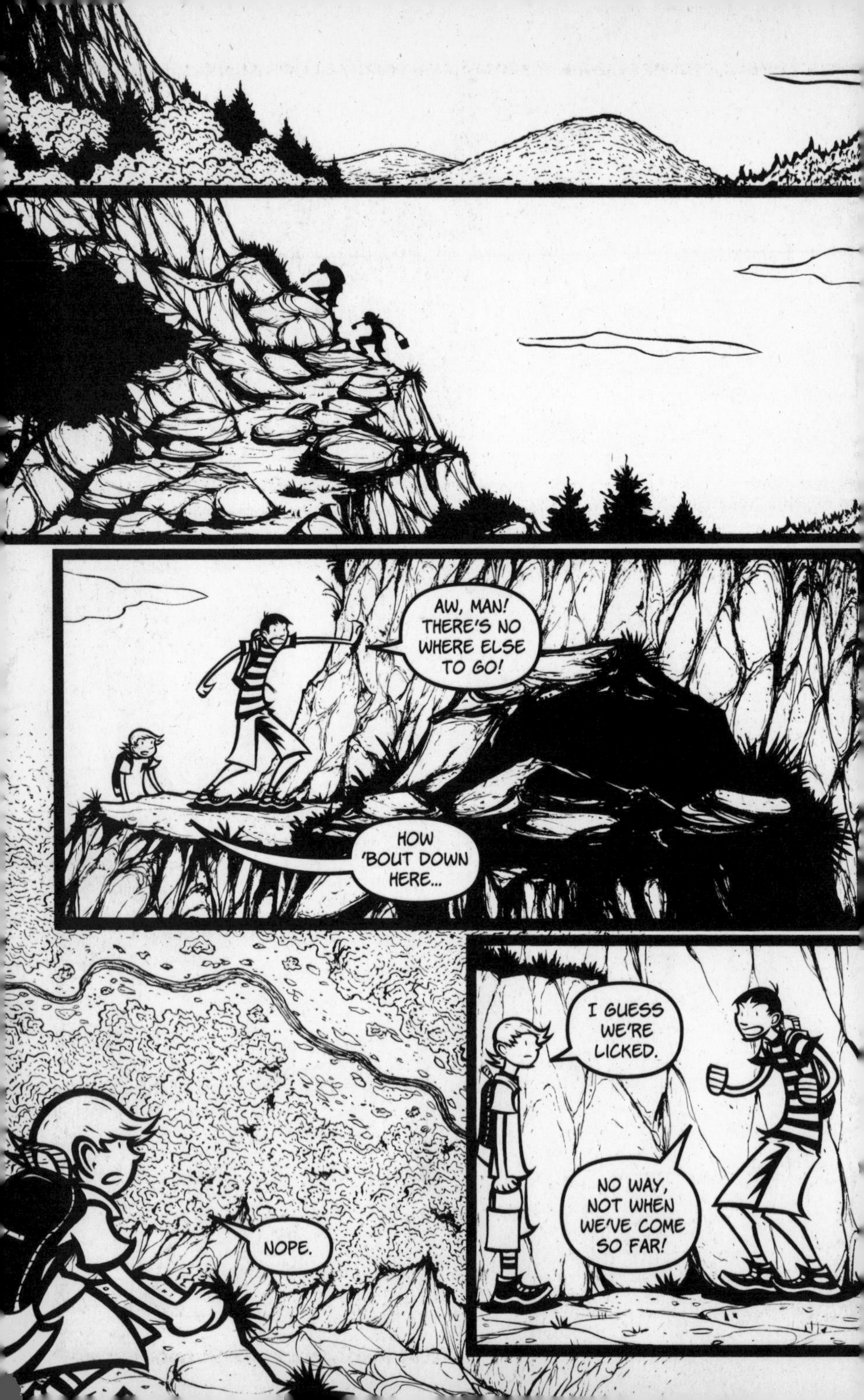
AW, MAN! THERE'S NO WHERE ELSE TO GO!
HOW 'BOUT DOWN HERE...
NOPE.
I GUESS WE'RE LICKED.
NO WAY, NOT WHEN WE'VE COME SO FAR!

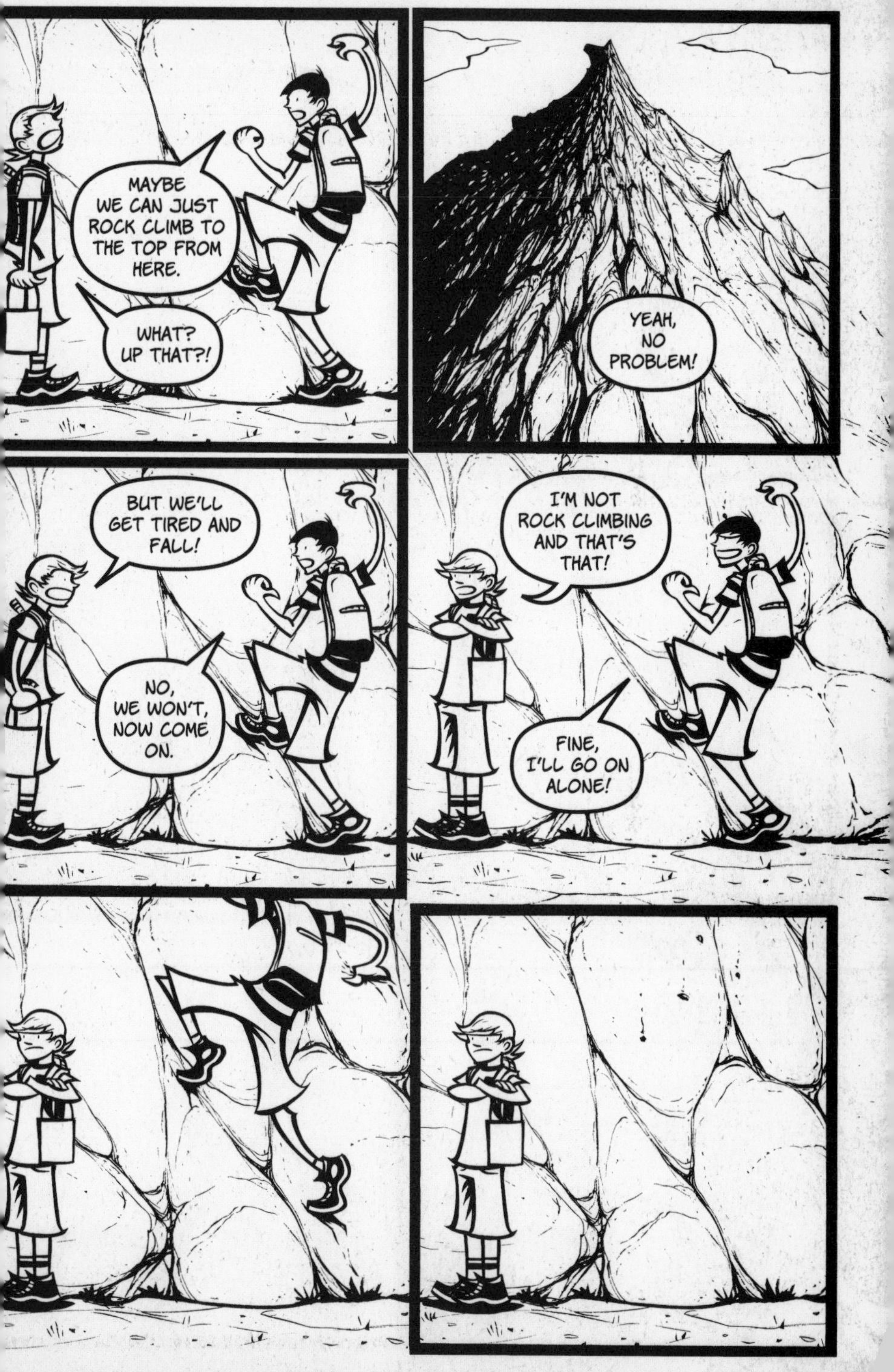
MAYBE WE CAN JUST ROCK CLIMB TO THE TOP FROM HERE.
WHAT? UP THAT?!
YEAH, NO PROBLEM!
BUT WE'LL GET TIRED AND FALL!
NO, WE WON'T, NOW COME ON.
I'M NOT ROCK CLIMBING AND THAT'S THAT!
FINE, I'LL GO ON ALONE!

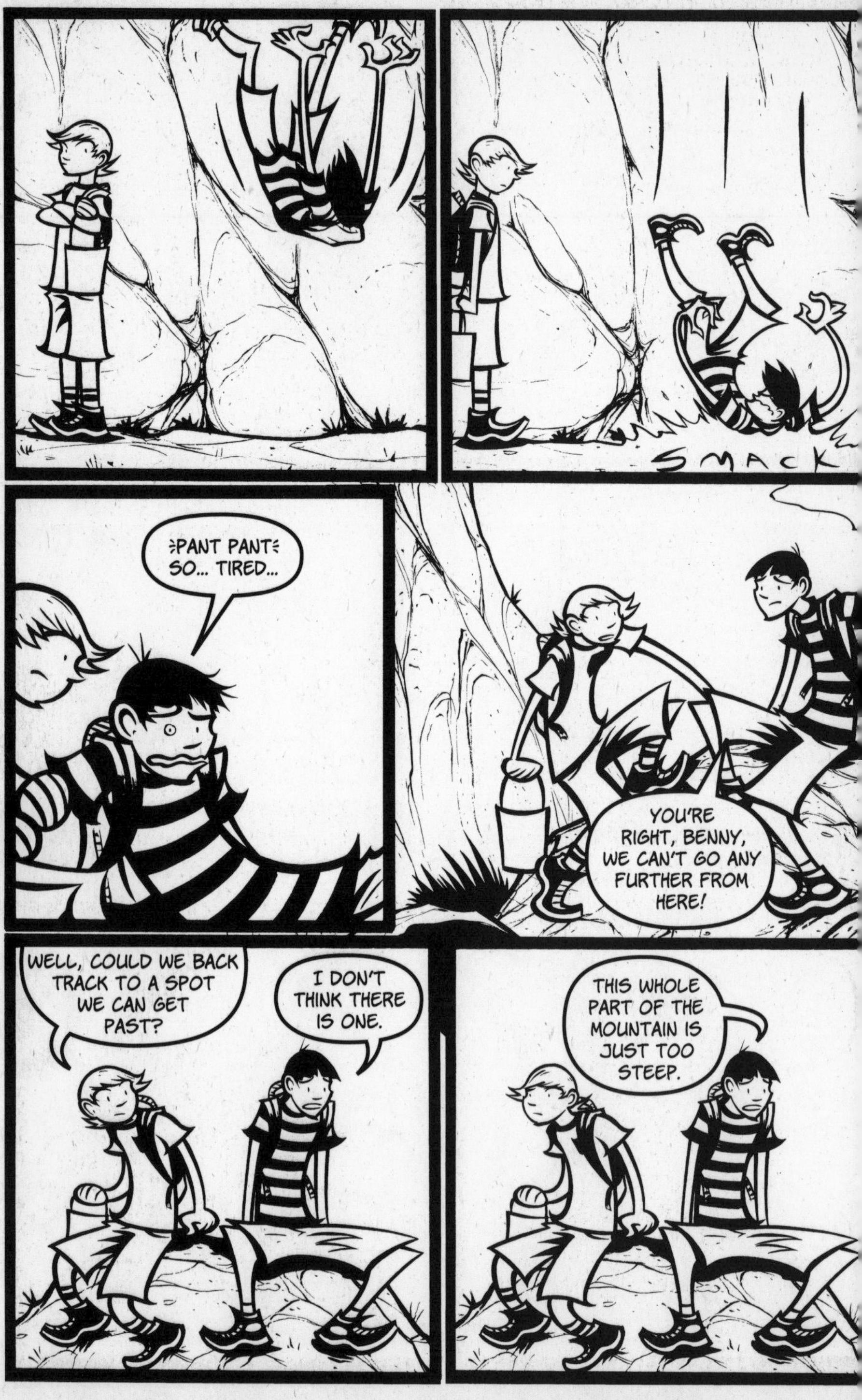
SMACK
PANT PANT
SO... TIRED...
YOU'RE RIGHT, BENNY, WE CAN'T GO ANY FURTHER FROM HERE!
WELL, COULD WE BACK TRACK TO A SPOT WE CAN GET PAST?
I DON'T THINK THERE IS ONE.
THIS WHOLE PART OF THE MOUNTAIN IS JUST TOO STEEP.

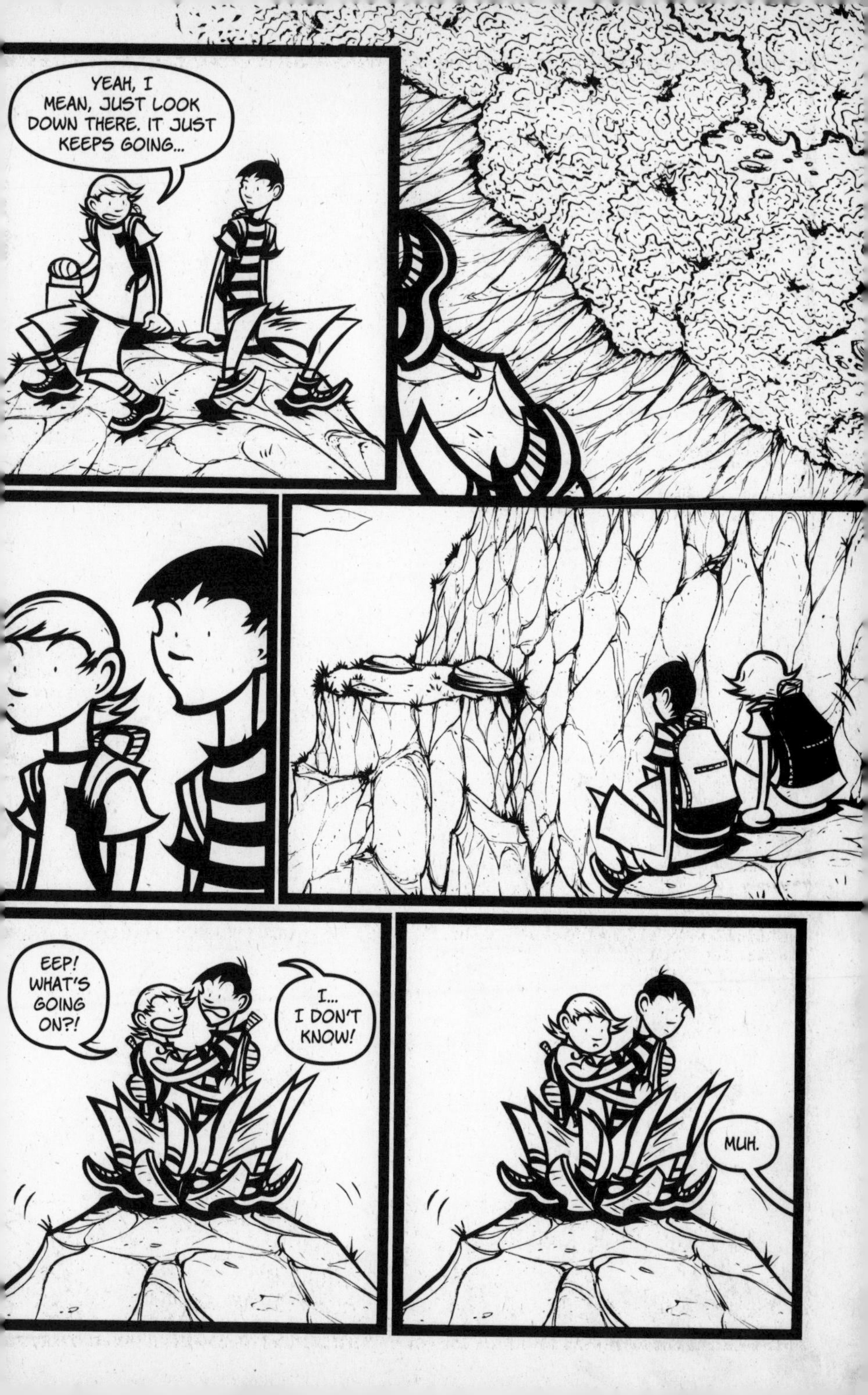
YEAH, I MEAN, JUST LOOK DOWN THERE. IT JUST KEEPS GOING...
EEP! WHAT'S GOING ON?!
I... I DON'T KNOW!
MUH.

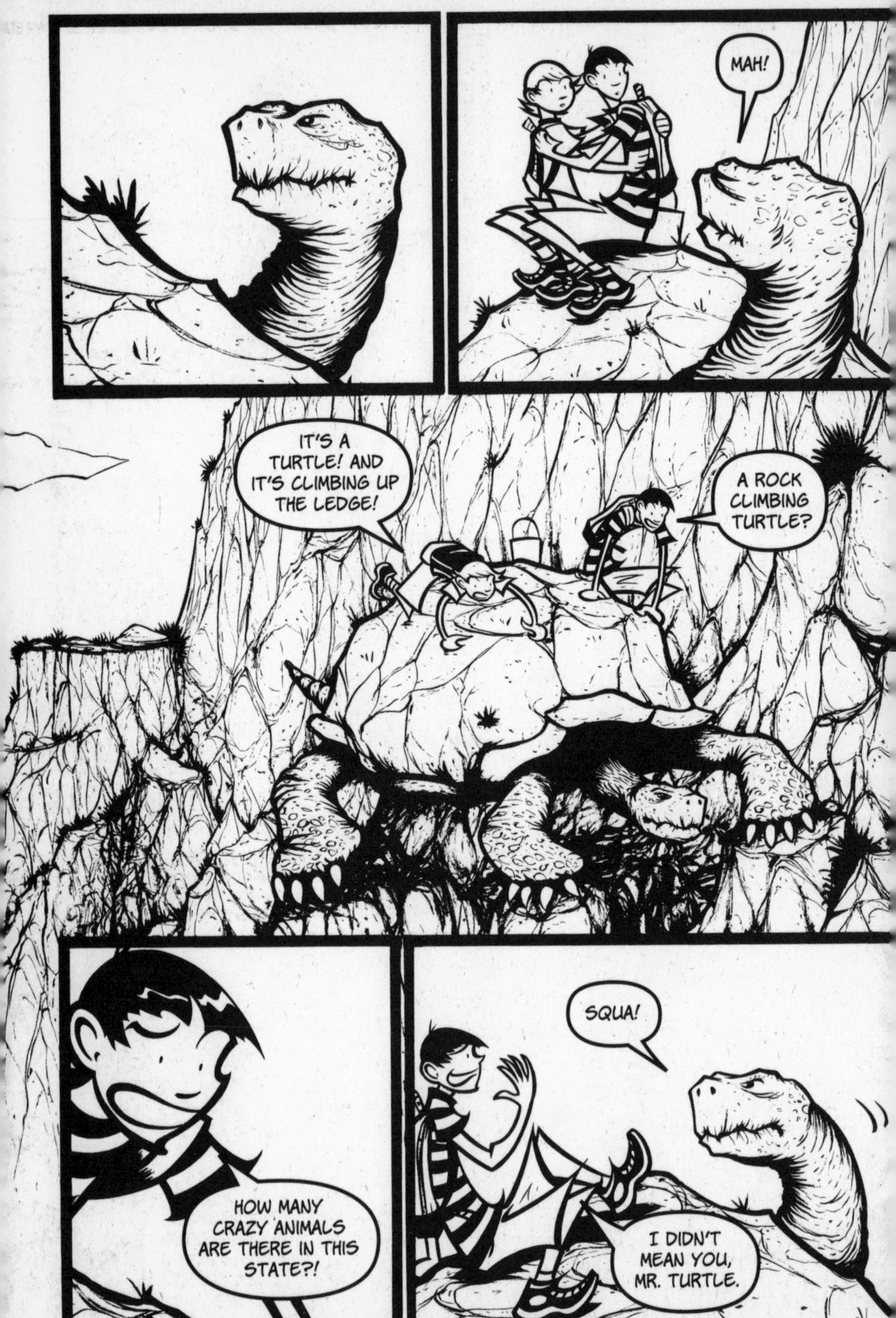
MAH!
IT'S A TURTLE! AND IT'S CLIMBING UP THE LEDGE!
A ROCK CLIMBING TURTLE?
HOW MANY CRAZY ANIMALS ARE THERE IN THIS STATE?!
SQUA!
I DIDN'T MEAN YOU, MR. TURTLE.

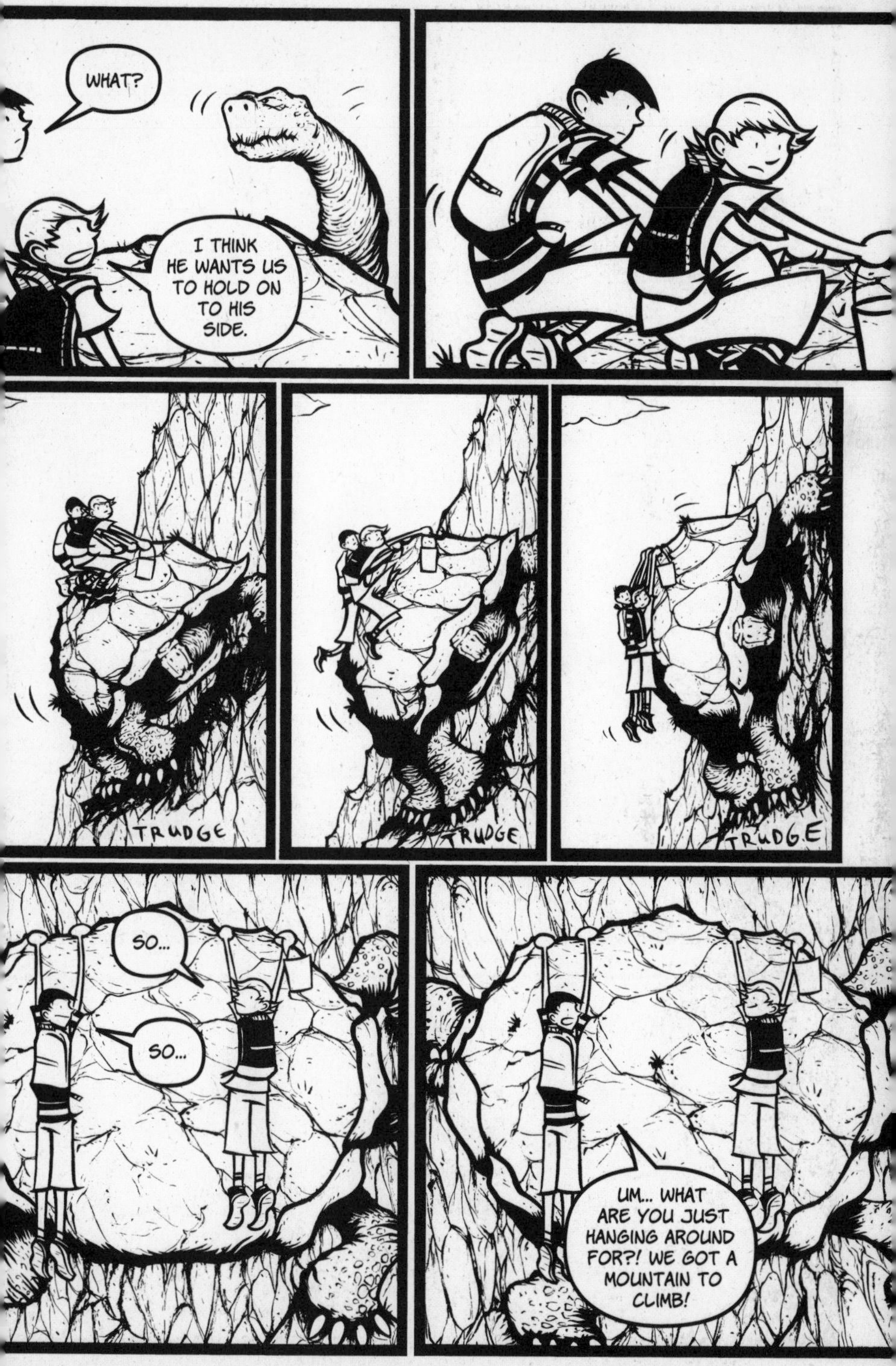
WHAT?
I THINK HE WANTS US TO HOLD ON TO HIS SIDE.
TRUDGE
TRUDGE
TRUDGE
SO...
SO...
UM... WHAT ARE YOU JUST HANGING AROUND FOR?! WE GOT A MOUNTAIN TO CLIMB!

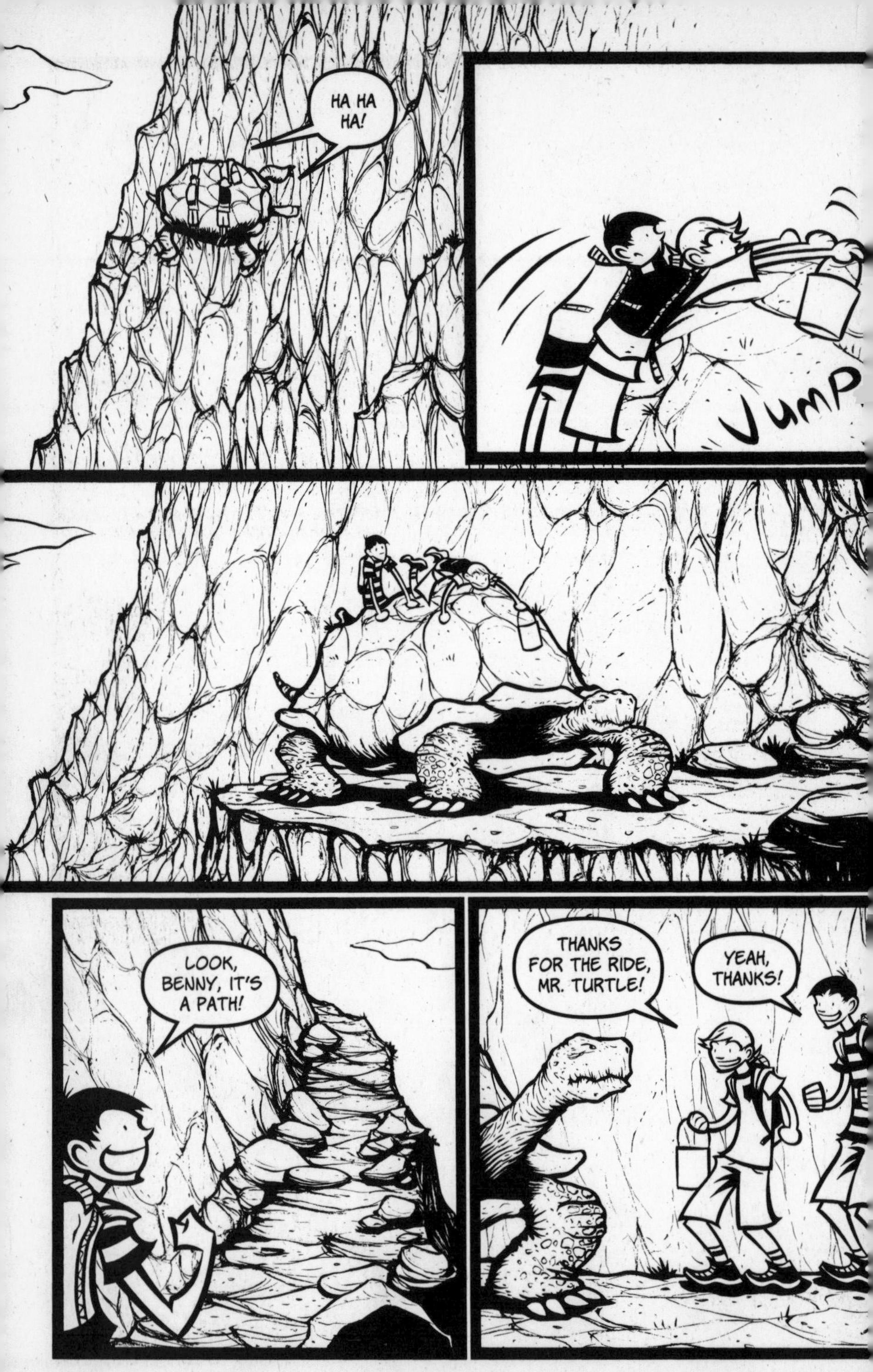
HA HA HA!
JUMP
LOOK, BENNY, IT'S A PATH!
THANKS FOR THE RIDE, MR. TURTLE!
YEAH, THANKS!

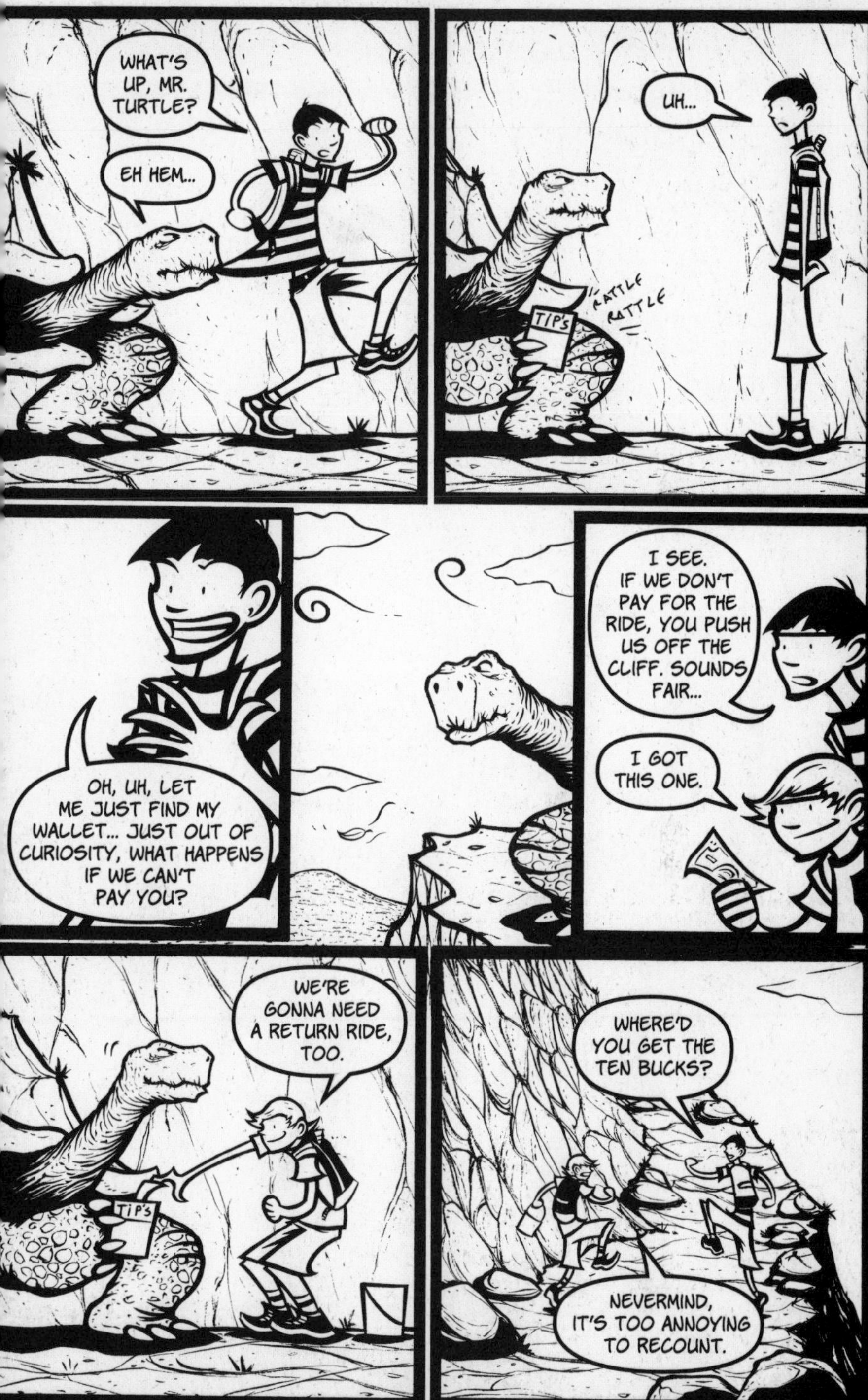
WHAT'S UP, MR. TURTLE?
EH HEM...
UH...
RATTLE RATTLE
TIP'S
OH, UH, LET ME JUST FIND MY WALLET... JUST OUT OF CURIOSITY, WHAT HAPPENS IF WE CAN'T PAY YOU?
I SEE. IF WE DON'T PAY FOR THE RIDE, YOU PUSH US OFF THE CLIFF. SOUNDS FAIR...
I GOT THIS ONE.
WE'RE GONNA NEED A RETURN RIDE, TOO.
TIP'S
WHERE'D YOU GET THE TEN BUCKS?
NEVERMIND, IT'S TOO ANNOYING TO RECOUNT.

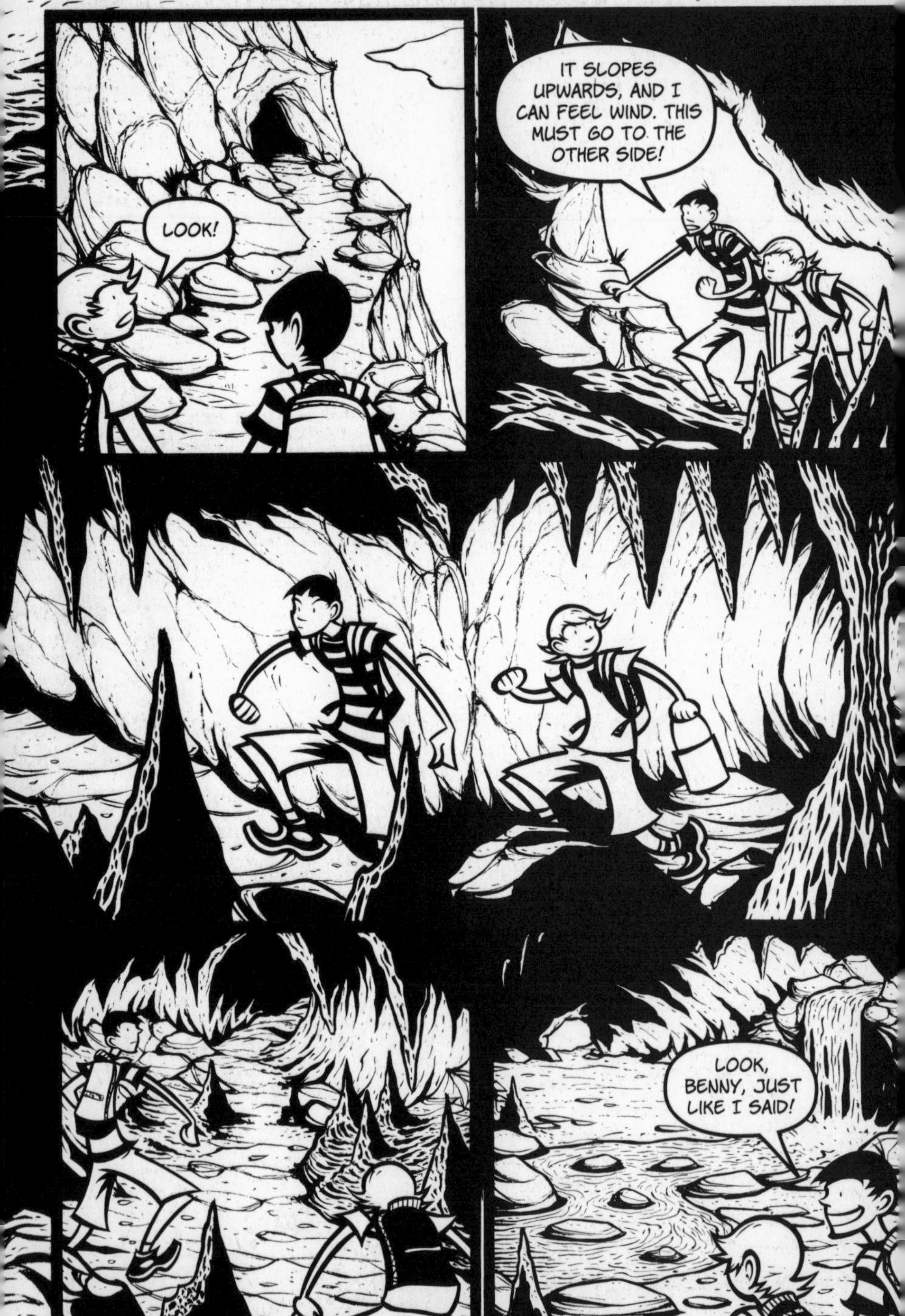
LOOK!
IT SLOPES UPWARDS, AND I CAN FEEL WIND. THIS MUST GO TO THE OTHER SIDE!
LOOK, BENNY, JUST LIKE I SAID!

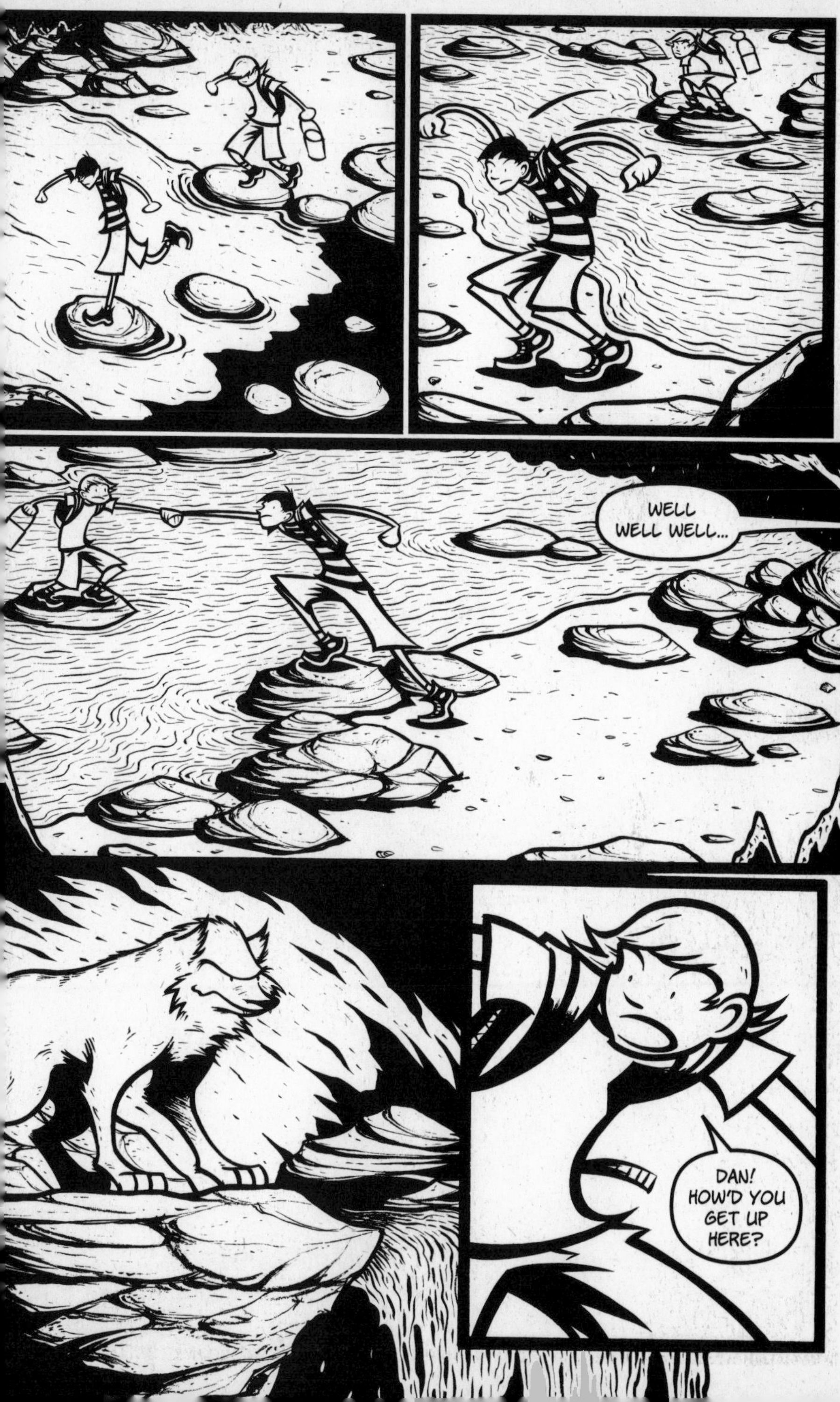
WELL
WELL WELL...
DAN!
HOW'D YOU
GET UP
HERE?

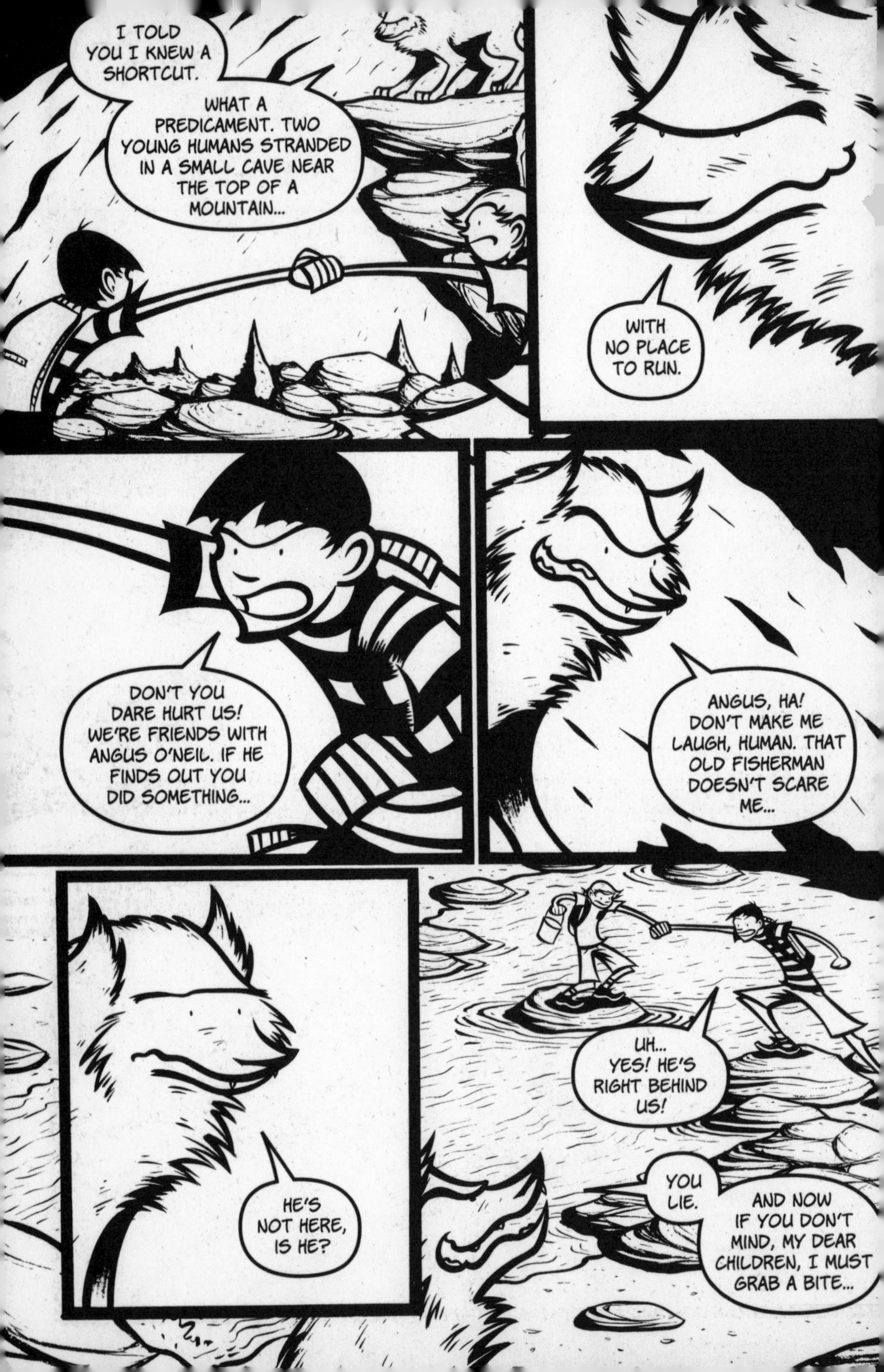
I TOLD YOU I KNEW A SHORTCUT.
WHAT A PREDICAMENT. TWO YOUNG HUMANS STRANDED IN A SMALL CAVE NEAR THE TOP OF A MOUNTAIN...
WITH NO PLACE TO RUN.
DON'T YOU DARE HURT US! WE'RE FRIENDS WITH ANGUS O'NEIL. IF HE FINDS OUT YOU DID SOMETHING...
ANGUS, HA! DON'T MAKE ME LAUGH, HUMAN. THAT OLD FISHERMAN DOESN'T SCARE ME...
UH... YES! HE'S RIGHT BEHIND US!
HE'S NOT HERE, IS HE?
YOU LIE.
AND NOW IF YOU DON'T MIND, MY DEAR CHILDREN, I MUST GRAB A BITE...

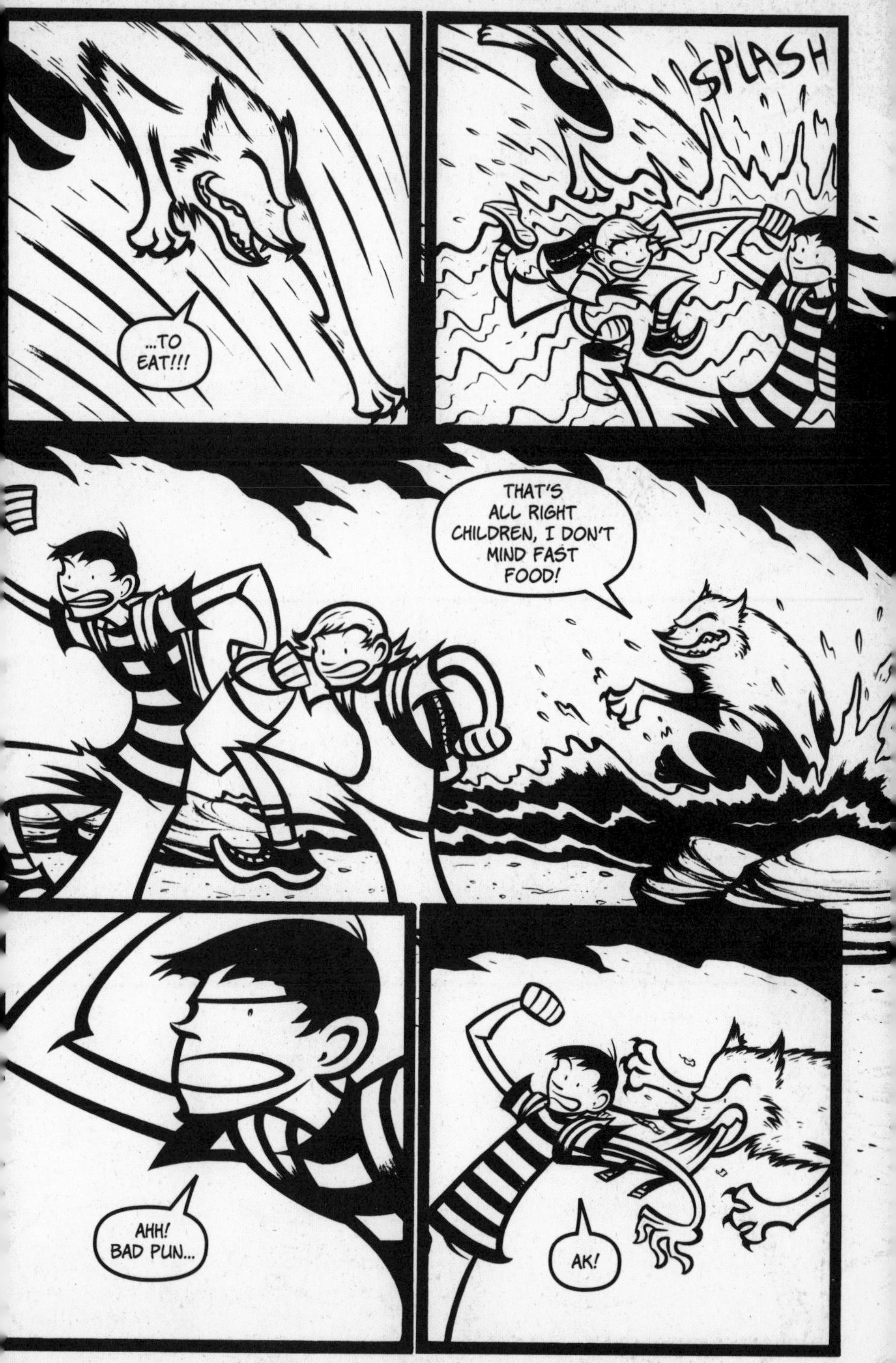
...TO EAT!!!
SPLASH
THAT'S ALL RIGHT CHILDREN, I DON'T MIND FAST FOOD!
AHH! BAD PUN...
AK!

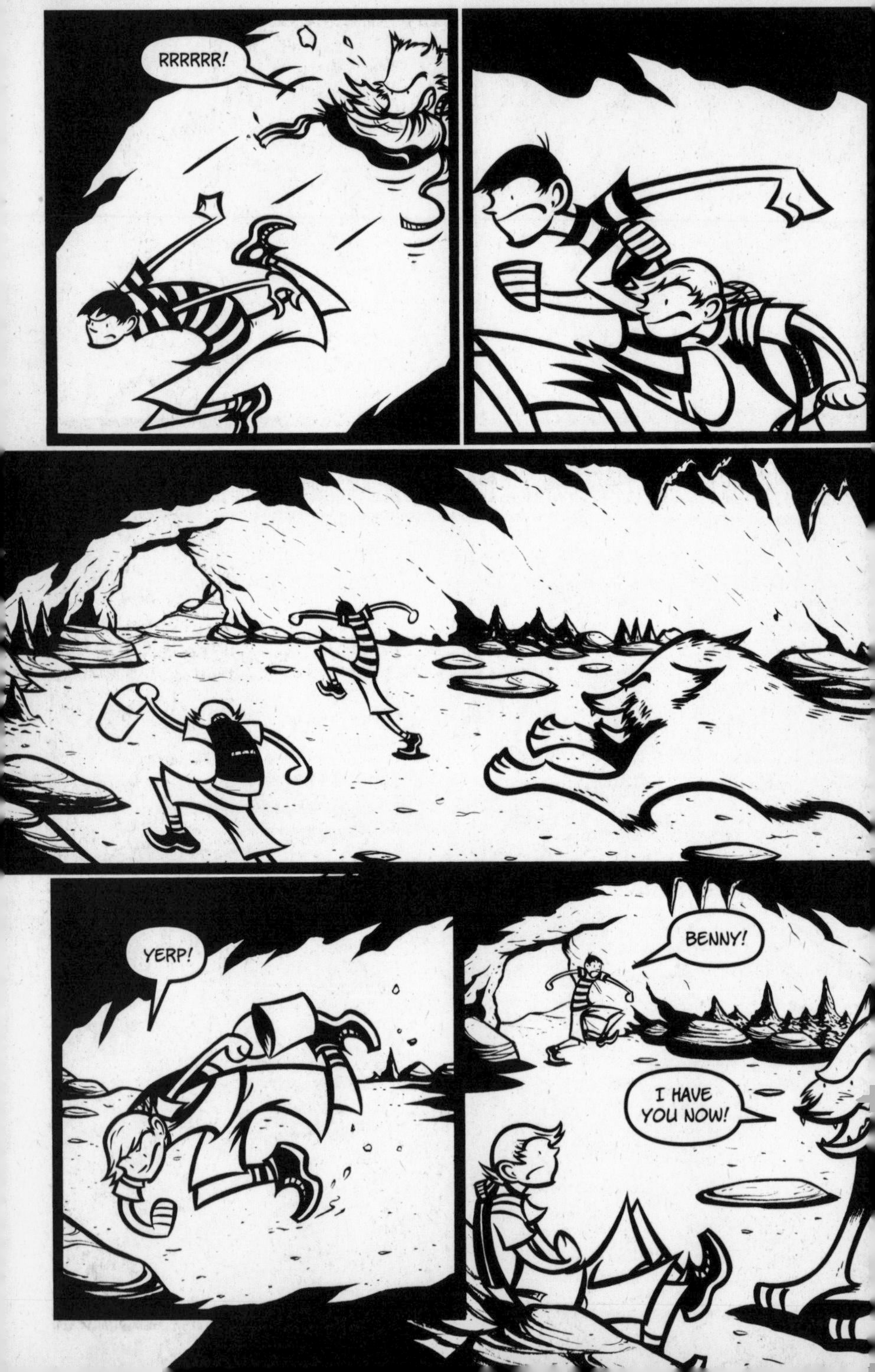
RRRRRR!
YERP!
BENNY!
I HAVE YOU NOW!

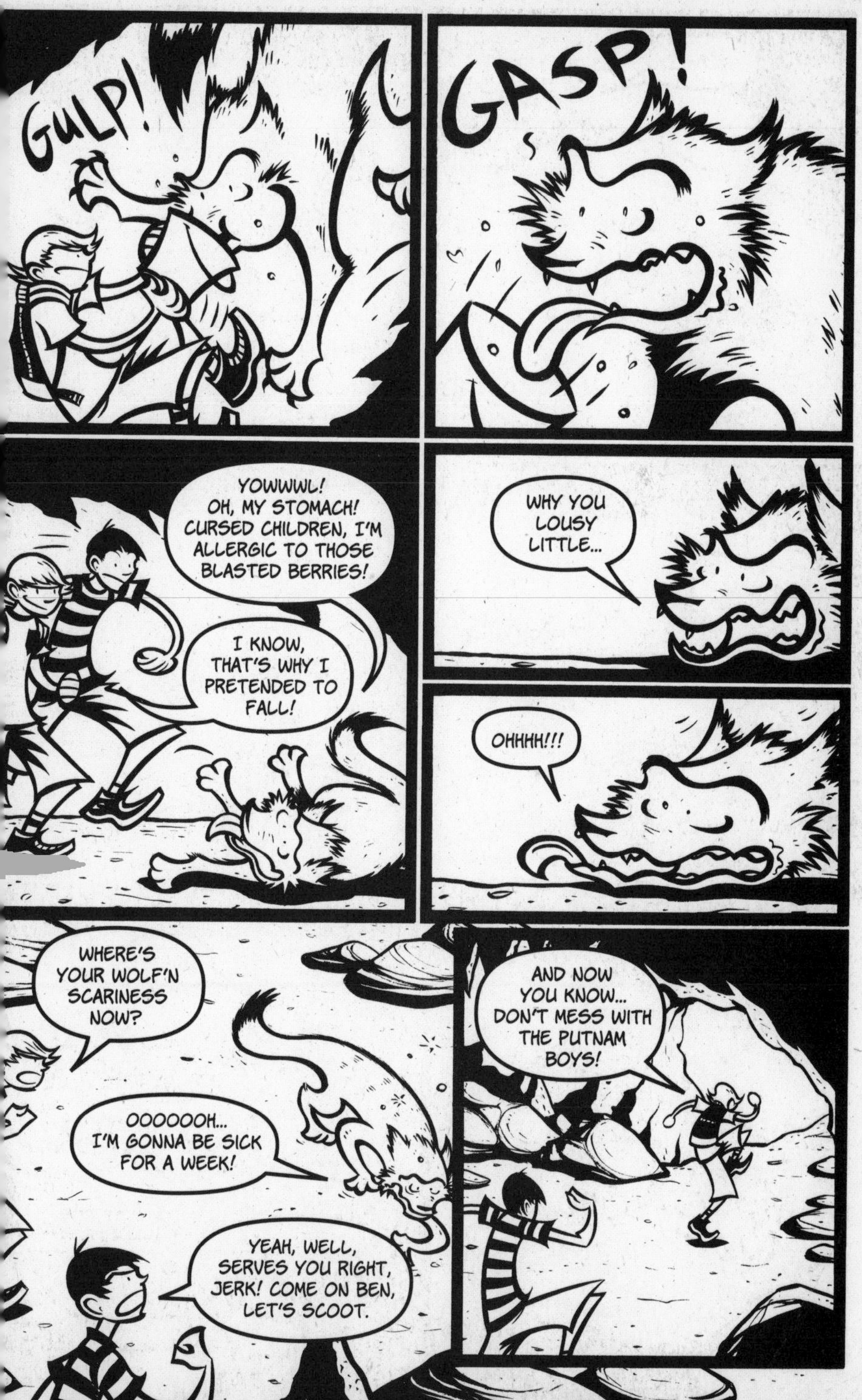
GULP!
GASP!
YOWWWL! OH, MY STOMACH! CURSED CHILDREN, I'M ALLERGIC TO THOSE BLASTED BERRIES!
I KNOW, THAT'S WHY I PRETENDED TO FALL!
WHY YOU LOUSY LITTLE...
OHHHH!!!
WHERE'S YOUR WOLF'N SCARINESS NOW?
OOOOOOH... I'M GONNA BE SICK FOR A WEEK!
YEAH, WELL, SERVES YOU RIGHT, JERK! COME ON BEN, LET'S SCOOT.
AND NOW YOU KNOW... DON'T MESS WITH THE PUTNAM BOYS!

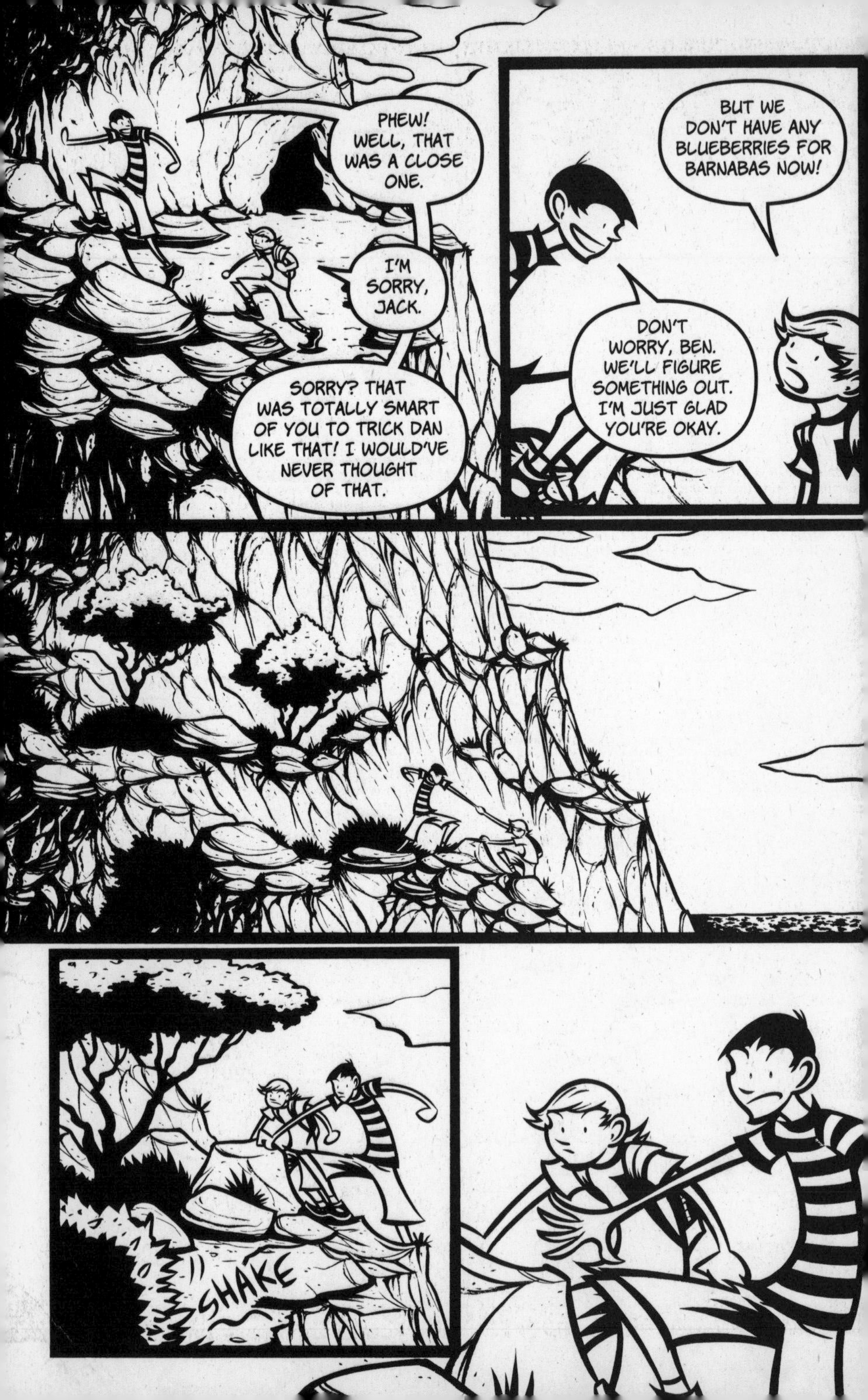
PHEW! WELL, THAT WAS A CLOSE ONE.
I'M SORRY, JACK.
SORRY? THAT WAS TOTALLY SMART OF YOU TO TRICK DAN LIKE THAT! I WOULD'VE NEVER THOUGHT OF THAT.
BUT WE DON'T HAVE ANY BLUEBERRIES FOR BARNABAS NOW!
DON'T WORRY, BEN. WE'LL FIGURE SOMETHING OUT. I'M JUST GLAD YOU'RE OKAY.
SHAKE

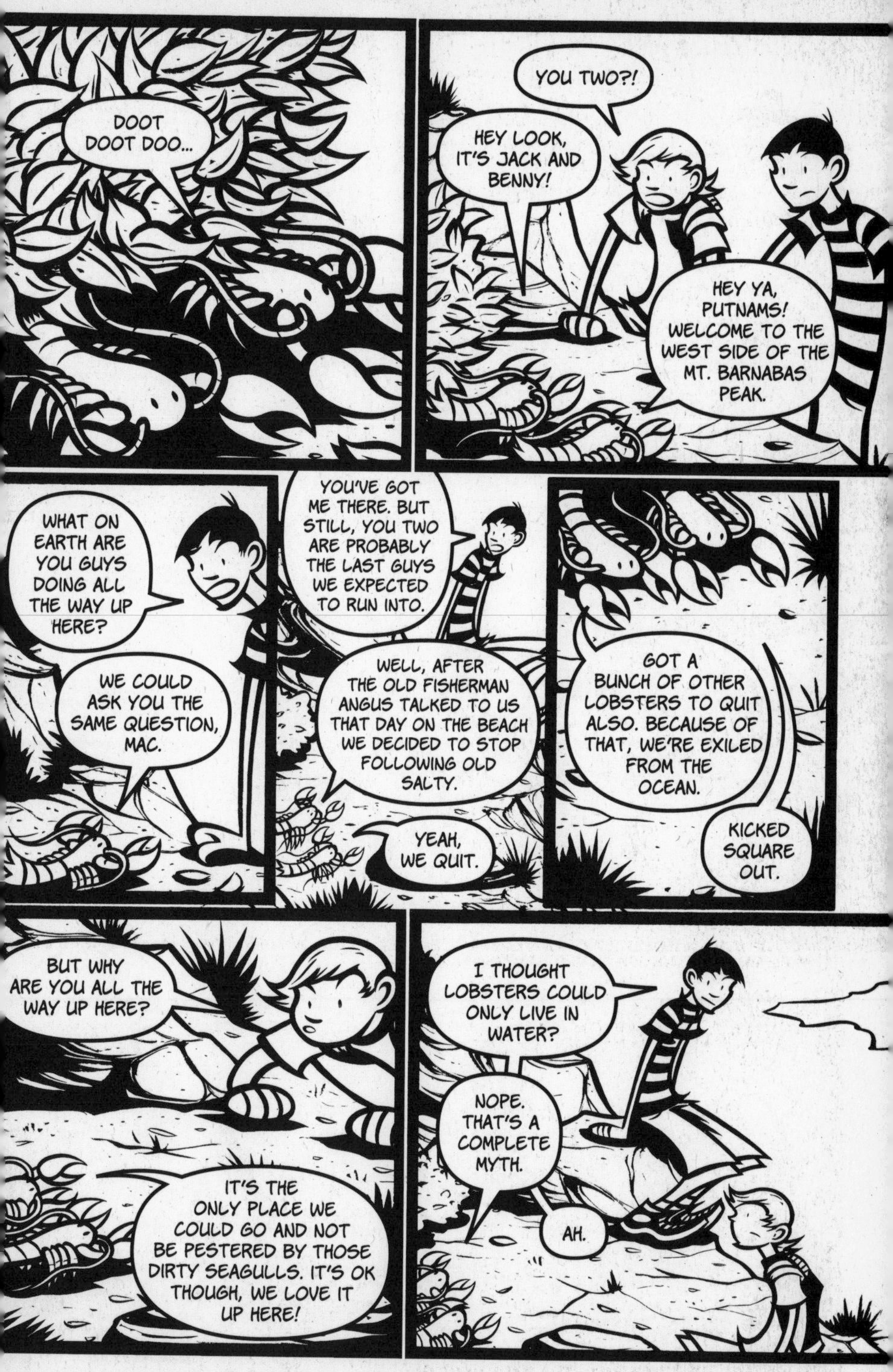
DOOT DOOT DOO...
YOU TWO?!
HEY LOOK, IT'S JACK AND BENNY!
HEY YA, PUTNAMS! WELCOME TO THE WEST SIDE OF THE MT. BARNABAS PEAK.
WHAT ON EARTH ARE YOU GUYS DOING ALL THE WAY UP HERE?
WE COULD ASK YOU THE SAME QUESTION, MAC.
YOU'VE GOT ME THERE. BUT STILL, YOU TWO ARE PROBABLY THE LAST GUYS WE EXPECTED TO RUN INTO.
WELL, AFTER THE OLD FISHERMAN ANGUS TALKED TO US THAT DAY ON THE BEACH WE DECIDED TO STOP FOLLOWING OLD SALTY.
YEAH, WE QUIT.
GOT A BUNCH OF OTHER LOBSTERS TO QUIT ALSO. BECAUSE OF THAT, WE'RE EXILED FROM THE OCEAN.
KICKED SQUARE OUT.
BUT WHY ARE YOU ALL THE WAY UP HERE?
IT'S THE ONLY PLACE WE COULD GO AND NOT BE PESTERED BY THOSE DIRTY SEAGULLS. IT'S OK THOUGH, WE LOVE IT UP HERE!
I THOUGHT LOBSTERS COULD ONLY LIVE IN WATER?
NOPE. THAT'S A COMPLETE MYTH.
AH.

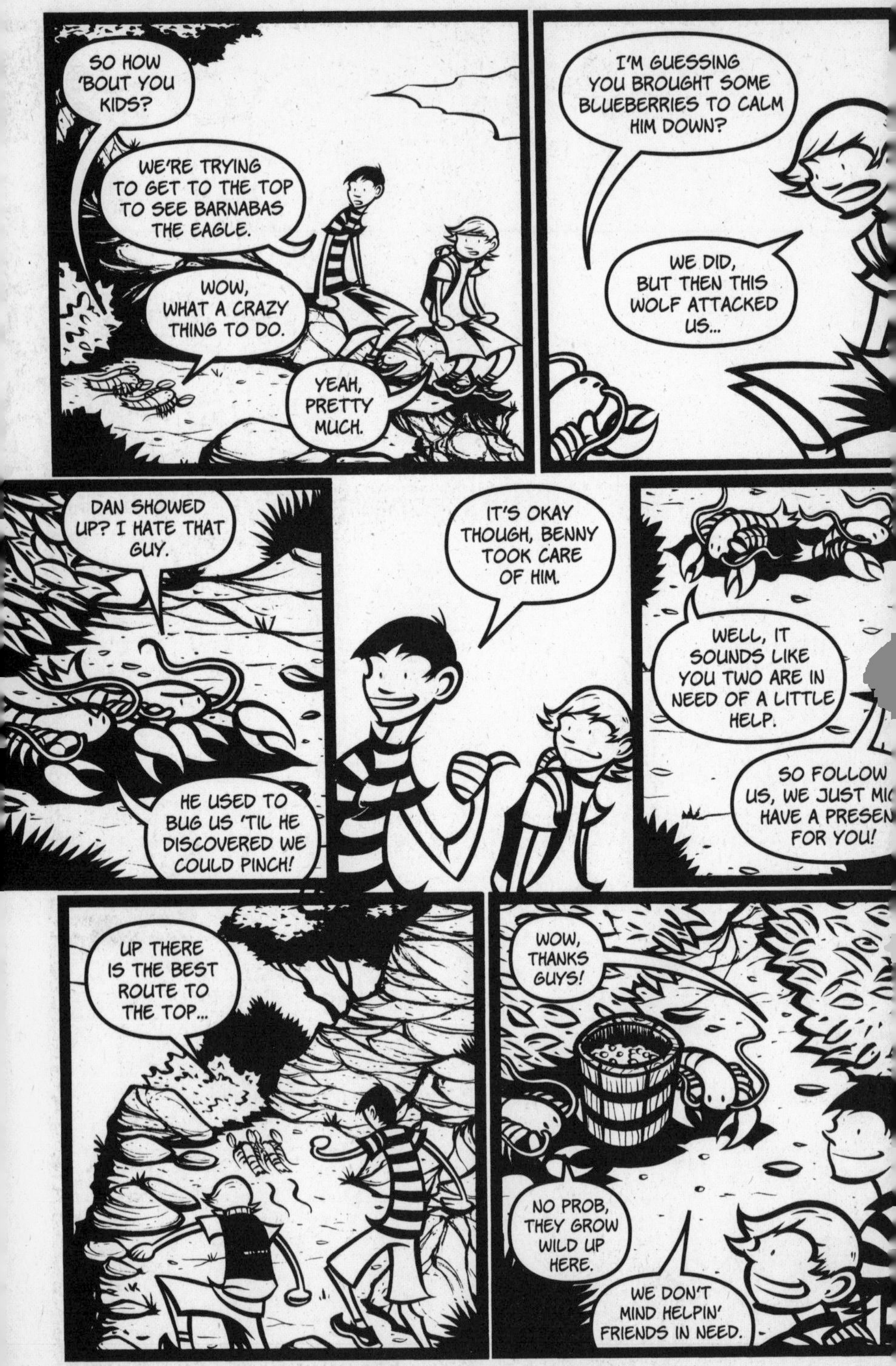
SO HOW 'BOUT YOU KIDS?
WE'RE TRYING TO GET TO THE TOP TO SEE BARNABAS THE EAGLE.
WOW, WHAT A CRAZY THING TO DO.
YEAH, PRETTY MUCH.
I'M GUESSING YOU BROUGHT SOME BLUEBERRIES TO CALM HIM DOWN?
WE DID, BUT THEN THIS WOLF ATTACKED US...
DAN SHOWED UP? I HATE THAT GUY.
HE USED TO BUG US 'TIL HE DISCOVERED WE COULD PINCH!
IT'S OKAY THOUGH, BENNY TOOK CARE OF HIM.
WELL, IT SOUNDS LIKE YOU TWO ARE IN NEED OF A LITTLE HELP.
SO FOLLOW US, WE JUST MI HAVE A PRESEN FOR YOU!
UP THERE IS THE BEST ROUTE TO THE TOP...
WOW, THANKS GUYS!
NO PROB, THEY GROW WILD UP HERE.
WE DON'T MIND HELPIN' FRIENDS IN NEED.

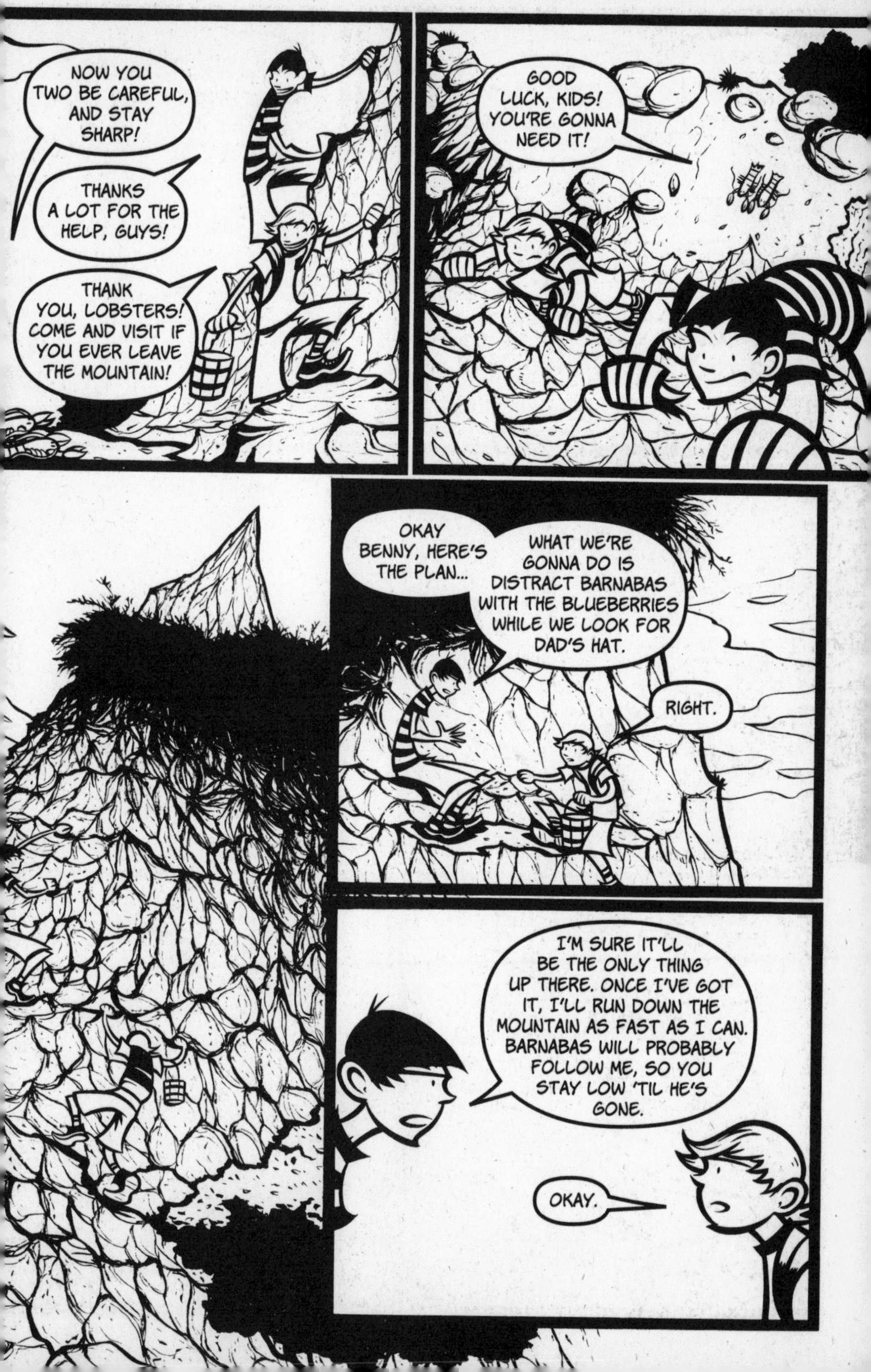
NOW YOU TWO BE CAREFUL, AND STAY SHARP!
THANKS A LOT FOR THE HELP, GUYS!
THANK YOU, LOBSTERS! COME AND VISIT IF YOU EVER LEAVE THE MOUNTAIN!
GOOD LUCK, KIDS! YOU'RE GONNA NEED IT!
OKAY BENNY, HERE'S THE PLAN...
WHAT WE'RE GONNA DO IS DISTRACT BARNABAS WITH THE BLUEBERRIES WHILE WE LOOK FOR DAD'S HAT.
RIGHT.
I'M SURE IT'LL BE THE ONLY THING UP THERE. ONCE I'VE GOT IT, I'LL RUN DOWN THE MOUNTAIN AS FAST AS I CAN. BARNABAS WILL PROBABLY FOLLOW ME, SO YOU STAY LOW 'TIL HE'S GONE.
OKAY.

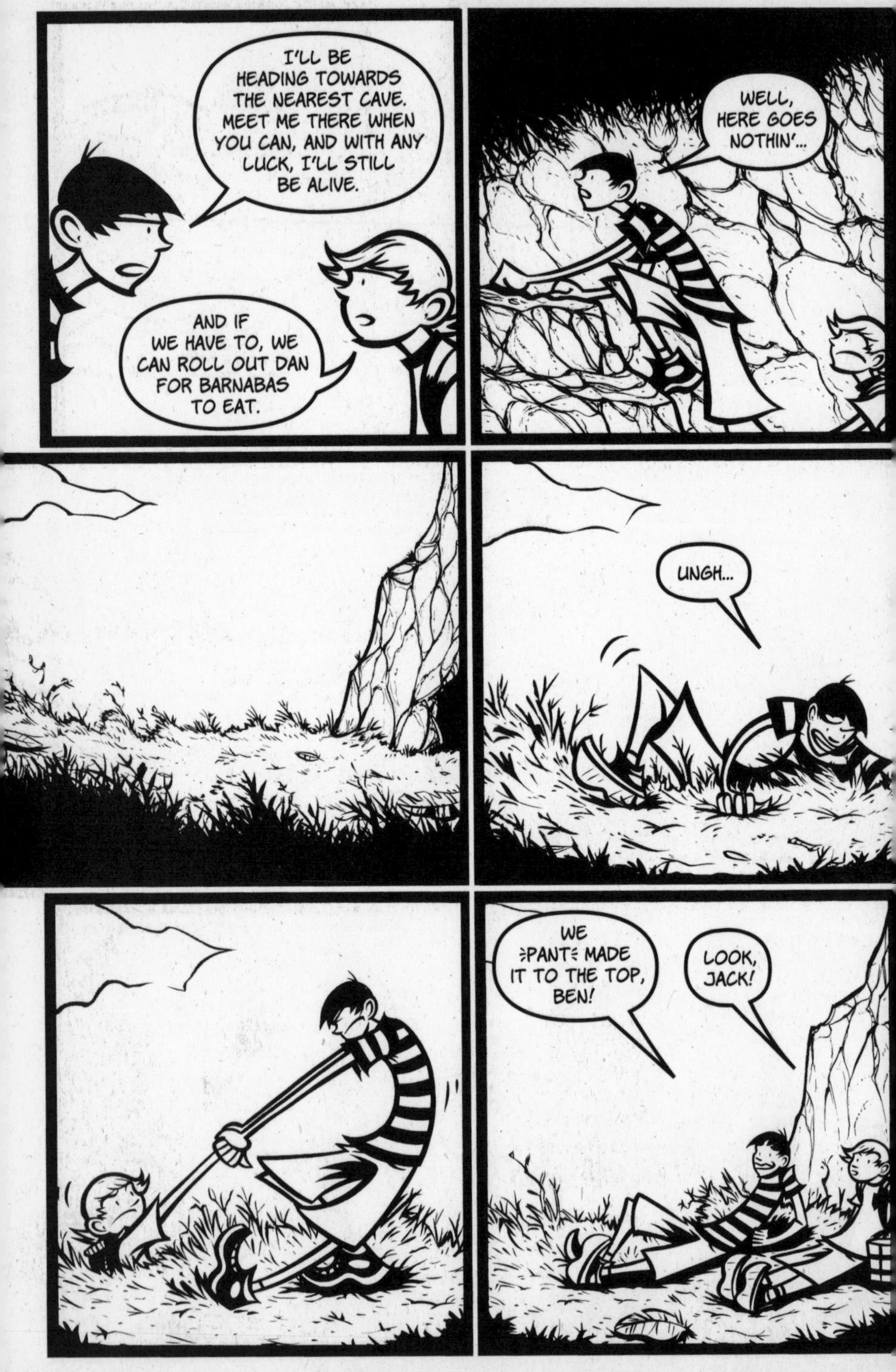
I'LL BE HEADING TOWARDS THE NEAREST CAVE. MEET ME THERE WHEN YOU CAN, AND WITH ANY LUCK, I'LL STILL BE ALIVE.
AND IF WE HAVE TO, WE CAN ROLL OUT DAN FOR BARNABAS TO EAT.
WELL, HERE GOES NOTHIN'...
UNGH...
WE *PANT* MADE IT TO THE TOP, BEN!
LOOK, JACK!

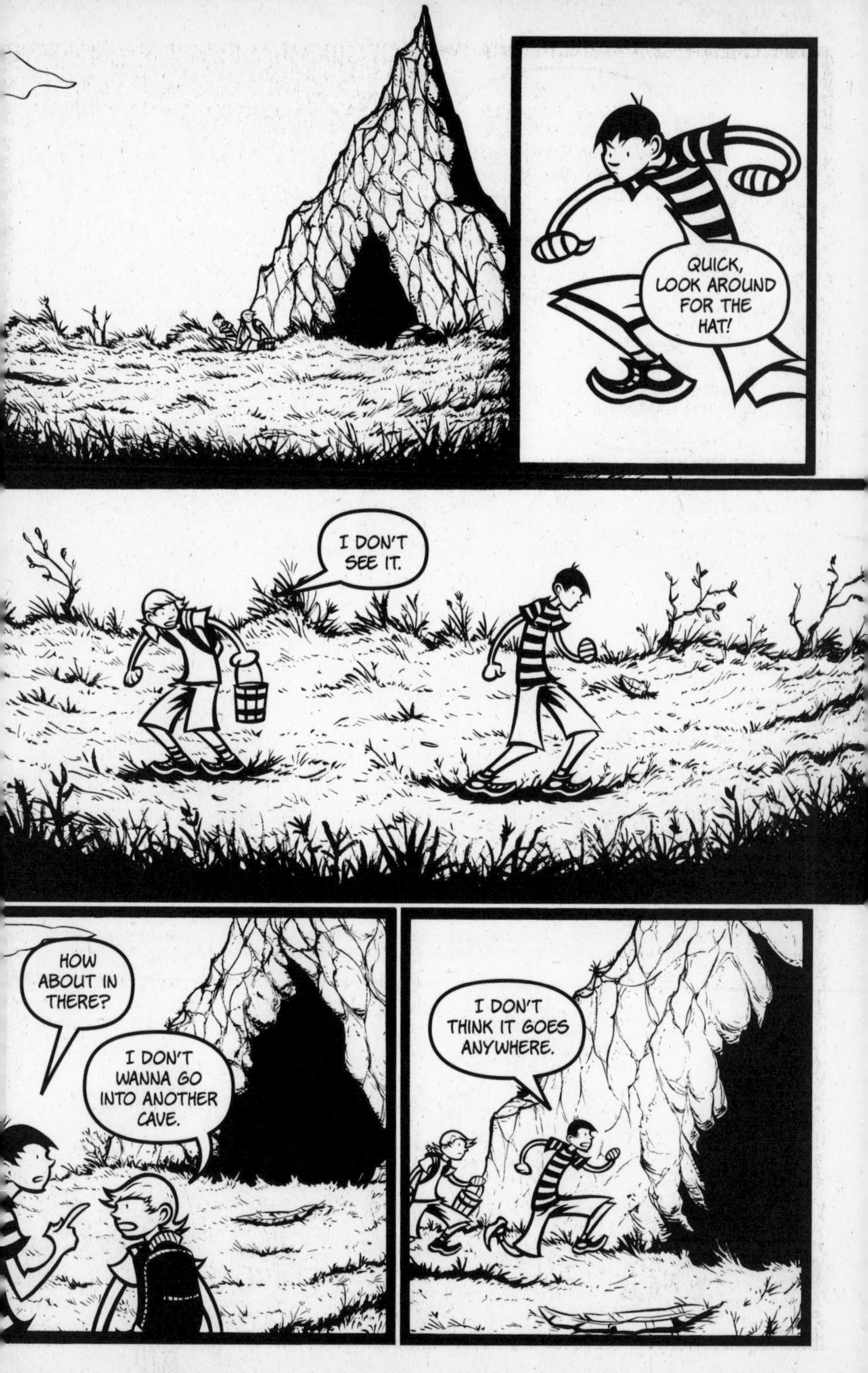
QUICK, LOOK AROUND FOR THE HAT!
I DON'T SEE IT.
HOW ABOUT IN THERE?
I DON'T WANNA GO INTO ANOTHER CAVE.
I DON'T THINK IT GOES ANYWHERE.

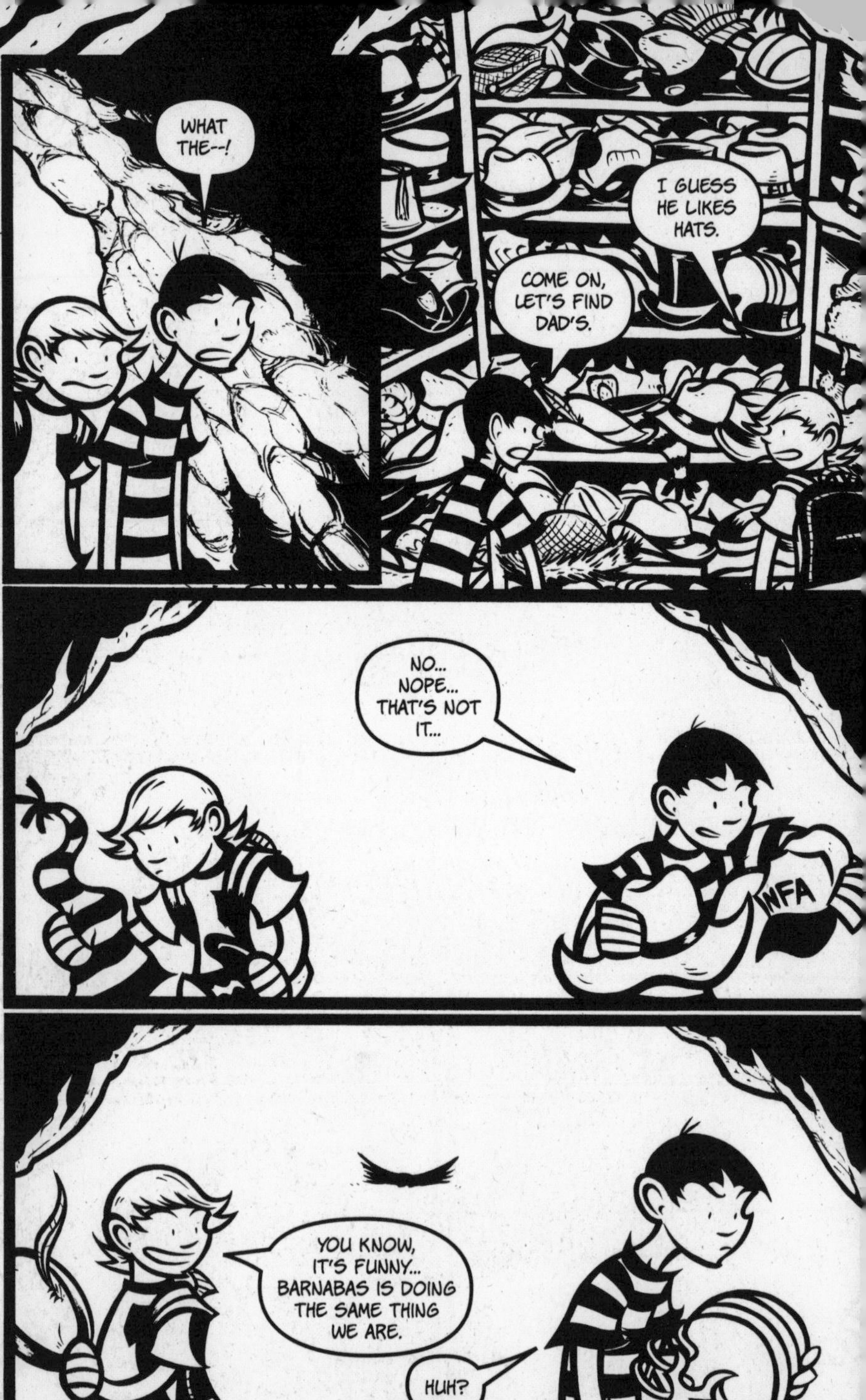
WHAT THE--!
I GUESS HE LIKES HATS.
COME ON, LET'S FIND DAD'S.
NO... NOPE... THAT'S NOT IT...
NFA
YOU KNOW, IT'S FUNNY... BARNABAS IS DOING THE SAME THING WE ARE.
HUH?

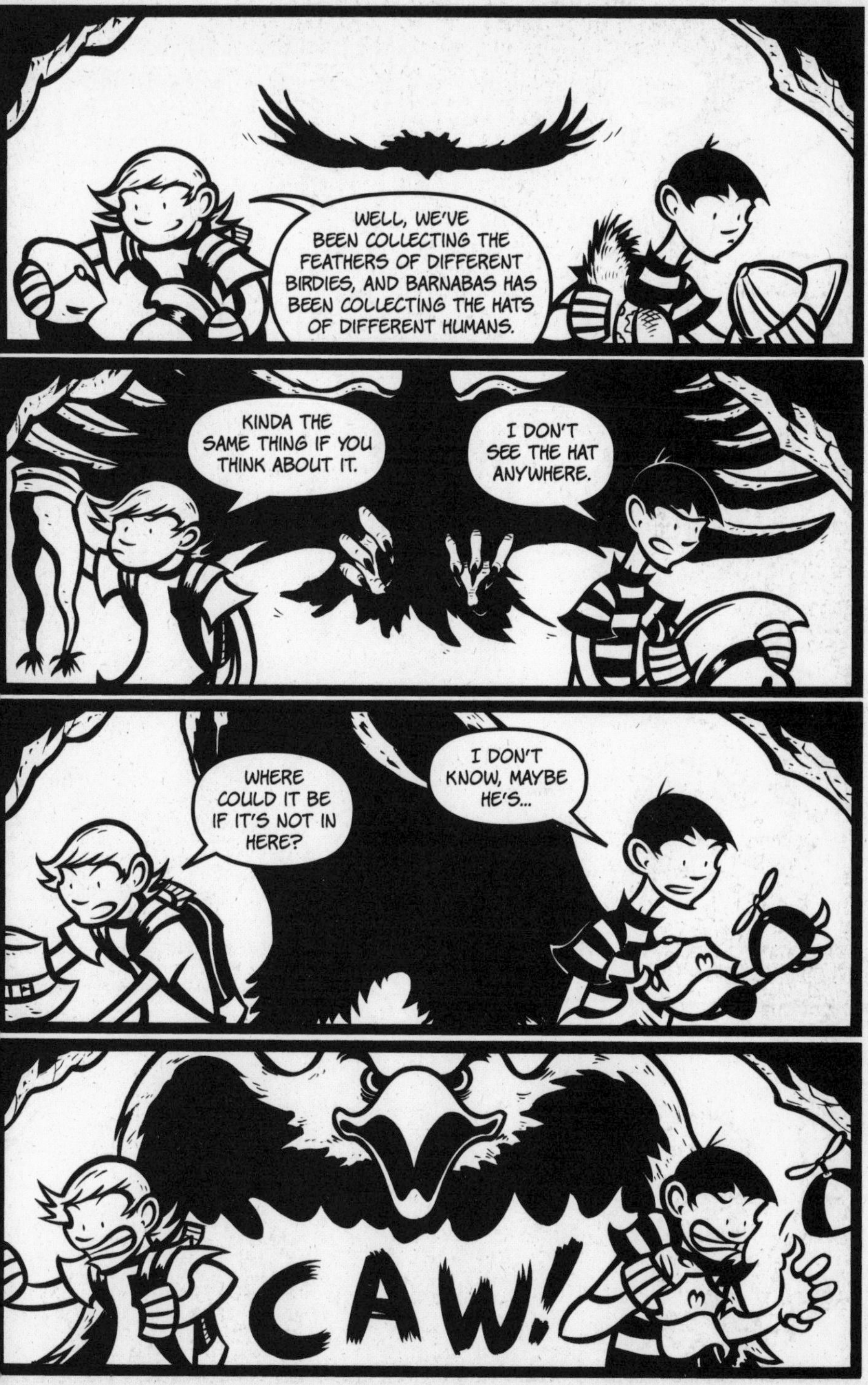
WELL, WE'VE BEEN COLLECTING THE FEATHERS OF DIFFERENT BIRDIES, AND BARNABAS HAS BEEN COLLECTING THE HATS OF DIFFERENT HUMANS.
KINDA THE SAME THING IF YOU THINK ABOUT IT.
I DON'T SEE THE HAT ANYWHERE.
WHERE COULD IT BE IF IT'S NOT IN HERE?
I DON'T KNOW, MAYBE HE'S...
CAW!

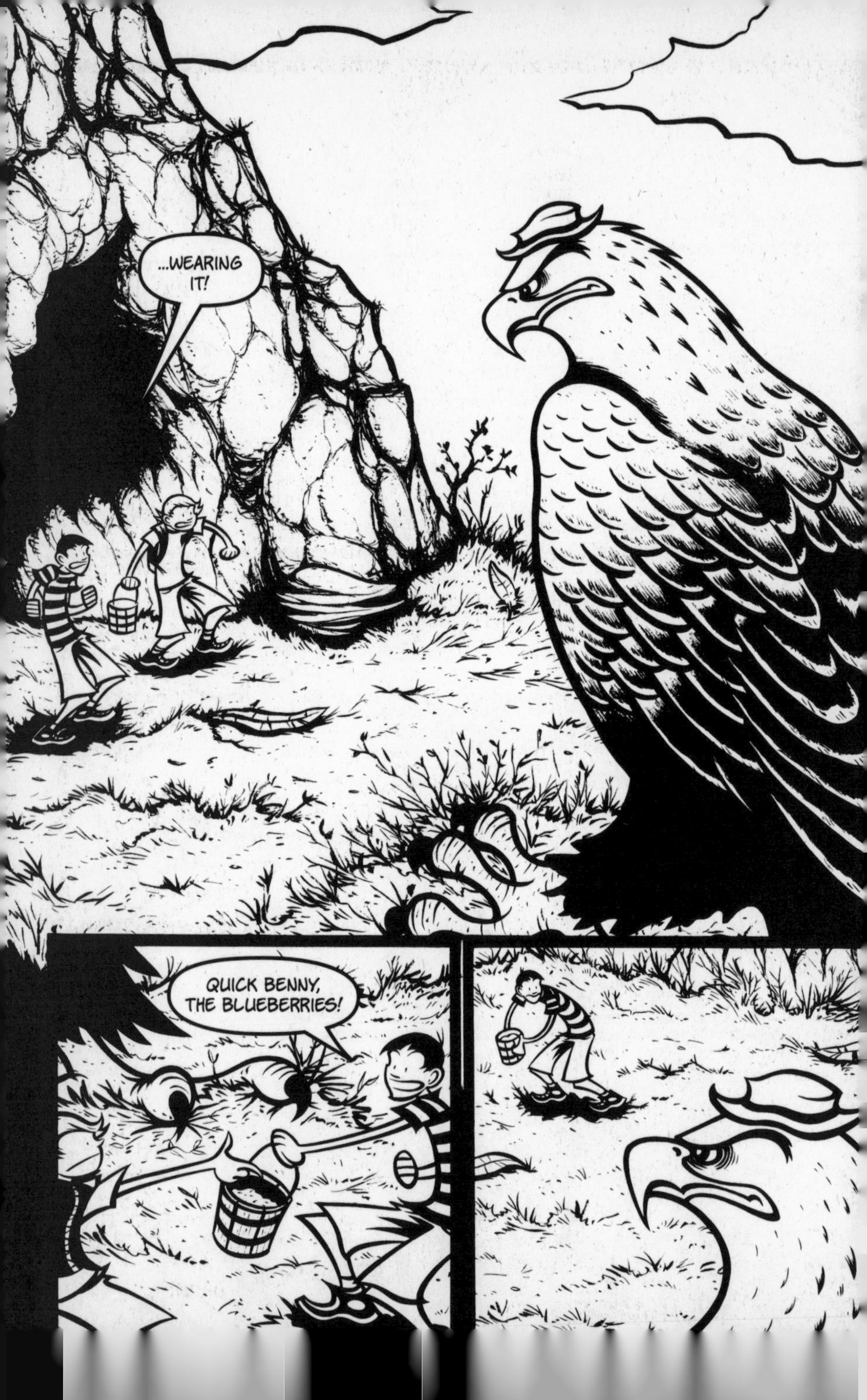
...WEARING IT!
QUICK BENNY, THE BLUEBERRIES!

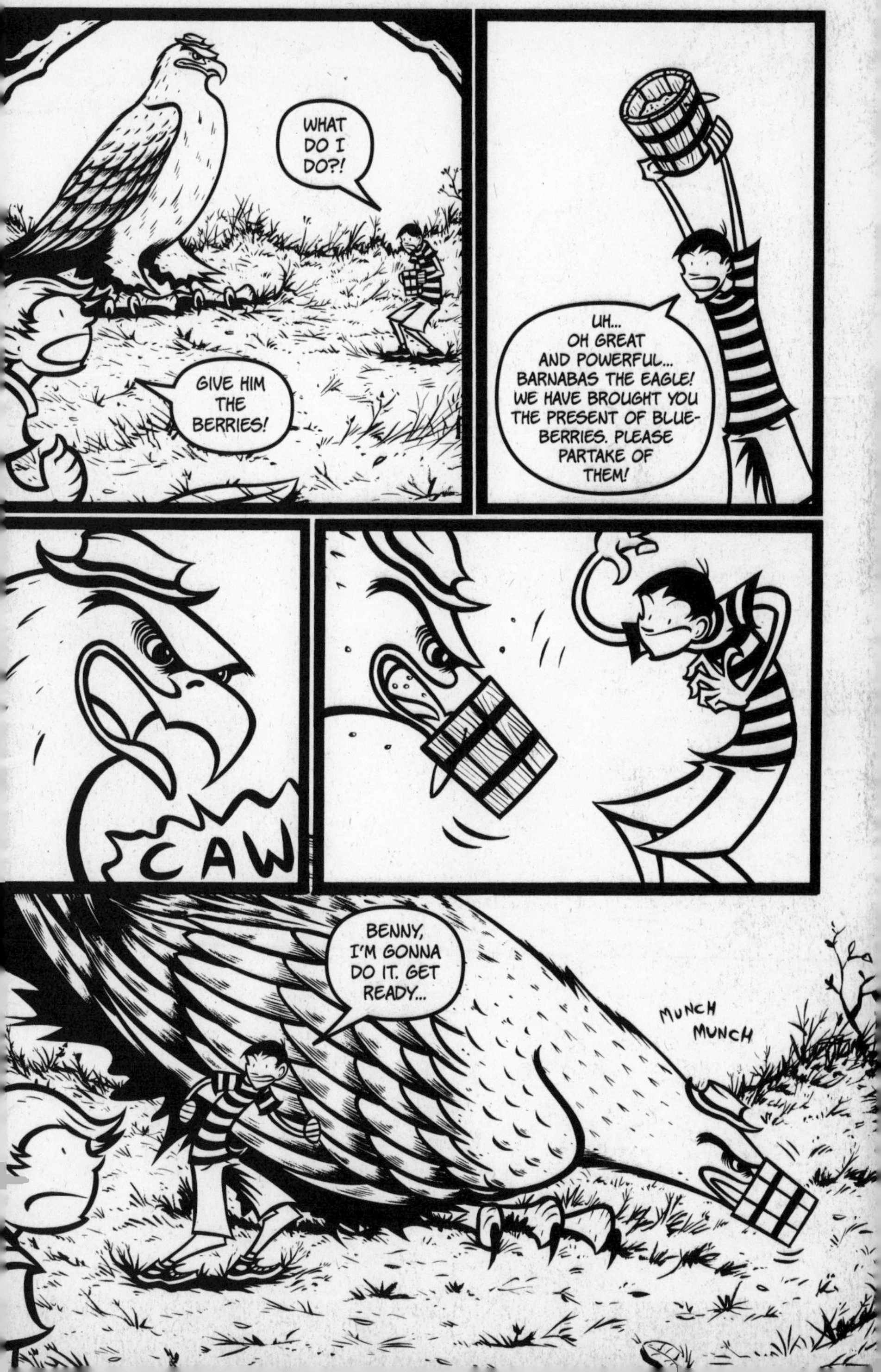
WHAT DO I DO?!
GIVE HIM THE BERRIES!
UH... OH GREAT AND POWERFUL... BARNABAS THE EAGLE! WE HAVE BROUGHT YOU THE PRESENT OF BLUE-BERRIES. PLEASE PARTAKE OF THEM!
CAW
BENNY, I'M GONNA DO IT. GET READY...
MUNCH MUNCH

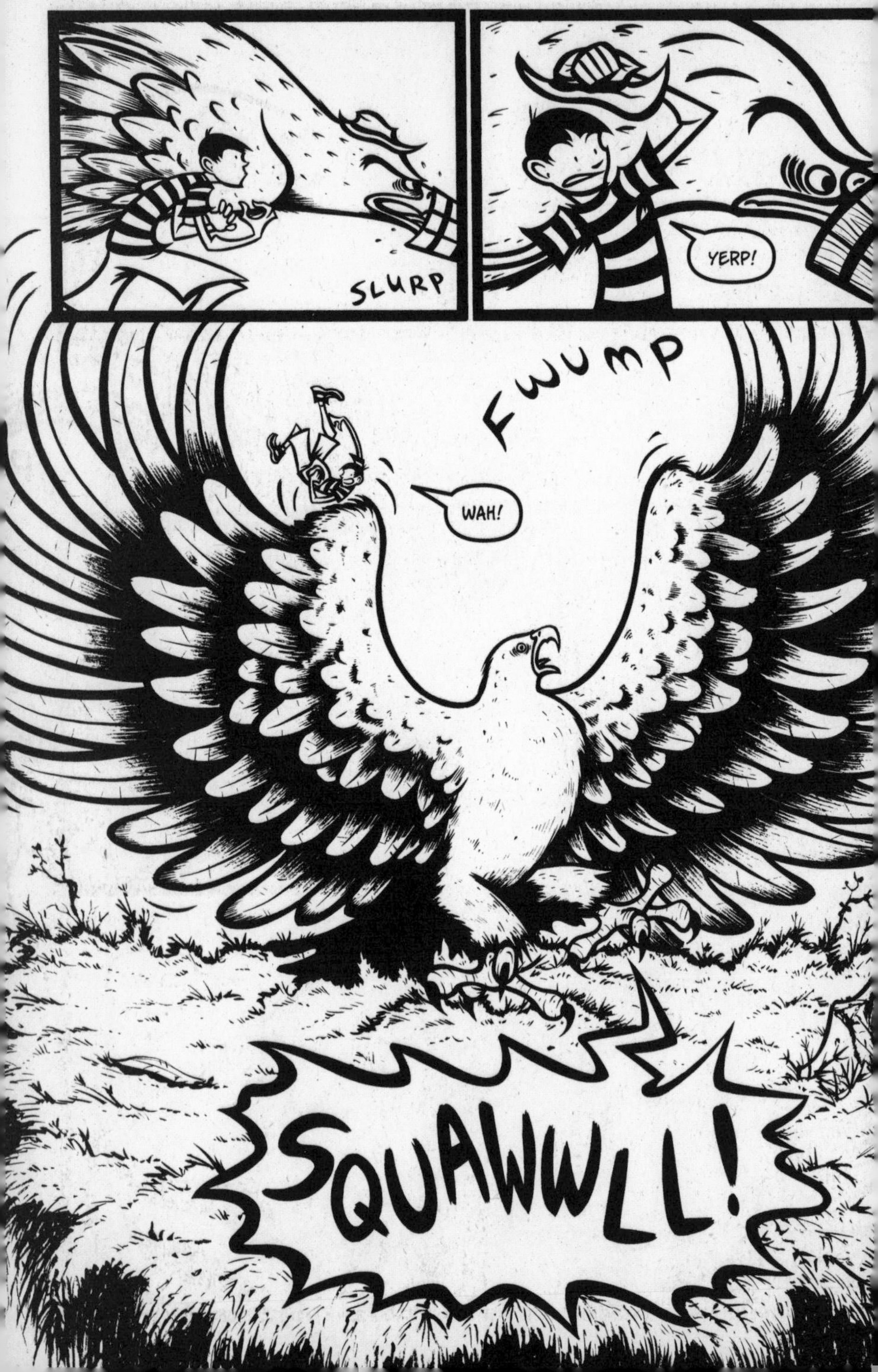
SLURP
YERP!
FWUMP
WAH!
SQUAWWLL!

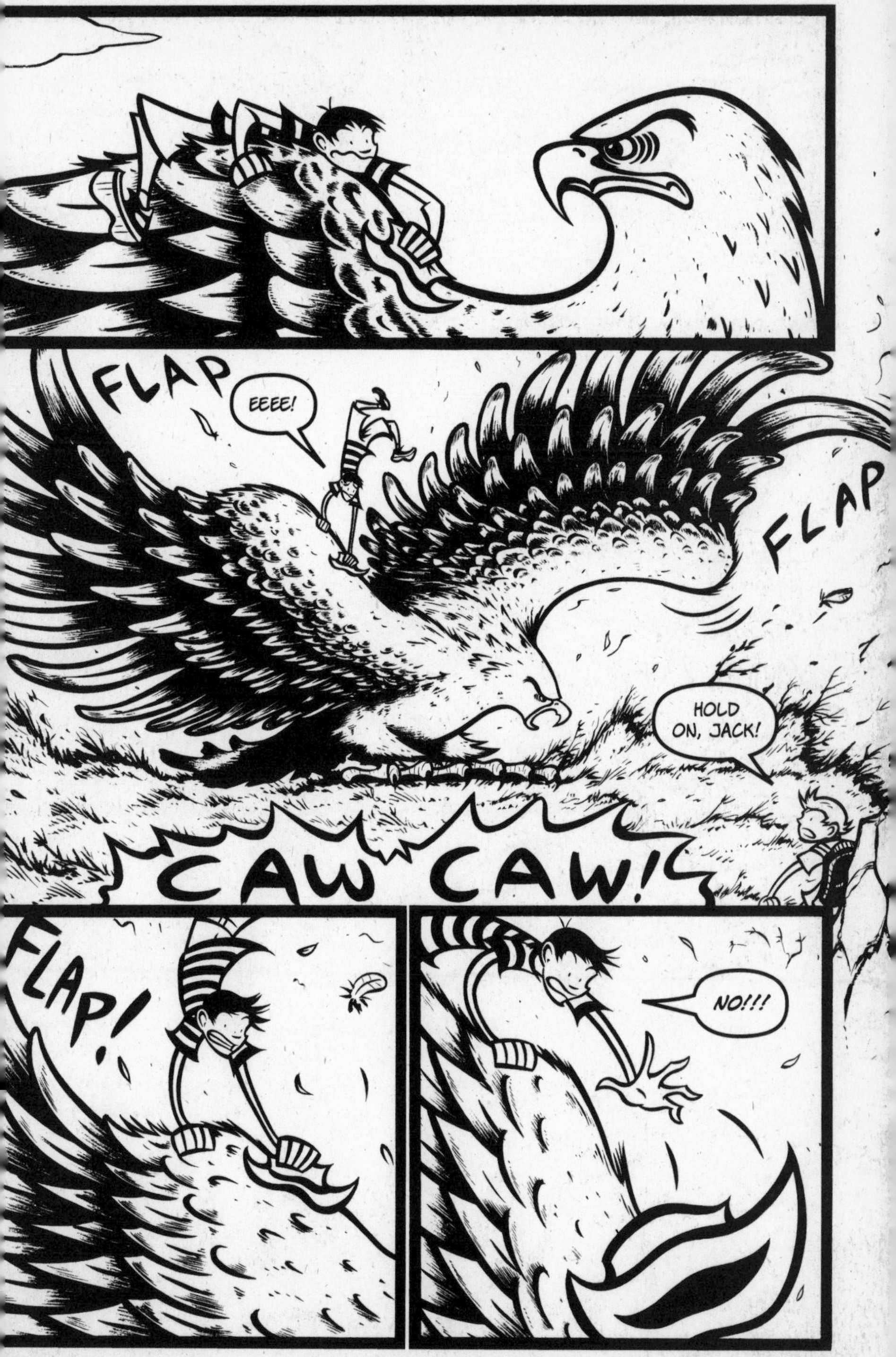
FLAP
EEEE!
FLAP
HOLD ON, JACK!
CAW CAW!
FLAP!
NO!!!

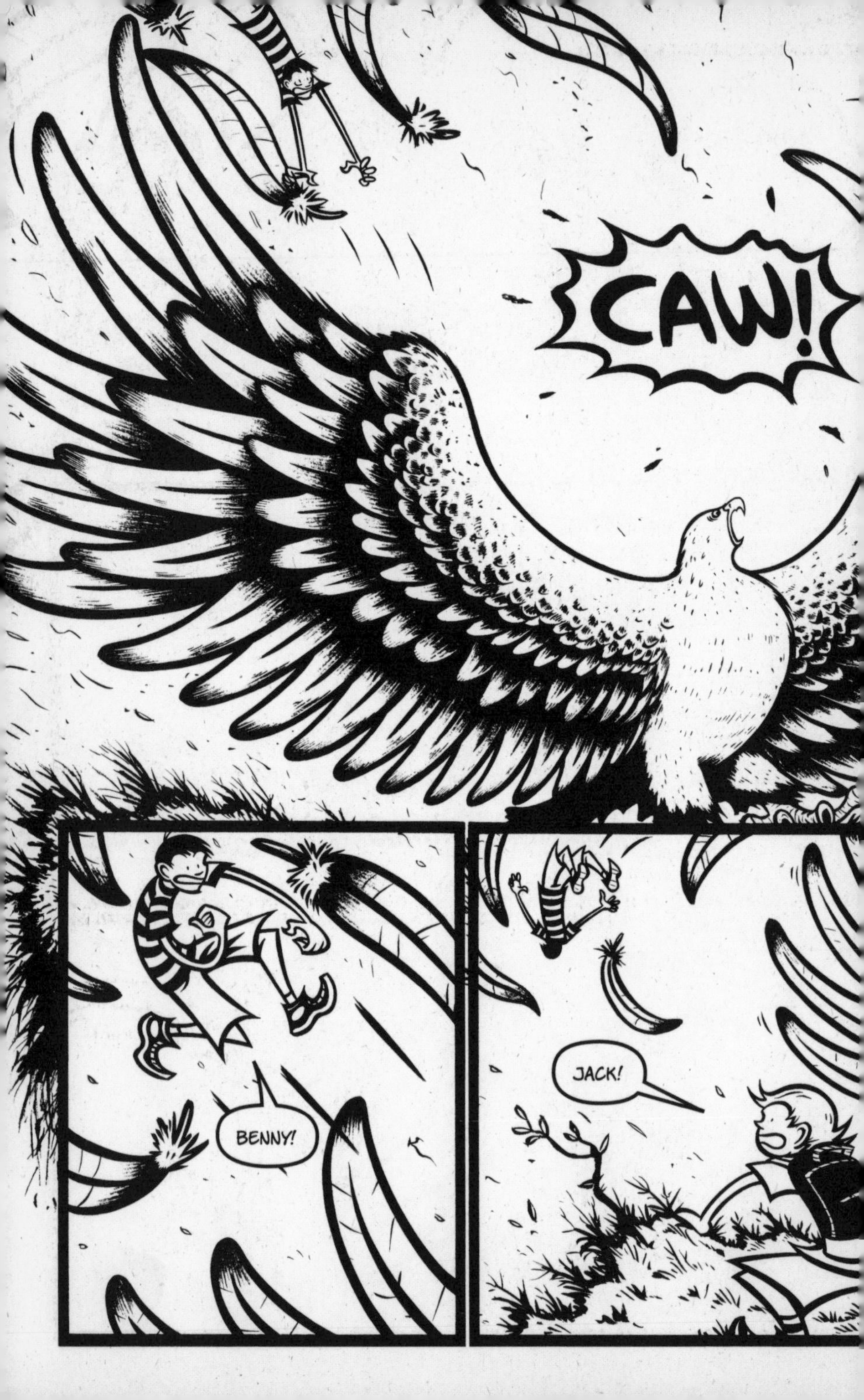
CAW!
BENNY!
JACK!

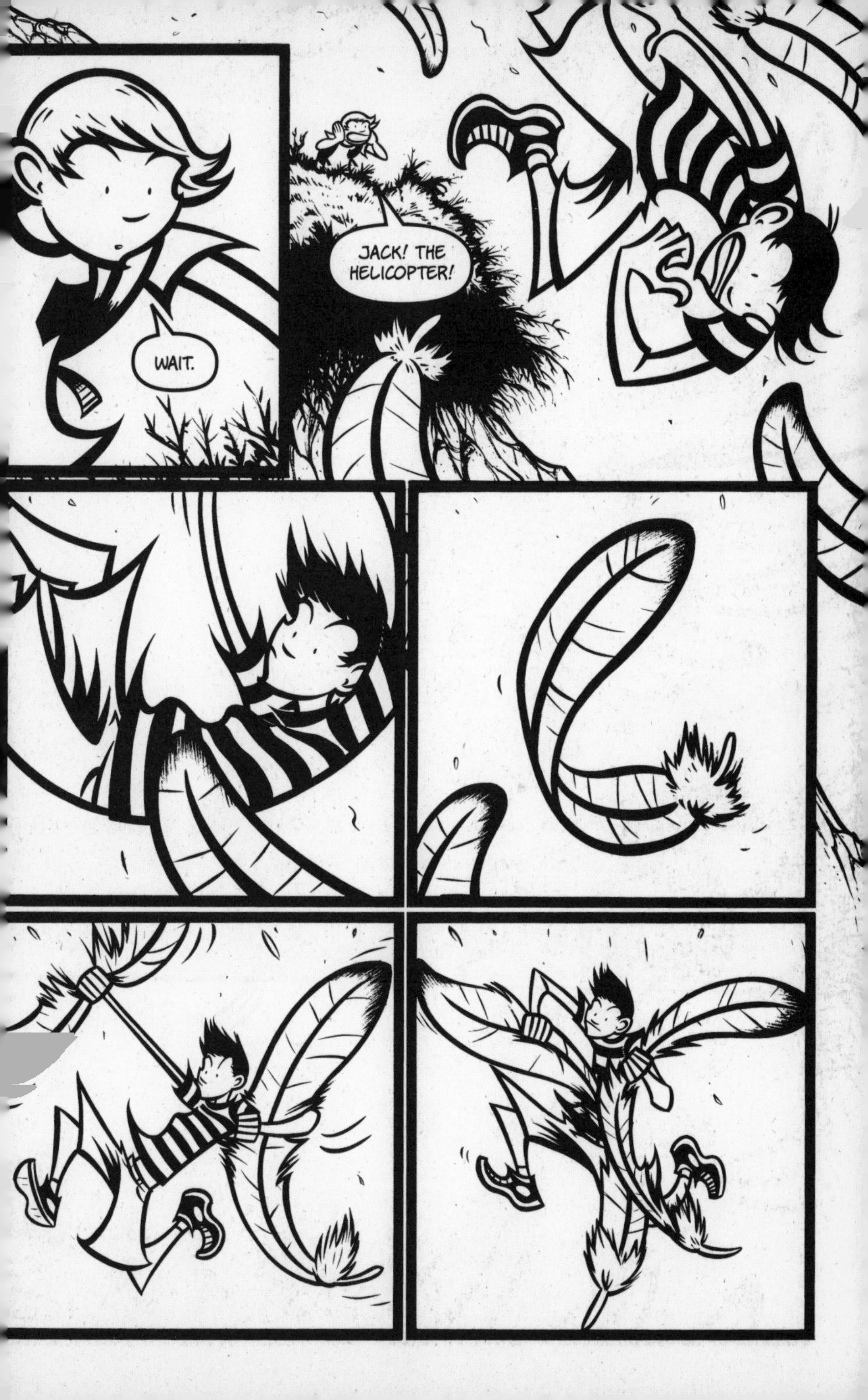
WAIT.
JACK! THE HELICOPTER!

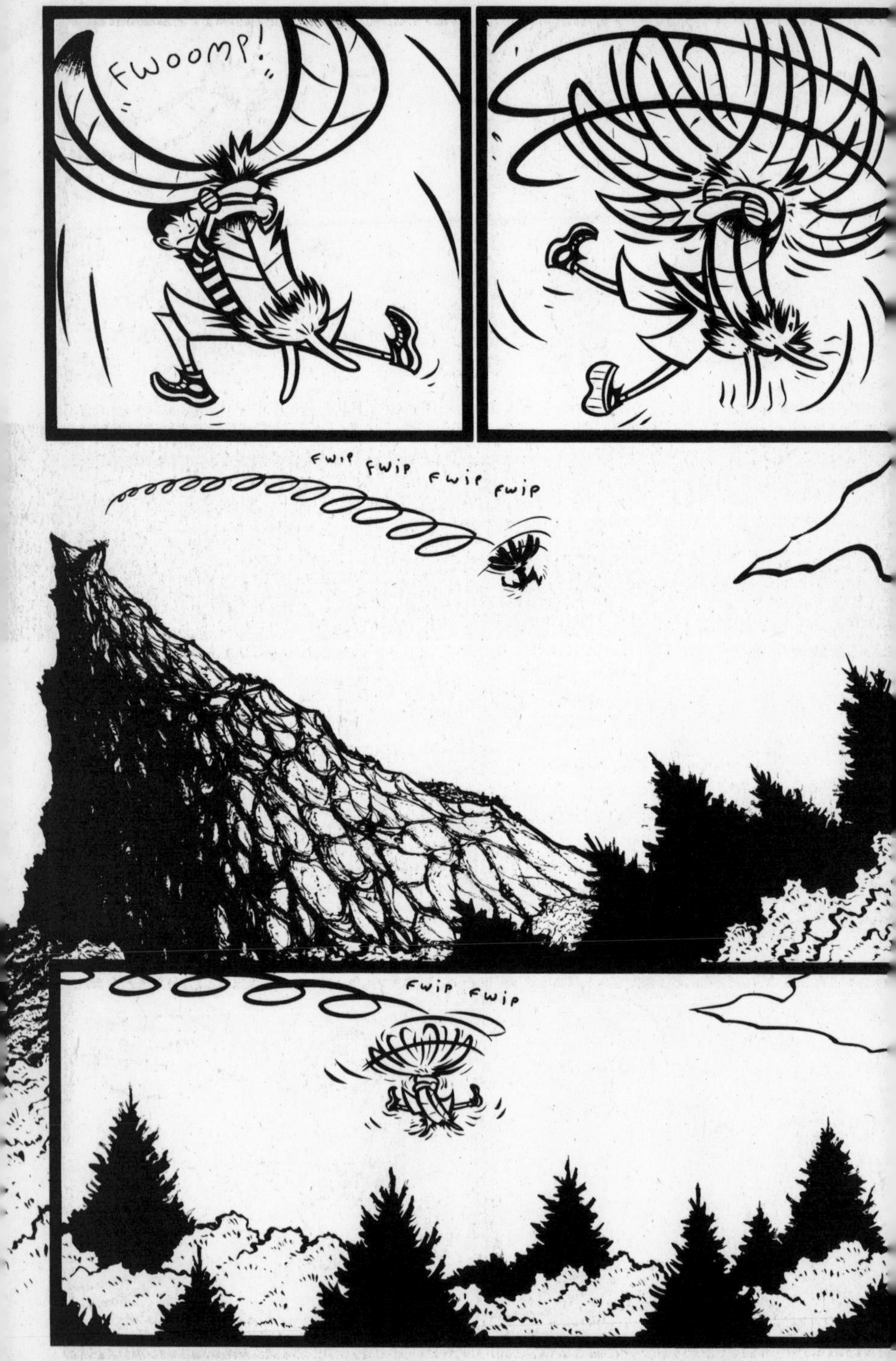
FWOOMP!
FWIP FWIP FWIP FWIP
FWIP FWIP

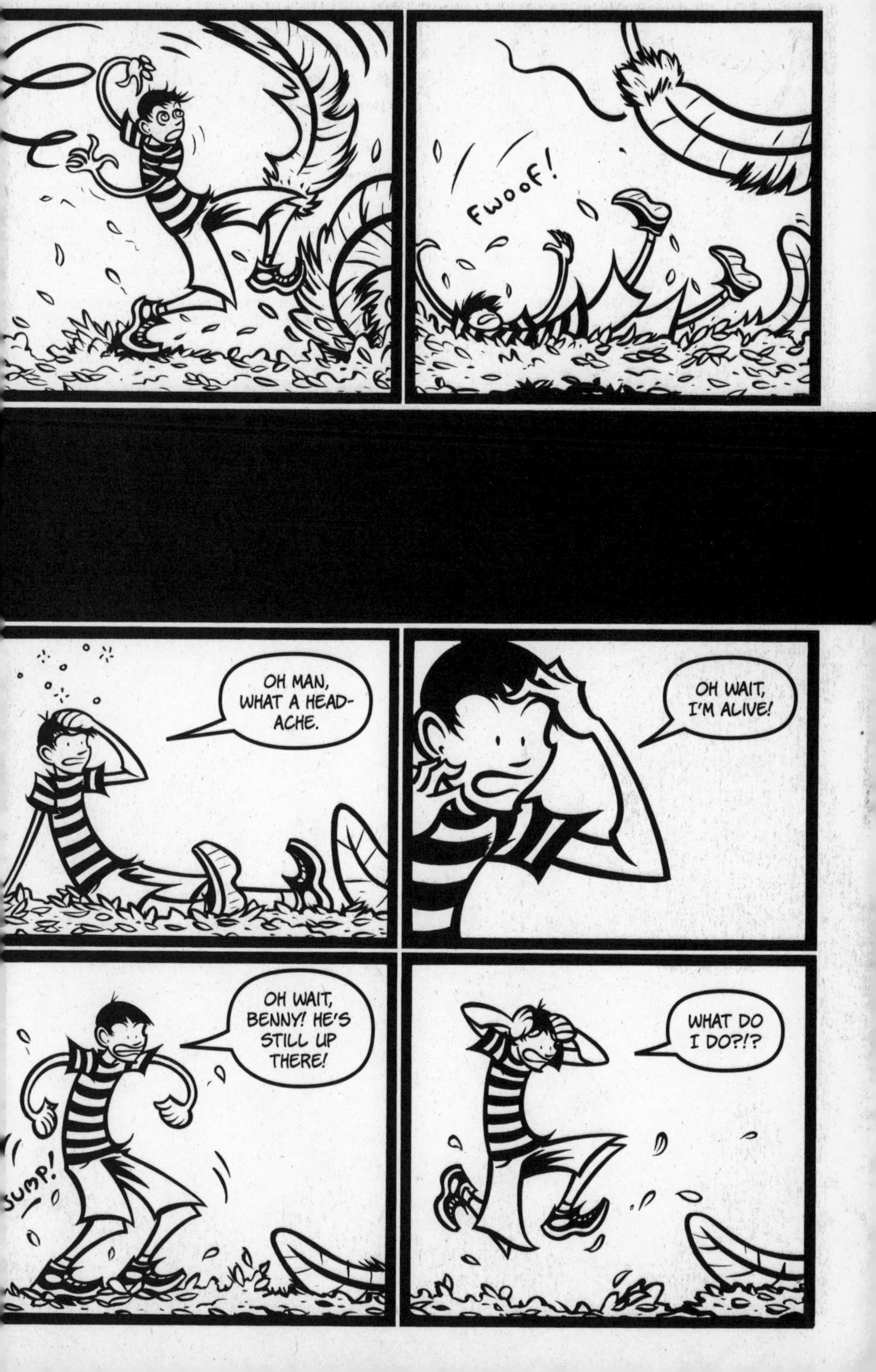
FWOOF!
OH MAN, WHAT A HEAD-ACHE.
OH WAIT, I'M ALIVE!
OH WAIT, BENNY! HE'S STILL UP THERE!
JUMP!
WHAT DO I DO?!?

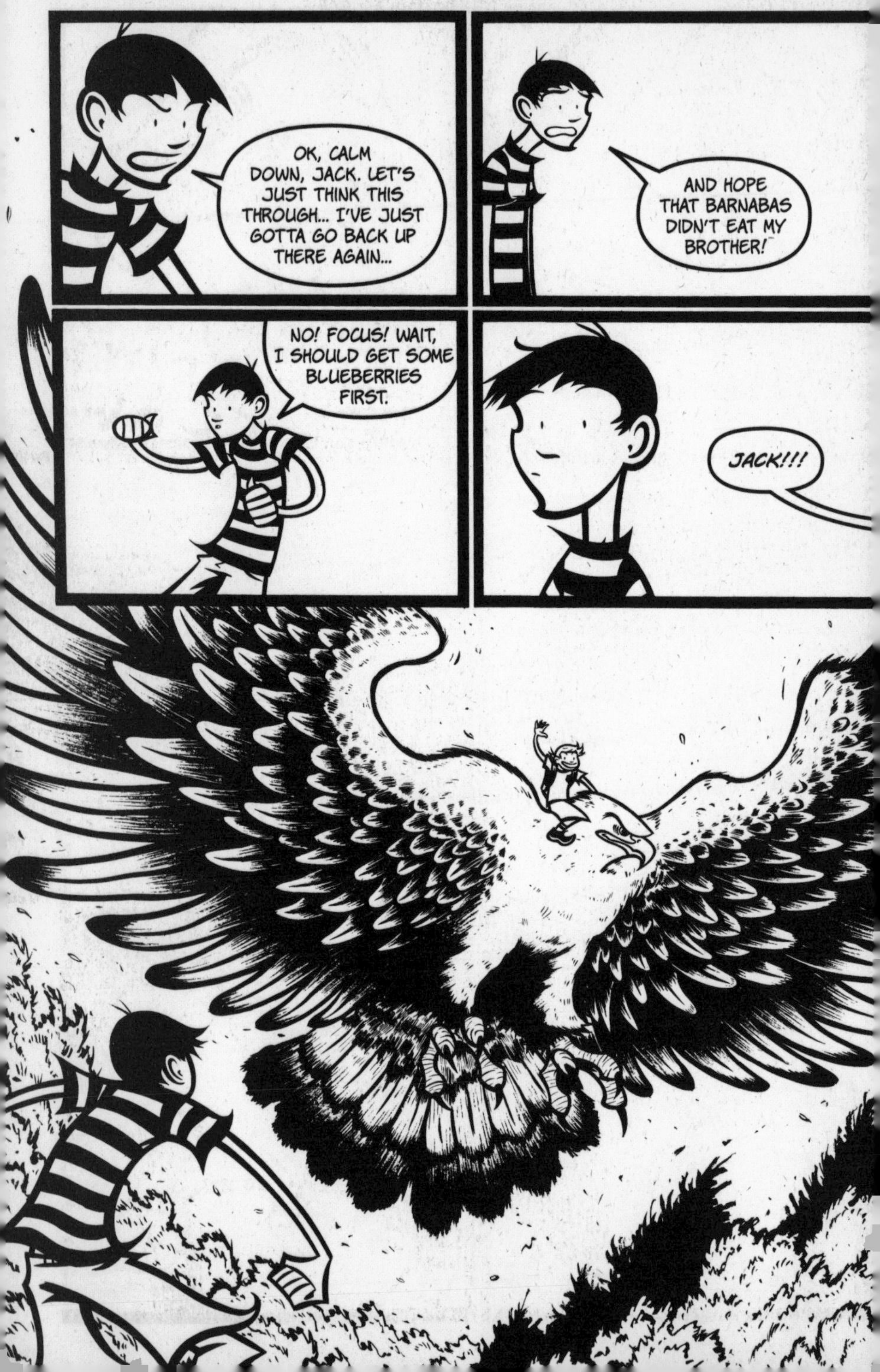
OK, CALM DOWN, JACK. LET'S JUST THINK THIS THROUGH... I'VE JUST GOTTA GO BACK UP THERE AGAIN...
AND HOPE THAT BARNABAS DIDN'T EAT MY BROTHER!
NO! FOCUS! WAIT, I SHOULD GET SOME BLUEBERRIES FIRST.
JACK!!!

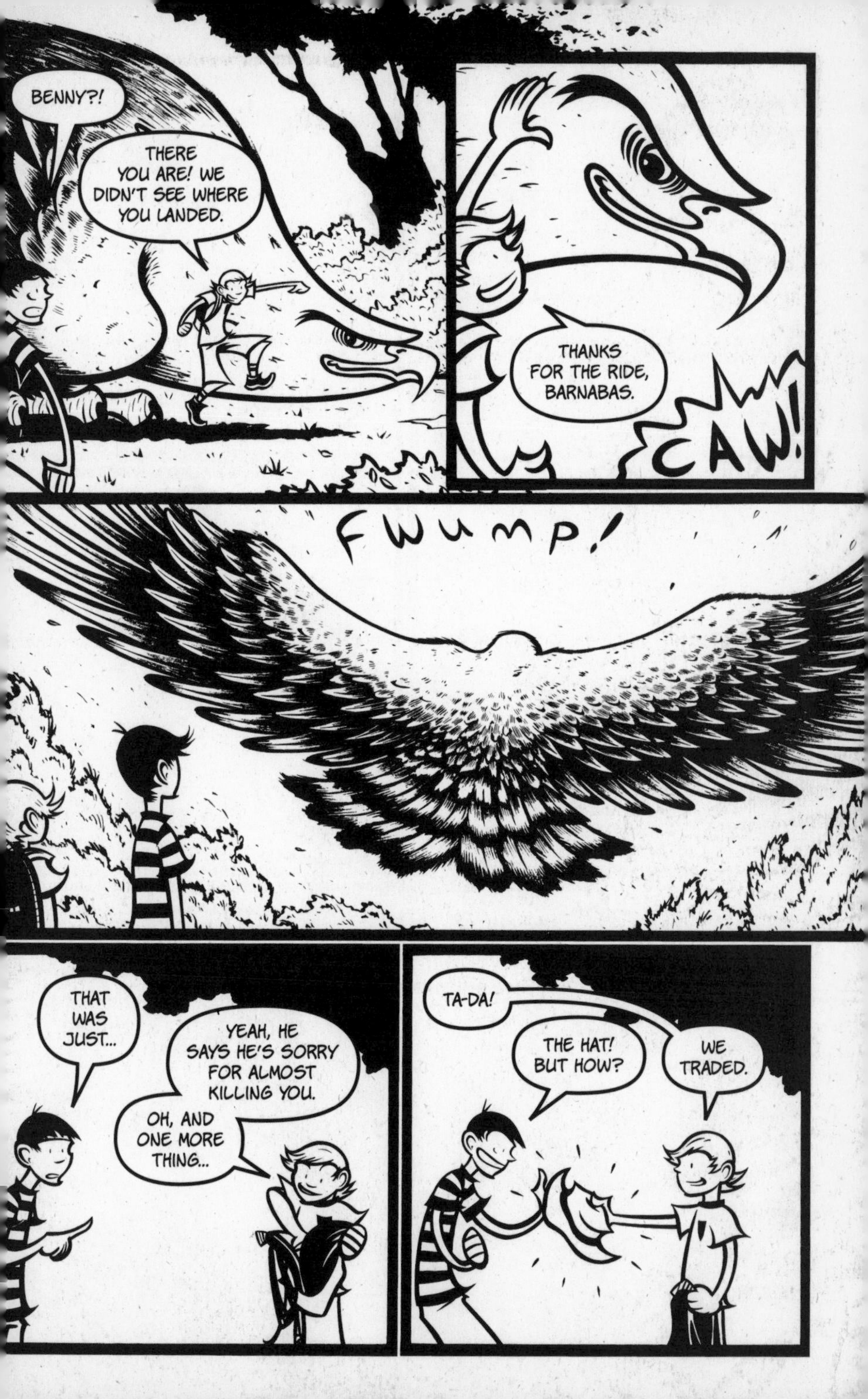
BENNY?!
THERE YOU ARE! WE DIDN'T SEE WHERE YOU LANDED.
THANKS FOR THE RIDE, BARNABAS.
CAW!
FWUMP!
THAT WAS JUST...
YEAH, HE SAYS HE'S SORRY FOR ALMOST KILLING YOU.
OH, AND ONE MORE THING...
TA-DA!
THE HAT! BUT HOW?
WE TRADED.

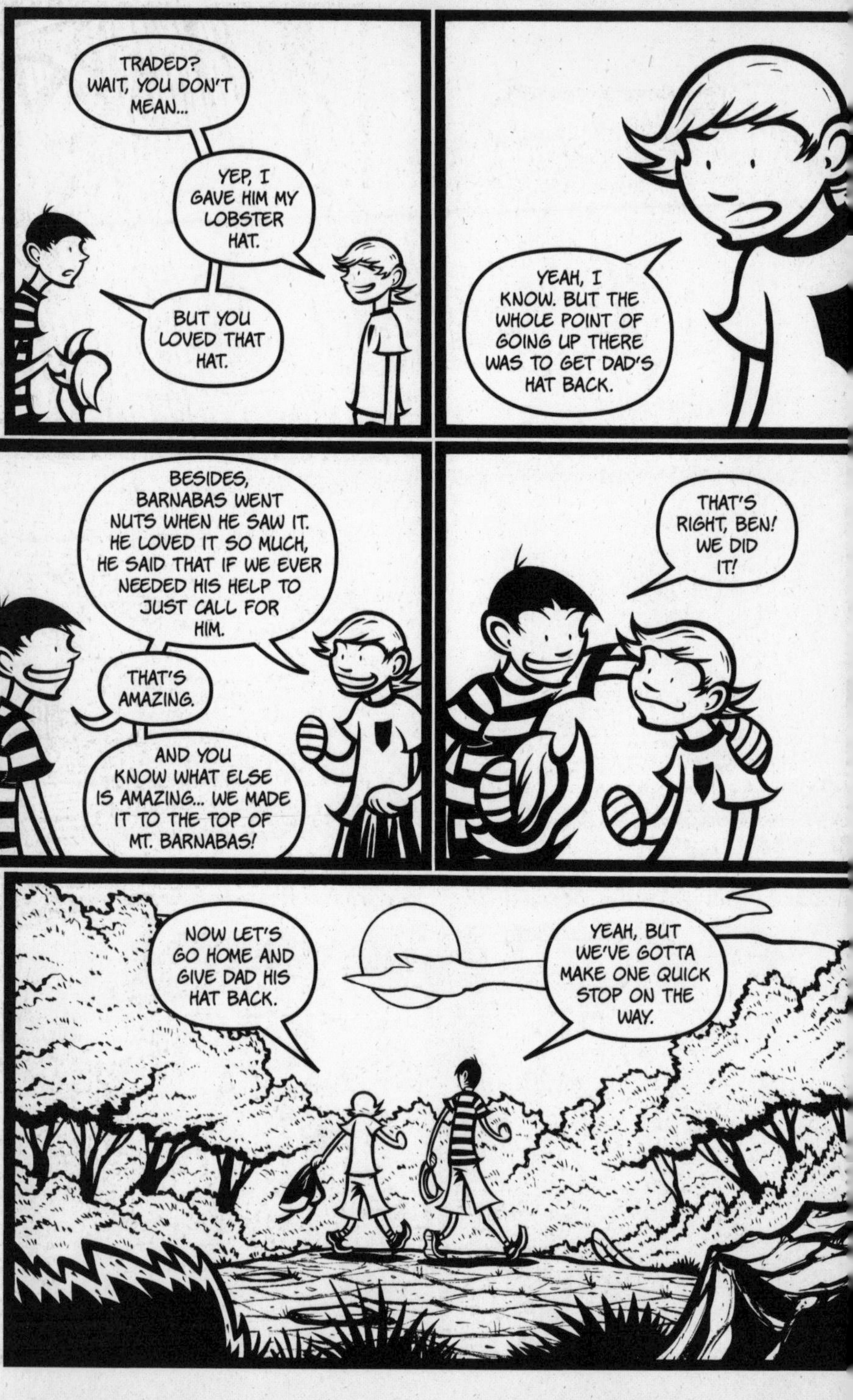
TRADED? WAIT, YOU DON'T MEAN...
YEP, I GAVE HIM MY LOBSTER HAT.
BUT YOU LOVED THAT HAT.
YEAH, I KNOW. BUT THE WHOLE POINT OF GOING UP THERE WAS TO GET DAD'S HAT BACK.
BESIDES, BARNABAS WENT NUTS WHEN HE SAW IT. HE LOVED IT SO MUCH, HE SAID THAT IF WE EVER NEEDED HIS HELP TO JUST CALL FOR HIM.
THAT'S AMAZING.
AND YOU KNOW WHAT ELSE IS AMAZING... WE MADE IT TO THE TOP OF MT. BARNABAS!
THAT'S RIGHT, BEN! WE DID IT!
NOW LET'S GO HOME AND GIVE DAD HIS HAT BACK.
YEAH, BUT WE'VE GOTTA MAKE ONE QUICK STOP ON THE WAY.

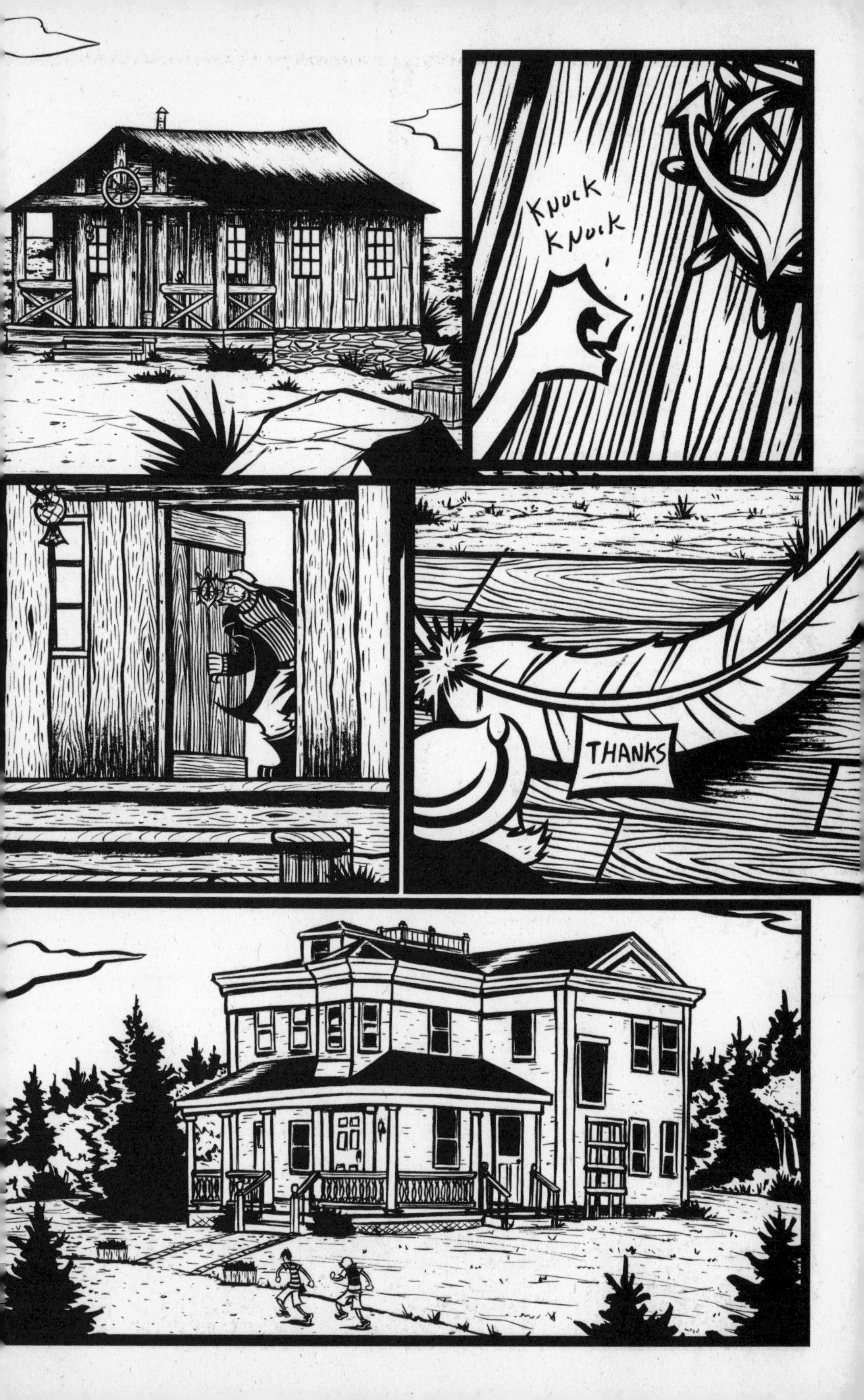

KNOCK KNOCK
THANKS

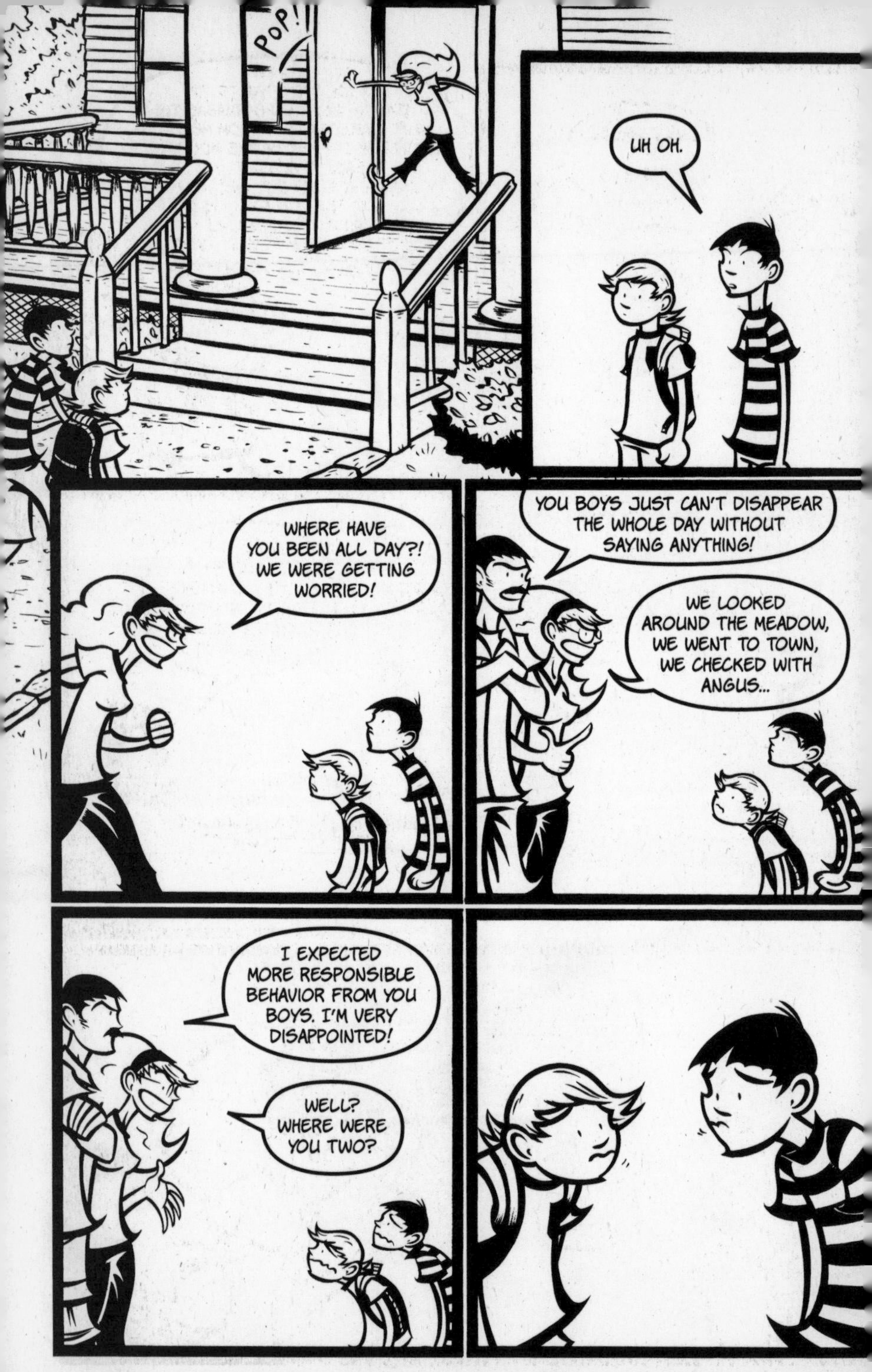
POP!
UH OH.
WHERE HAVE YOU BEEN ALL DAY?! WE WERE GETTING WORRIED!
YOU BOYS JUST CAN'T DISAPPEAR THE WHOLE DAY WITHOUT SAYING ANYTHING!
WE LOOKED AROUND THE MEADOW, WE WENT TO TOWN, WE CHECKED WITH ANGUS...
I EXPECTED MORE RESPONSIBLE BEHAVIOR FROM YOU BOYS. I'M VERY DISAPPOINTED!
WELL? WHERE WERE YOU TWO?

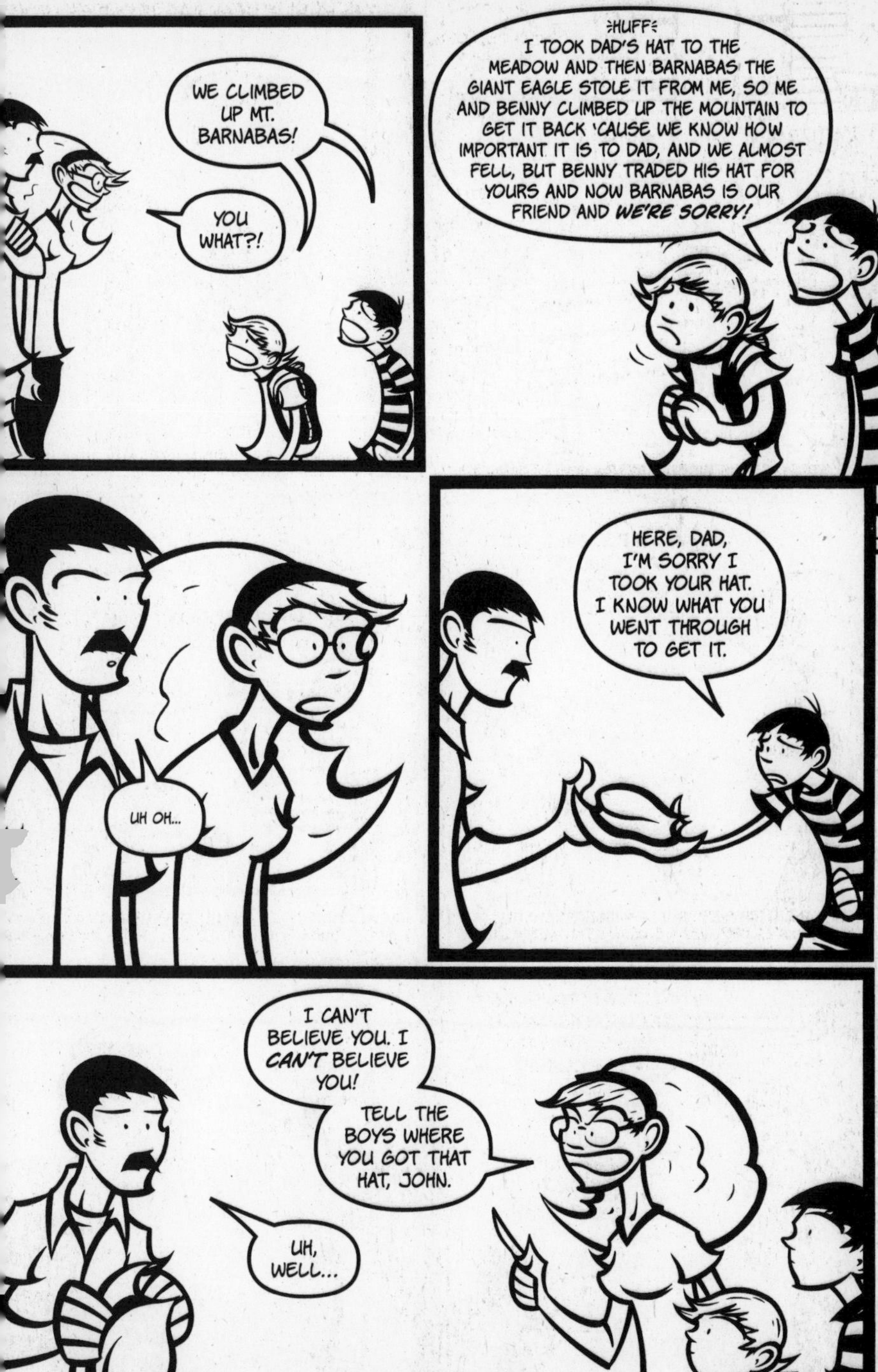
WE CLIMBED UP MT. BARNABAS!
YOU WHAT?!
⪫HUFF⪪ I TOOK DAD'S HAT TO THE MEADOW AND THEN BARNABAS THE GIANT EAGLE STOLE IT FROM ME, SO ME AND BENNY CLIMBED UP THE MOUNTAIN TO GET IT BACK 'CAUSE WE KNOW HOW IMPORTANT IT IS TO DAD, AND WE ALMOST FELL, BUT BENNY TRADED HIS HAT FOR YOURS AND NOW BARNABAS IS OUR FRIEND AND *WE'RE SORRY!*
UH OH...
HERE, DAD, I'M SORRY I TOOK YOUR HAT. I KNOW WHAT YOU WENT THROUGH TO GET IT.
I CAN'T BELIEVE YOU. I *CAN'T* BELIEVE YOU!
TELL THE BOYS WHERE YOU GOT THAT HAT, JOHN.
UH, WELL...

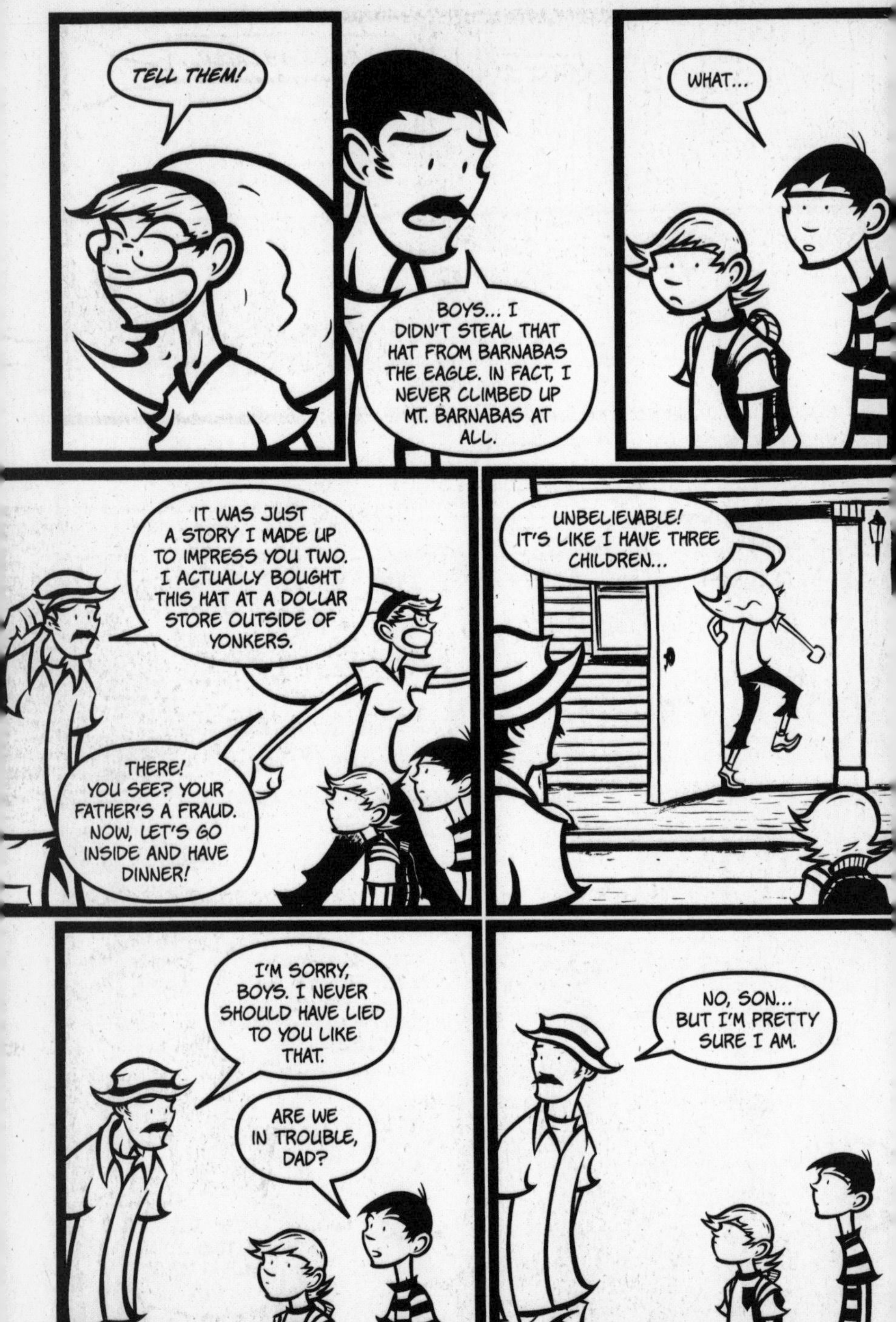
TELL THEM!
BOYS... I DIDN'T STEAL THAT HAT FROM BARNABAS THE EAGLE. IN FACT, I NEVER CLIMBED UP MT. BARNABAS AT ALL.
WHAT...
IT WAS JUST A STORY I MADE UP TO IMPRESS YOU TWO. I ACTUALLY BOUGHT THIS HAT AT A DOLLAR STORE OUTSIDE OF YONKERS.
THERE! YOU SEE? YOUR FATHER'S A FRAUD. NOW, LET'S GO INSIDE AND HAVE DINNER!
UNBELIEVABLE! IT'S LIKE I HAVE THREE CHILDREN...
I'M SORRY, BOYS. I NEVER SHOULD HAVE LIED TO YOU LIKE THAT.
ARE WE IN TROUBLE, DAD?
NO, SON... BUT I'M PRETTY SURE I AM.

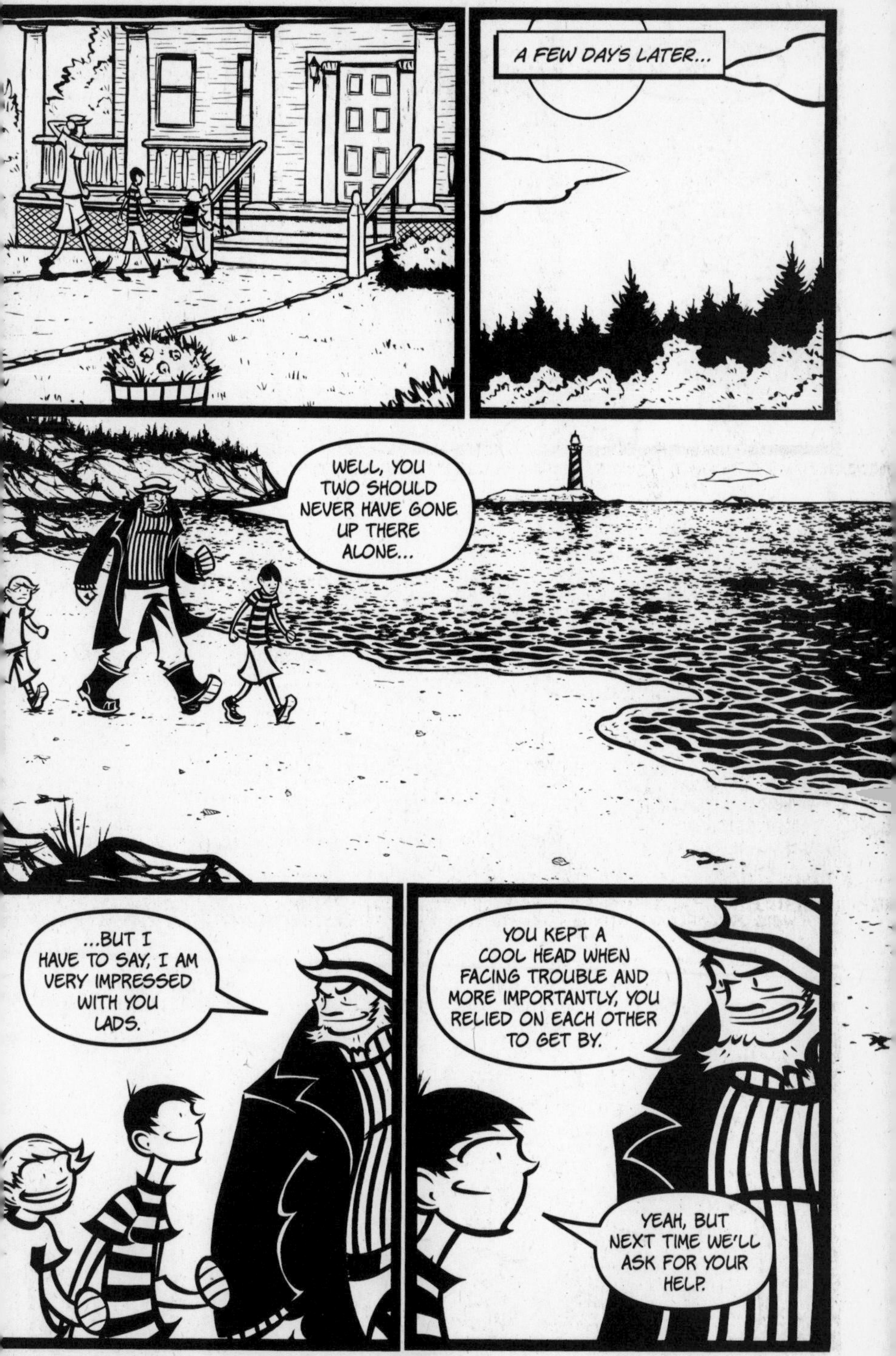
A FEW DAYS LATER...
WELL, YOU TWO SHOULD NEVER HAVE GONE UP THERE ALONE...
...BUT I HAVE TO SAY, I AM VERY IMPRESSED WITH YOU LADS.
YOU KEPT A COOL HEAD WHEN FACING TROUBLE AND MORE IMPORTANTLY, YOU RELIED ON EACH OTHER TO GET BY.
YEAH, BUT NEXT TIME WE'LL ASK FOR YOUR HELP.

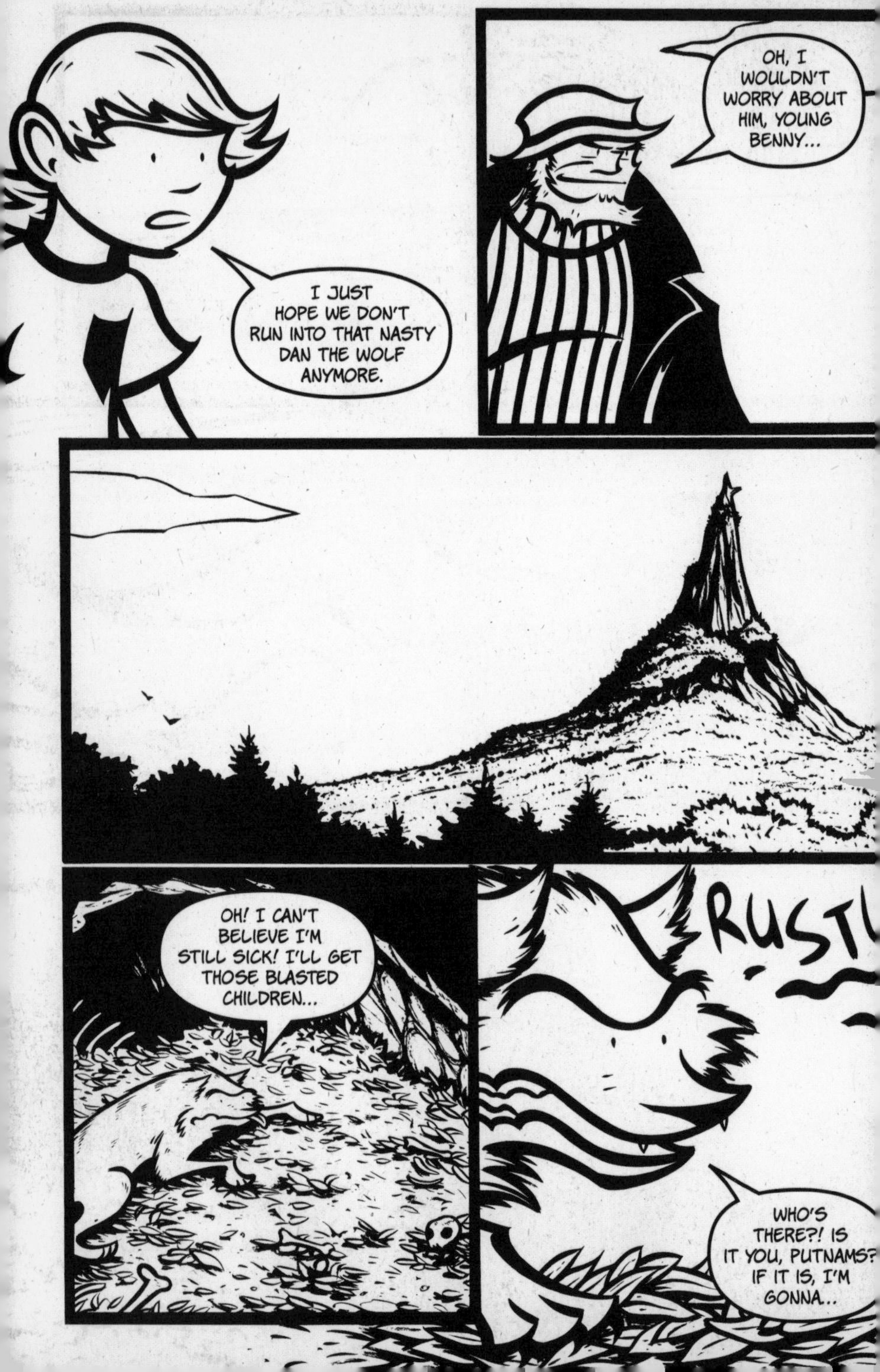
I JUST HOPE WE DON'T RUN INTO THAT NASTY DAN THE WOLF ANYMORE.
OH, I WOULDN'T WORRY ABOUT HIM, YOUNG BENNY...
OH! I CAN'T BELIEVE I'M STILL SICK! I'LL GET THOSE BLASTED CHILDREN...
WHO'S THERE?! IS IT YOU, PUTNAMS? IF IT IS, I'M GONNA...

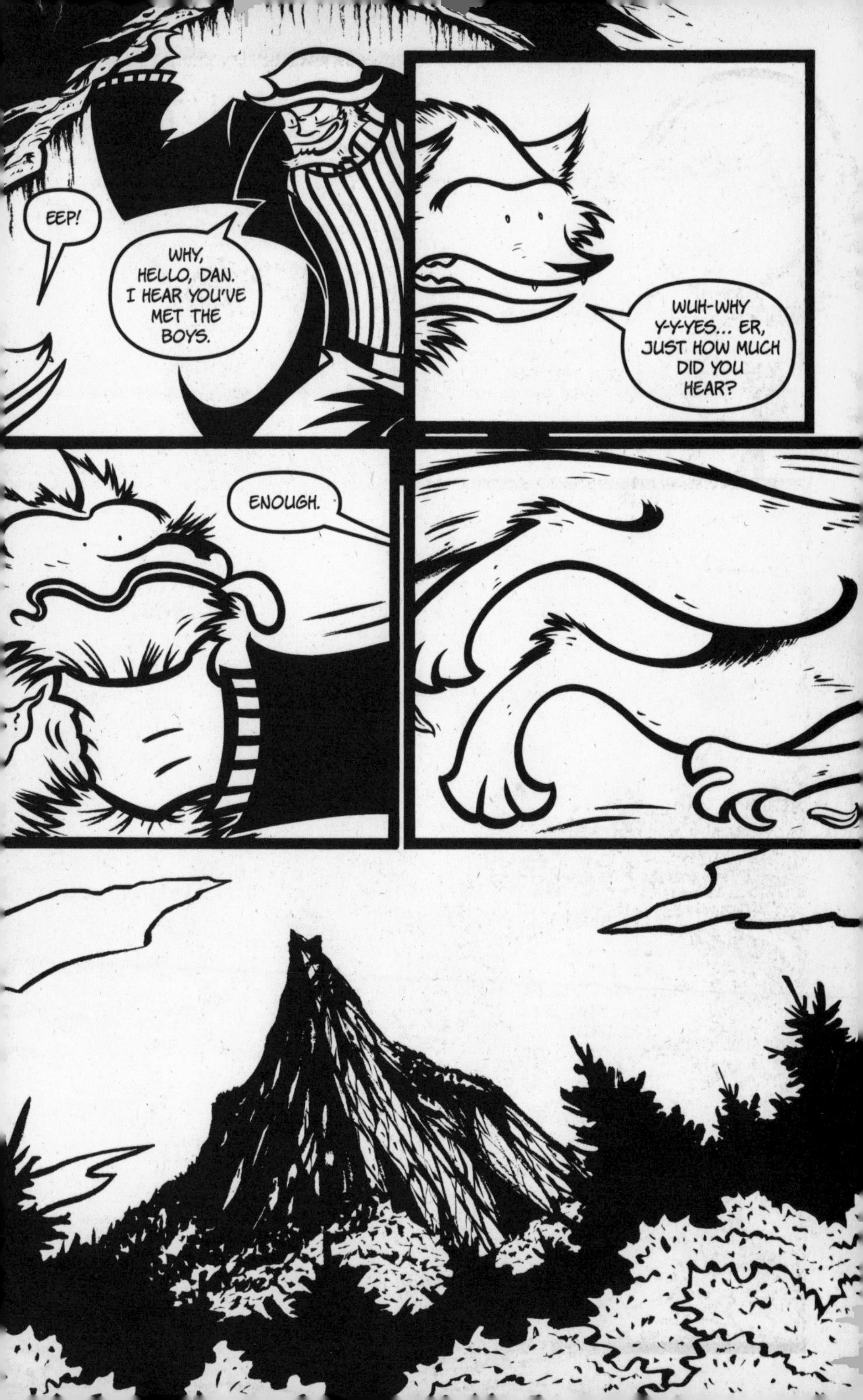
EEP!
WHY, HELLO, DAN. I HEAR YOU'VE MET THE BOYS.
WUH-WHY Y-Y-YES... ER, JUST HOW MUCH DID YOU HEAR?
ENOUGH.

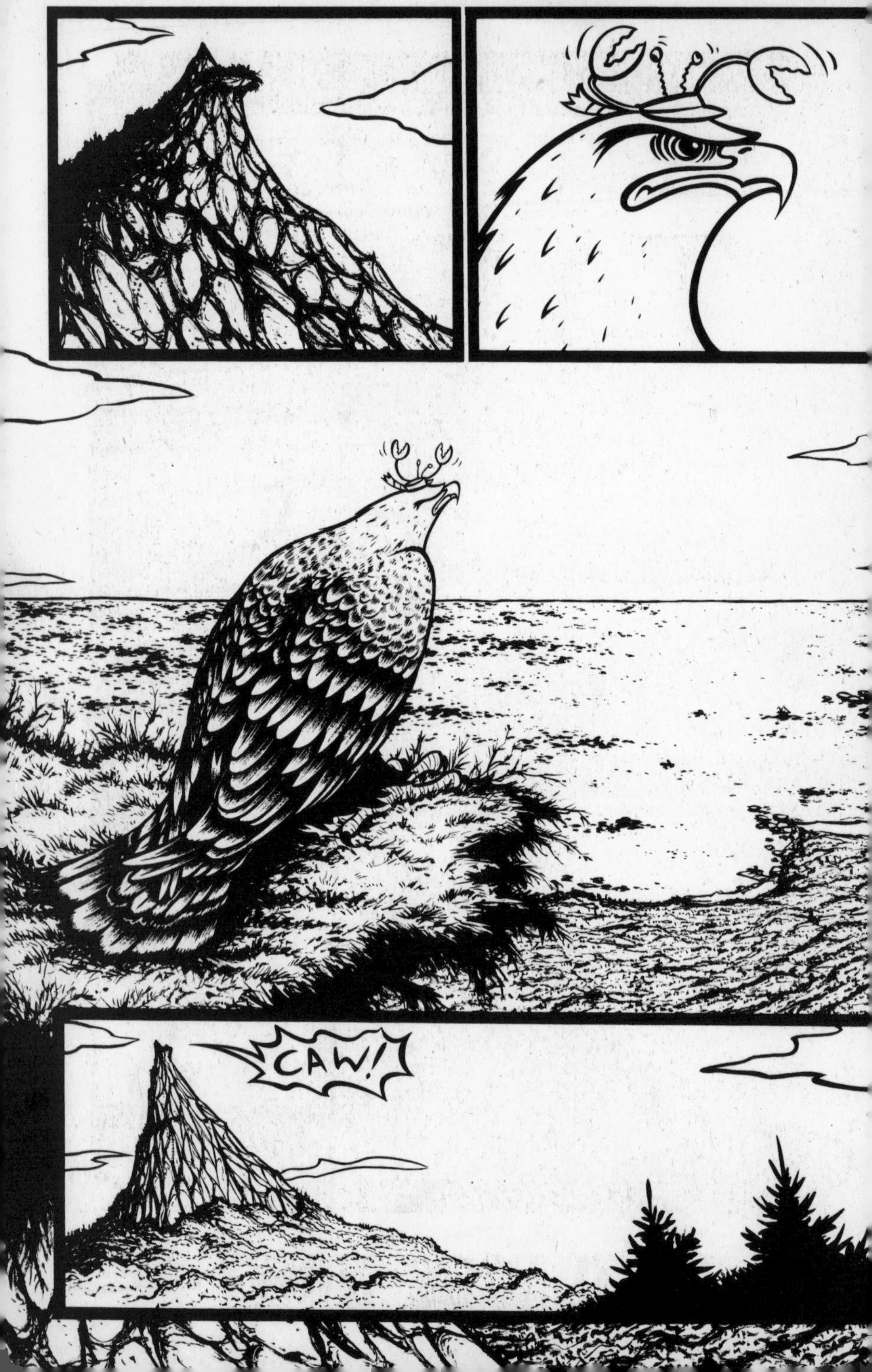
CAW!

OTHER BOOKS FROM MATTHEW LOUX...

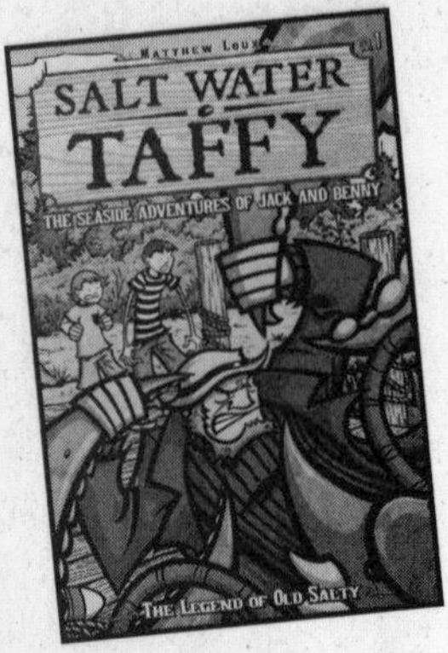
MATTHEW LOUX
SALT WATER TAFFY
THE SEASIDE ADVENTURES OF JACK AND BENNY
THE LEGEND OF OLD SALTY

SALT WATER TAFFY™
VOL. 1:
"THE LEGEND OF OLD SALTY"
written & illustrated by
Matthew Loux
96 pages • $5.99 US
ISBN: 978-1-932664-94-2

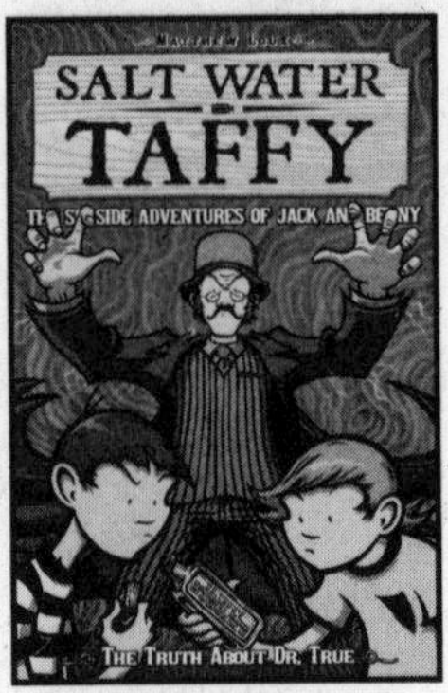
MATTHEW LOUX
SALT WATER TAFFY
THE TRUTH ABOUT DR. TRUE

SALT WATER TAFFY™
VOL.3:
"THE TRUTH ABOUT DR. TRUE"
written & illustrated by
Matthew Loux
96 pages • $5.99 US
ISBN: 978-1-934964-04-0

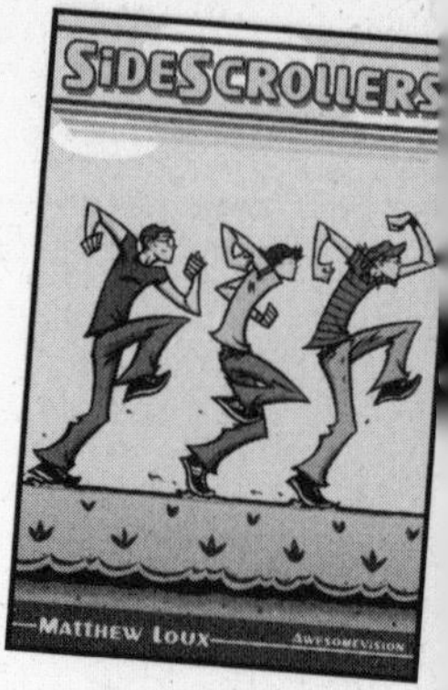
SIDESCROLLERS
MATTHEW LOUX
AWESOMEVISION

SIDESCROLLERS™
Written & illustrated by
Matthew Loux
216 pages • $11.99 US
ISBN: 978-1-932664-50-8

YASLA's "Top 10 Great Graphic Novels for Teens!"

OTHER BOOKS FROM ONI PRESS...

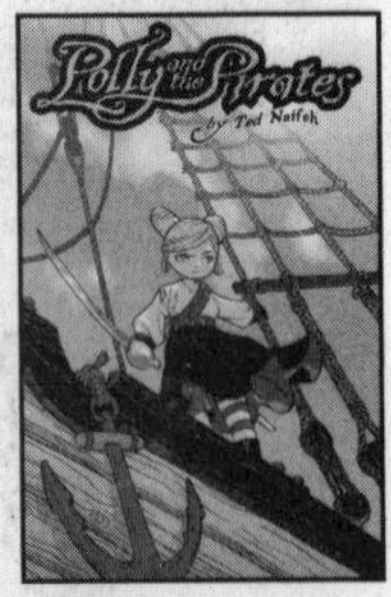
Polly and the Pirates
by Ted Naifeh

POLLY & THE PIRATES™
VOL. 1
Written & illustrated by
Ted Naifeh
176 pages • $11.95 US
ISBN: 978-1-932664-46-1

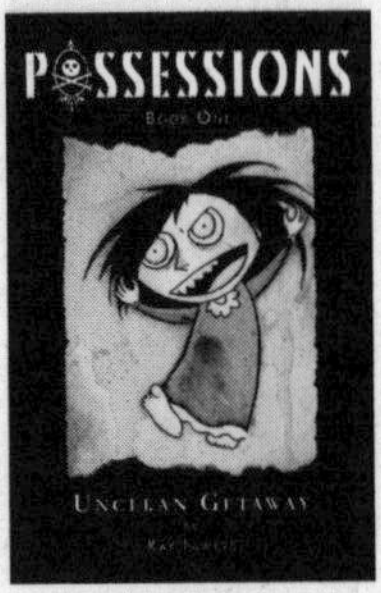
POSSESSIONS
UNCLEAN GETAWAY

POSSESSIONS ™
VOL. 1 UNCLEAN GETAWAY
Written & illustrated by
Ray Fawkes
88 pages • $5.99 US
ISBN: 978-1-934964-36-1

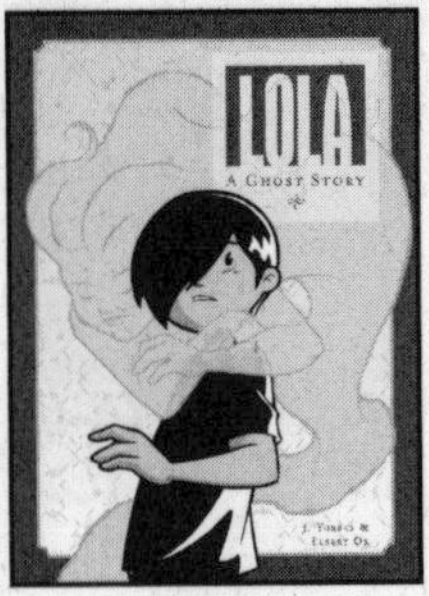
LOLA
A GHOST STORY

LOLA™
A GHOST STORY
Written by J. Torres
illustrated by Elbert Or
112 pages • $14.95 US
ISBN: 978-1-934964-33-0

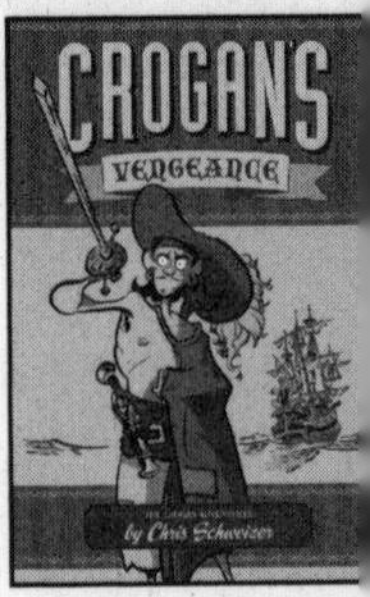
CROGANS
VENGEANCE
by Chris Schweizer

CROGAN'S VENGEANCE
Written & illustrated by
Chris Schweizer
Hardcover
192 pages • $14.99 US
ISBN: 978-1-934964-06-4

AVAILABLE AT FINER COMICS SHOPS EVERYWHERE. FOR A COMICS STORE NEAR YOU, CALL 1-888-COMIC-BOOK OR VISIT WWW.COMICSHOPS.US.

FOR MORE ONI PRESS TITLES AND INFORMATION VISIT WWW.ONIPRESS.COM.